2004

W9-DGB-363

WORLD CLASS
ELEMENTARY SCHOOLS

HOW TO ORDER THIS BOOK

BY PHONE: 800-233-9936 or 717-291-5609, 8AM–5PM Eastern Time

BY FAX: 717-295-4538

BY MAIL: Order Department
Technomic Publishing Company, Inc.
851 New Holland Avenue, Box 3535
Lancaster, PA 17604, U.S.A.

BY CREDIT CARD: American Express, VISA, MasterCard

BY WWW SITE: http://www.techpub.com

PERMISSION TO PHOTOCOPY–POLICY STATEMENT

Authorization to photocopy items for internal or personal use, or the internal or personal use of spe-
cific clients, is granted by Technomic Publishing Co., Inc. provided that the base fee of US $3.00 per
copy, plus US $ .25 per page is paid directly to Copyright Clearance Center, 222 Rosewood Drive,
Danvers, MA 01923, USA. For those organizations that have been granted a photocopy license by
CCC, a separate system of payment has been arranged. The fee code for users of the Transactional
Reporting Service is 1-56676/97 $5.00 + $ .25.

WORLD CLASS ELEMENTARY SCHOOLS

AGENDA FOR ACTION

LIBRARY
UNIVERSITY OF ST. FRANCIS
JOLIET, ILLINOIS

Richard M. Haynes
Western Carolina University

Donald M. Chalker
Western Carolina University

TECHNOMIC
PUBLISHING CO., INC.
LANCASTER · BASEL

World Class Elementary Schools
a **TECHNOMIC** publication

Published in the Western Hemisphere by
Technomic Publishing Company, Inc.
851 New Holland Avenue, Box 3535
Lancaster, Pennsylvania 17604 U.S.A.

Distributed in the Rest of the World by
Technomic Publishing AG
Missionsstrasse 44
CH-4055 Basel, Switzerland

Copyright © 1997 by Technomic Publishing Company, Inc.
All rights reserved

No part of this publication may be reproduced, stored in a
retrieval system, or transmitted, in any form or by any means,
electronic, mechanical, photocopying, recording, or otherwise,
without the prior written permission of the publisher.

Printed in the United States of America
10 9 8 7 6 5 4 3 2 1

Main entry under title:
    World Class Elementary Schools: Agenda for Action

A Technomic Publishing Company book
Bibliography: p.
Includes index p. 309

Library of Congress Catalog Card No. 96-61848
ISBN No. 1-56676-290-1

372.973
H424

To our wives, with love and admiration:
Dianne Linton Haynes and Harriet Jean Chalker

Why should anyone care if the United States has world-class schools? The answer is everyone who pays for them; anyone who attends them; and the teachers who teach in them. Although we no longer have the Cold War to divert our attention from the needs of American education, Haynes and Chalker point out we cannot allow the nation to be outclassed in the fierce economic battles that loom ahead in the 21st century. Our economic position is linked to our investment in and our battle to transform our schools to prepare intelligent citizens, traders, engineers, scientists, and humanitarians.

The World Economic Forum in Geneva and the International Institute for Management and Development in Lausanne, Switzerland, recently released competitive rankings of the world's economies. They are shown below:

(1) United States
(2) Singapore
(3) Hong Kong
(4) Japan
(5) Switzerland
(6) Germany
(7) Netherlands
(8) New Zealand
(9) Denmark

(10) Norway

(11) Taiwan

(12) Canada

(13) Austria

(14) Australia

(15) Sweden

(16) Finland

(17) France

(18) United Kingdom

(19) Belgium

(20) Chile

The United States owes its number one ranking to high marks in domestic economic strength, internationalization, and management. Industry in the United States has been very aggressive in developing new technologies, from computers to telecommunication.

Although the U.S. economy is strong, its schools remain backward, particularly from the perspective of governance. As Chalker and Haynes (1994) noted in their first book, *World Class Schools: New Standards for Education,* America lacks a national, focused curriculum. It lacks a consensus about what American students should know in the 21st century.

It is doubtful if American education can rise to the challenge of the 21st century hobbled by an archaic system of governance in which 14,000 school boards decide when and if American curricula can be revamped. American educational reformers seem to want to balkanize the system even further by site-basing curriculum decisions to neighborhood referenda. Contrary to politically correct notions, most neighborhood citizens know very little about what is coming in the 21st century. Their own education is out-of-date by 20−30 years. What do the locals know about the challenges in the Pacific Rim?

The "Asian Tigers" of South Korea, Hong Kong, Singapore, and Taiwan's real gross domestic product growth as an annual average percentage from 1994−2003 will be 7.6 percent, whereas the gross national product of the rich industrial countries of the world is expected to be 2.7 percent in the same time period. The 21st century will be the "Asian Century."

I am appalled that the United States has decentralized some of its most important decisions about the future to those with the most provincial credentials who do not want to deal with the following trends occurring in front of our eyes: Islam is the fastest growing religion in the United States; the Hispanic population is the fastest growing minority population and Spanish the most rapidly growing language; the white population is shrinking; we lead the world in one-parent families with the father missing; 135,000 American students bring guns to school each day; and 50 percent of our adults are functionally illiterate. Although American business has become internationalized and global, American education remains isolated, provincial, and anti-intellectual, held in place by the lowest local school board common denominator.

Consider this book Haynes and Chalker's second wake-up call. A recent ranking of the nations' wealth, based on their natural resources, machinery, buildings, and other man-made capital, and human resources, showed the United States was not even in the top 10. These are the rankings of the world's 15 wealthiest countries ranked by per capita wealth expressed in thousands of U.S. dollars.

(1) Australia

(2) Canada

(3) Luxembourg

(4) Switzerland

(5) Japan

(6) Sweden

(7) Iceland

(8) Qatar

(9) United Arab Emirates

(10) Denmark

(11) Norway

(12) United States

(13) France

(14) Kuwait

(15) Germany

The message is clear. The United States is being eclipsed in natural wealth by international competitors. We remain strong because of our global management strength, our ability to embrace change especially as it pertains to technology, and our domestic strength. If American business had the same problems as American education, we would have lost our competitive edge some time ago, and our standard of living would have slipped even further than it has.

I urge the reader to read carefully Haynes and Chalker's comparisons and conclusions. In the end it will not be our technology that fails us. It will be our parochial isolationism, our cultural backwardness, and our anti-intellectualism that permeate our schools. We must think globally and act locally. That requires a vision based on world-class standards and not the cultural tunnel vision found in elitist concepts of the 19th century.

The stakes are too high to pussyfoot around. We are indebted to Haynes and Chalker for their tenacity and their courage to define the agenda in clear terms.

FENWICK W. ENGLISH, PH.D.
Vice Chancellor, Academic Affairs
Indiana University-Purdue University
at Fort Wayne, Indiana

This book is a sequel to the authors' book published in 1994, *World Class Schools: New Standards for Education.* Many gracious people made this current book possible by sharing time and expertise with the authors. The availability of abundant research and literature on the subject of international education was equally important. The authors have appropriately credited the copyrighted materials and appreciate the generous sharing of information by experts, authors, and publishing companies.

The Alliance of Business Leaders and Educators (ABLE), College of Education and Allied Professions, Western Carolina University, made possible much of the travel and research necessary to conduct the world-class elementary school research. We thank the ABLE Advisory Board for including our project in their strategic plan. The authors thank Gurney Chambers, Dean of the College of Education and Allied Professions, and Phil Monk, ABLE Coordinator, for their encouragement and support. The authors appreciate the Office of Academic Affairs, Western Carolina University, for providing a Canadian study grant that allowed us to research schools in three Canadian provinces and for supporting our work. We sincerely thank our colleagues in the Department of Administration, Curriculum, and Instruction for providing research used in the study and for continuing to listen politely to constant talk about world-class education standards. Office assistants, Phyllis Cogdill and Rebecca Hoyle, and graduate assistant, Brian Shaw, provided excellent technical support. Bill Studenc, WCU Public Affairs, delivered our message to the media. The able assistance of Chuck Morris aided us in the use of technology that was vital to our project.

While conducting the world-class research for elementary schools, many individuals in Washington Embassies graciously received us and helped us understand their country's elementary or primary schools. We thank the following embassy individuals:

- Mr. Bernard Brahm, French Embassy
- Mr. John Krug, Federal Republic of Germany Embassy
- Ms. Dorit Eldar, Embassy of Israel
- Mr. Junsuck Park, Korean Embassy
- Dr. Chen-ching Li, Taipei Economic and Cultural Office in the United States
- Dr. Norman London, Canadian Embassy

Both authors traveled to Canada to learn more about our closest neighbor. We met gracious hosts and world-class educators as we visited. We especially thank the following persons who hosted our stay and scheduled our visits: Wif Innerd, University of Windsor; Gerry Connelly, Toronto Board of Education; and Joe Draper, Ontario Institute for Studies in Education who assisted Don Chalker. Tom Rich, Nova Scotia Department of Education and Culture; Dr. Keith Sullivan, Dean, College of Education, Dalhousie University in Halifax, Nova Scotia; and Dr. Donald Weeren, Faculty of Education, Saint Mary's University in Halifax, Nova Scotia; Bryon James, Tom Hanley and his staff in the New Brunswick Ministry of Education assisted Dick Haynes. The principals and staffs of many schools opened their doors graciously; we thank those who shared with us: Lord Lansdowne Public School and Annette Street Public School, Toronto; Dougall Public School, Princess Anne School, Eastwood School, Windsor; Brookhouse School in Dartmouth, Nova Scotia; and Keswick Ridge School in New Brunswick. Additionally, we thank the Japan School of Raleigh, North Carolina, for generously supplying materials and for including us in the activities of the school.

This book would not have been possible without those who graciously helped us with the first book. We thanked them in the acknowledgements for that volume and drew on our learning from them as we worked on this book.

The authors taught a course in comparative education while writing this book. We thank our graduate students who shared ideas with us about world-class schools and who contributed to the research used in this book. Each of our students interviewed a student from one of the world-class countries, and the authors used the results of the interviews throughout the book. Other foreign students interviewed were associated with the University of North Carolina at Asheville, Western Carolina University, and local public schools. The authors reference the names of contributing world-class students appropriately throughout the book.

We express our admiration and respect for educators throughout the United States for helping keep this country a world-class nation. Both authors drew heavily from previous school experience as teachers and administrators in Florida, Michigan, North Carolina, and Ohio. The public school teachers and administrators of western North Carolina remain our most important tie to excellence in education, and we thank them all.

Included in the combined families of the two authors are the following education experts: parents, teachers, teacher assistants, school administrators, and students. We listen to them and make use of their experience. We thank them for their patience, love, support, and encouragement.

Finally, we thank our contributing authors, photographers, and suppliers of additional materials. First, the Moyer family: Francis (Tony), Frances, Marie, and Anna who write of their experiences in Japanese schools; second, Dr. Clive McGee, Director, Centre for Primary Education, The University of Waikato, Hamilton, New Zealand, who writes about the very successful primary schools in New Zealand; and third, Dr. Joan Elliot, Fulbright Scholar of Korean Elementary Education, University of North Carolina at Asheville. Photographs for this book were generously provided by Dr. Clive McGee of New Zealand, Dorit Eldar of Israel, Dr. Joan Elliot of Korea, Tony Moyer of Japan, The Ministry of Education in Taiwan, Republic of China, Earnest Jones of Germany, and Malcolmb Loughlin of England. Report cards were contributed by Jean Llelwyn of Dartmouth, Nova Scotia, Canada, Tony Moyer of Japan, and Dr. Chen-ching Li of Republic of China. The ClipArt used to identify World Class Quotes, Reflections on Research, and Best Practice were used with permission from T/Maker Company, Mountain View, California. Our thanks additionally go to Dr. Fenwick English for his encouragement and suggestions for framing this text conceptually and for contributing the foreword to this book.

The world continues to grow smaller, and American educators must study the condition of education in other developed nations. Such a study will change the views of educators just as the search for a world-class elementary school changed our view of education. If we remain open to the outside world, our schools can become world-class.

Chapter 1

DEFINING WORLD-CLASS SCHOOLS

All who have meditated on the art of governing mankind have been convinced that the fate of empires depends on the education of youth.
— Aristotle

This chapter introduces the definition of world-class schools, and it summarizes the initial findings on what world-class school standards are. The authors selected 10 nations representative of the finest education systems on the Earth. Careful study of those nations' schools led to the concept of afterthoughts. This chapter explains the research and what world-class standards are. The need for a "level playing field" exists so that comparisons among nations are valid. The chapter explores the organization and design of the text and its progression and also presents two fundamental world-class rules to guide the reader.

The goal of developing world-class schools fills the minds of educators, the mouths of politicians, and the hearts of parents. "Global education and global competition [must] go hand-in-hand. There must be some idea in our country of the world-class standards of excellence we need to really meet the challenges of the future" explained the President of the United States while addressing the National PTA Legislative Conference (1994). Many school systems across the country promise a world-class education for their students. But what does that mean? Demands to reach world-class standards reappear each time comparative international studies of student achievement are released, with the United States seldom ranking among the top third. This is the first book published that both defines what a world-class elementary school is and provides guidance for those wishing to lead their schools to meet these lofty standards.

SETTING WORLD-CLASS STANDARDS

Given the expectations that America will have world-class schools— along with the assumption that it doesn't have them now—some real meaning must be given to the term. In their earlier work (Chalker and Haynes, 1994) the authors provide the first substantive definition of world-class schools. Although their research revealed voluminous references to world-class schools, no attempt at defining the term existed prior to that book. This chapter presents a brief review of the earlier world-class standards along with a synopsis of the most fundamental findings of the earlier study.

Leveling the Playing Field

Once the authors concluded that no meaningful definition of world-class schools existed, they decided to create one. There were lengthy discussions with numerous educators to determine what they thought the term meant and how they felt about international student achievement comparisons. Many educators complained that there needed to be a ''level playing field'' for the comparisons to be valid, yet no definition of a level playing field exists. There was a consensus that the term *world-class schools* needs defining. So the authors read the most recent international achievement comparisons, the materials referenced by the authors of those studies, and all of the comparative education test reports they could find. The result of that research was frustration because of the inconsistencies among the various studies. For example, in the second international student achievement comparisons in science and mathematics, Japan did not rank first. Because Japanese schools are most often compared with the United States to show how poor American education is, the expectation is that Japan will always beat the United States in such tests. In this case, Japan did not participate in these international tests. The nations of Taiwan and the Republic of Korea (South Korea) were the leaders in this comparison.

The researchers realized the need for a common core of nations, with the same questions asked uniformly of each country. There was great care to use only comparative information, using the same reporting year and the same question for all countries. In this way a level playing field results in which the nations and comparisons were uniform.

Selecting Nations

To create the level playing field the authors selected a cohort of 10 nations with the able assistance of Dr. Franklin Parker, a distinguished visiting scholar at Western Carolina University and an internationally known authority on comparative education. Table 1.1 lists the 10 nations and the reasons for selecting each nation.

Researching the Nations

With the level playing field of nations set, the authors requested information about the education system from each nation's embassy or

TABLE 1.1 Ten nations selected for defining world-class schools.

Nation	Reason Selected
Canada	America's cultural cousin; vast expenditure on education
France	World's most copied school system
Federal Republic of Germany (former West Germany)	Home of great educators; a birthplace of compulsory education; Europe's most dynamic economy
Great Britain	Huge reform movement started 1988; high literacy rate
New Zealand	World's most literate society; leader in reading and mathematics education
Taiwan	World leader in science and math acheivement; among the most dynamic economies
State of Israel	Combines one of the oldest and newest education systems in the world; made the desert bloom
Japan	Nation most commonly cited as educationally superior to the United States; dynamic economy
Republic of Korea (South Korea)	World leader in science and math acheivement; among the most dynamic economies
United States	World leader in higher education; dominance in Nobel laureates

consulate. They focused on *input* variables, rather than *outputs* from the school systems. This was an important decision because the authors were looking for causes of educational outcomes rather than the indicators of different achievement. By examining input variables they wanted to determine causes of the different outcomes.

The input variables cluster under correlates of effective schools, in nine categories. Within each category is a common set of questions ensuring a level playing field for the comparison. Table 1.2 lists the nine correlates and the questions asked in each area.

With the nations selected for study and the questions ready to ask, the authors contacted the embassy or consulate of each nation asking for specific information about their nation's schools. The authors arranged interviews with each education officer or cultural attaché in an embassy or consulate. The structured interviews were particularly useful because the embassy personnel were both experts on their nation's schools and parents with children enrolled in American schools, thereby enriching the perspective of these individuals. The research, including extensive additional reading, concluded with interviews of students from each country.

Setting World-Class Standards

Much of the resulting data was numeric, yielding a matrix with one axis listing the 10 countries and the other axis detailing answers to each research question. That allowed the authors to develop a column of comparative questions yielding the level playing field educators so frequently requested. These data (days in the school year, for example) allowed a mean score to be derived. That mean score (204 days of school per year, for example) became the world-class standard for that research area. The study concluded by deriving a U.S. deviation from each world-class standard.

The research presented in this book is largely unique. There was an effort to use the most current comparative data available. Therefore, much of the research available to the authors came as a result of assistance from each nation's embassy in Washington, through organizations such as UNESCO, and from extensive interviewing of educational specialists and students from each country. The authors worked with several brainstorming groups to ferret out the most likely questions elementary school principals need answered. An unusually useful book resulted from this effort.

TABLE 1.2 Nine effective schools correlates and within each correlate the common questions asked.

Effective Schools Correlate	Questions Examined
1. Education expenditure	Percent of GNP spent on education
	Per capita GNP
	Percent GDP increased in 5 years
	Per pupil expenditure in public schools
	Per capita income
2. Time on task	Average days in school year
	Average minutes of instruction per school day
	Average hours of instruction in a school year
	Span of compulsory education
	Average minutes of math and science instruction per week, age 13
3. Class size	Average class size, age 13
	Primary and secondary per pupil ratio
4. Teachers	Teacher preparation
	Classroom climate
	Percent of time teacher teaches math or science, age 13
5. Student data	Percent of students reaching final grade offered
	Percent of students spending 4 or more hours on math or science homework weekly, age 13
	Percent of students who spend 2 or more hours on homework daily, age 13
	Percent of students who watch 5 or more hours of television daily

(continued)

TABLE 1.2 (continued).

Effective Schools Correlate	Questions Examined
6. Curriculum and instruction	Names of course offerings for elementary, middle, and upper schools
	Time allotments for teaching each subject at each level
7. Evaluation	Purpose of student assessment
	How assessment is prepared
	Use of test results
8. Educational governance	National, state or local control
	Who controls curriculum and instruction
	Percent of students in private education at three levels
9. Home and community	National literacy rate
	Parent involvement
	Ratio of TV sets and newspapers per 1000
	Cram schools
	Student suicide rate by age and gender per 100,000
	Divorce rate per 1000

Afterthoughts

As the earlier (1994) study concluded, the authors reflected on the meaning of the lessons learned with the world-class standards. These reflections, called afterthoughts, are in Table 1.3.

ORGANIZATION OF THIS BOOK

This book is for elementary school principals and other elementary school leaders who want to create world-class elementary schools in a deliberate, structured manner. The book is for practical use, and it contains several features to facilitate that process. There are two basic world-class rules that need consideration before launching into any effort to develop world-class elementary schools. The rules are in Table1.4.

Chapters in the Book

The book follows a logical and orderly design. Following this chapter is an overview of the American elementary school and its evolution, in a historical and philosophical form.

Pre-school youngsters learn at Dougall Public School in Windsor, Canada. One of the authors was struck by the multi-cultural setting of this table of happy students (photo by Chalker).

TABLE 1.3 Afterthoughts on world-class schools.

1. Class size: The United States offers world-class size. The quest for smaller classes can only be justified on the basis of teacher comfort and/or the presence of disruptive and nonfocused students.
2. Curriculum: Cultural variables among the nations studied appeared to explain more about the variable performance of students than does an analysis of the curriculum. Those cultures that stress the work education requires had better performance records than the systems that did not stress the relationship between effort and learning.
3. Education expenditure: The United States appears generous in amounts spent on education, given the fact that it is no longer the world's wealthiest country. The question remains, "Does the United States spend wisely on education when compared with other world-class countries?"
4. Governance: The United States needs a national education authority that defines the term "educated American." A national curriculum is needed.
5. Parents, home, and community: Meaningful change in the outcomes of education in the United States requires fundamental change in the way parents and teachers unite to instill an "education ethic" in each student.
6. Student assessment: Each nation attempts to define what students should know. A majority of the world-class nations define this knowledge through the use of national goals, a national curriculum, and national testing. The most successful national testing programs do not attempt to test knowledge at several levels, but instead, focus on one or two levels. The United States appears to test more frequently but places less emphasis on test results. Essay testing is the international norm.
7. Education ethic: Among the world-class nations studied, those with the most successful education systems have students who are serious about learning and view learning as hard work. Successful students view the outcome of education as preparation for life's work and believe that success in school establishes success in life.
8. Teachers: American teachers work longer with more hours of instruction than their international counterparts. Both the pay level and the pay range of American teachers is lower than the world-class average. Before the United States addresses preparation shortages, the equity issue between states and individual locales needs to be resolved. The best way to increase teacher pay is to increase the length of the school year for teachers and students. The low self-esteem associated with American teachers will only be resolved when gifted athletes and musicians are put on a par with gifted teachers.
9. Time on task: The length of the American school year is too short. A longer year could be phased in, 5 days per year, until at least 205 teaching days are involved.

Source: Chalker and Haynes (1994). Reprinted with the permission of the publisher.

TABLE 1.4 Two rules for developing world-class elementary schools.

1. Just because something is a world-class standard does not mean it will work or be desired as part of American education. Americans want schools that produce internationally competitive students who are still uniquely American.
2. Just because something is an American idea or practice does not mean it is not world-class. After all, the overwhelming majority of Nobel laureates since the end of World War II have been products of U.S. education.

Following Chapter 2 are six chapters that present elements of world-class education in this order: curriculum and instruction, teaching, governance, assessment, students, concluding with a chapter on parents, homes, and communities. Each chapter follows a similar format, beginning with a shaded box containing an abstract of the chapter to acquaint the reader with the chapter contents. That precedes a narrative that provides a global perspective of the chapter's topic. The chapters conclude with an agenda for developing a world-class elementary school.

Reflections on Research

Throughout the chapters are ''Reflections on Research'' cameos, which review findings on various topics such as successful homework, best testing practices, and ability grouping. The reader can quickly get a summary of the research from the effective schools' movement as it parallels the world-class perspective. These sections are presented in double-ruled boxes. Each chapter ends with cited references and a list of recommended reading for those wanting to study further a particular issue.

World-Class Quotes

The authors included quotes that came from international educators during structured interviews. These quotations contain ideas, concepts, or insights into a particularly interesting concept from that person's nation. For example, an intern in the New Zealand embassy told one of the authors that he could not understand why U.S. educators make a single day so important in the life of a child. Asked what day he was referring to, the intern replied, ''The day a child turns sixteen, three

Children enjoying school playtime in the Republic of Korea. Many U.S. educators think children in Asian schools are in sweatshops, when they are happier in school than many U.S. students are (photo by Elliott).

things happen: compulsory attendance ends, the right to drive begins, and child labor laws end'' (Ryan, 1994).

World-Class Ideas

As particularly useful ideas were presented from various nations, the authors were often struck with the paradigm change the idea contained. For instance, eastern Pacific Rim teachers have a ''teachers' room'' in the center of their schools. Instead of having teachers work in the isolation of their rooms, teachers work together, commonly planning lessons and reflecting on the cause of teaching successes. U.S. teachers plan in isolation, teach in isolation, and reflect in isolation. No wonder U.S. teachers are lonely.

Chapters on New Zealand and Japan

With the brainstorming and discussion the authors have conducted with U.S. educators, they have noticed an obsession with two particular countries: New Zealand and Japan. New Zealand interests U.S. elementary educators because of the many ideas that have come from the world's most literate nation: Reading Recovery, whole language teaching, site-based management, etc. Japan is of interest as much for the misinformation about it (the terrible suicide rate is about half that of comparable U.S. student groups, for example) as for the "whipping boy" mentality that Japanese schools are always better than U.S. schools (they are not). Chapter 9 was written by Dr. Clive McGee who is the director of the Primary Education Centre at the University of Waikato in Hamilton, New Zealand. McGee presents his explanation why New Zealand elementary schools are successful, along with ideas to help U.S. elementary schools to improve. Chapter 10 was written by Tony Moyer's family. Moyer is the deputy director of the North Carolina Japan Center. Moyer, his wife, and two daughters lived in Tokyo for many years. Their older daughter spent 6 years in a Japanese elementary school. The Moyers reflect on what they learned about Japanese education and what it could mean to U.S. educators. The final chapter includes the primary implications for those wanting to develop world-class elementary schools.

The Final Chapter

The concluding chapter includes an overview of what world-class elementary schools could look like in the United States. It suggests some staff development and planning ideas that should assist whatever form of a school improvement plan an individual school or school system chooses to employ. The chapter concludes with a checklist for planning an agenda for action as the reader crafts a unique form of a world-class elementary school.

Scanning, Reading, or Using the Book as a Basis for Further Study

The book is designed for three types of readers: (1) those who scan for the main idea, (2) those who read reflectively, and (3) those who want to open the door to the good ideas from educators around the world.

The reader may scan the book, reading the shaded box that begins every chapter. Scan the chapter by reading the figures or other charts, and boxed features. Then turn to the agenda that concludes most chapters. Scan the agenda by reading the numbered italic items that organize it.

For those *reading the book,* read it as written. Each chapter contains a quotation at the beginning, then the abstract, and major headings in bold type that introduce the topic that follows. Use the final chapter as a basis for staff development and creating an image of the best world-class school for a particular community and student body.

This book may be a springboard for further study. Each chapter cites the references used and suggestions for further reading.

However the book is used, the authors hope that a world-class elementary school is the result.

REFERENCES

Chalker, D. M. and R. M. Haynes. 1994. *World Class Schools: New Standards for Education.* Lancaster, PA: Technomic Publishing Company, Inc.

McAdams, R. P. 1993. *Lessons from Abroad: How Other Countries Educate Their Children.* Lancaster, PA: Technomic Publishing Company, Inc.

Ryan, I. 1994. Interview, May 12, 1994.

Steffy, B. and F. English. 1997. *Curriculum and Assessment for World-Class Schools.* Lancaster, PA: Technomic Publishing Company, Inc.

THE HISTORICAL IMPACT OF WORLD-CLASS EDUCATION ON ELEMENTARY EDUCATION IN AMERICA

Paradigms are about patterns of behavior and the rules and regulations we use to construct these patterns. We use those patterns first to establish boundaries, and then to direct us on how to solve problems.

—Barker, 1994

Although the history of education does not necessarily provide the elementary school leader an agenda for developing world-class education, it does provide necessary foundations that must be understood before the elementary school leader attempts a contemporary agenda. Chapter 2 first addresses the historical development of American elementary education by focusing on the development of paradigms throughout history that impact elementary education. Three purposes form the foundation for the chapter:

(1) The chapter acquaints the school leader with educational practices from America's past.

(2) The chapter reassesses educational and cultural traditions that impact on current practices in elementary education.

(3) The chapter encourages the school leader to predict future educational developments in American elementary education.

It is not possible or practical to review in this chapter the complete history of American elementary schools. The chapter, therefore, focuses on events that form significant educational paradigms within the parameters of American elementary education today. This focus allows the student of elementary education to develop a sound historical knowledge base from which to evaluate and judge current educational practice in our elementary schools.

13

Second, Chapter 2 briefly addresses similar and dissimilar historical developments in the world-class countries of Canada, Germany, New Zealand, and South Korea. The authors selected these countries because they offer different but effective practices rooted in the history of each country. Each country offers a piece of the puzzle needed to identity world-class education. A knowledge of historical paradigms in countries experiencing success in their educational system gives American elementary educators data with which to make essential comparisons.

HISTORICAL PARADIGMS OF AMERICAN EDUCATION

In 1993, the Douglas County Schools in Colorado adopted the theme, ''The Road to World Class.'' The system bought into the national idea of making American education world-class. The Douglas County Schools are out front but not alone. Throughout America the idea of world-class schools permeates the educational scene. This chapter supplies the historical paradigms needed to explore the development of world-class elementary schools. Future chapters compose ideas useful in developing paradigm shifts necessary to keep education relevant and successful. As Barker (1993) claims, ''We may run out of today, but we'll never run out of tomorrow.''

American pioneers charted the road to world-class education, and the road has continued under construction throughout the history of the United States. Construction continues today. The past controls our future in all segments of life, and education is no exception. The road to world-class contains both potholes and smooth surfaces. Educators cannot control the past, but they can use the past to ensure smooth sailing in the future. To ensure future smooth sailing down the road to world-class, the road should be paved with current knowledge and wisdom that is rooted in America's historical educational paradigms, and educators should have the power to shift those paradigms when necessary. Several of these paradigms are presented in the following paragraphs.

A paradigm is a pattern that eventually serves as a model. Transformational leaders in America's elementary schools must examine historical paradigms and determine which are useful today and which inhibit the establishment of world-class schools. Transformational leaders must also understand the historical paradigms that drive successful educational systems in other countries. Following a look at America's histori-

TABLE 2.1 *The elementary school in the United States, 1990.*

Number of elementary schools:	58,000
Number of elementary students:	29,522,000
Elementary grades:	Grades 1–6 (middle schools commonly have grade 6)
Length of elementary school year:	178 (average)
Length of elementary school day:	5.5 hours (average)

Source: Valverde (1994).

cal paradigms, this chapter briefly examines the historical paradigms that drive four of the educational systems in the world-class countries identified by Chalker and Haynes (1994) in their companion book, *World Class Schools: New Standards for Education.* The countries presented are Germany, Republic of Korea, New Zealand, and Canada.

Individualism

A strong sense of individualism brought the first settlers to America. Individual survival, individual development, and individual reliance on self characterized early settlers. Adults in the home desiring to socialize children to a new environment but also desiring to retain old family values conducted the first colonial primary schooling. Colonists regarded the family as fundamental to a healthy religious and civil society. Parents taught their children to read the Bible, and chores introduced them to the world of work. The community expected children to embrace the values of piety and respect for adults (Gutek, 1983). Parents and grandparents taught values to children often based on the "golden rule." Parental control of the learning environment was essential, and every home provided a unique educational environment.

By the latter part of the 17th century, pragmatism caused many families to form "Dame Schools." Women interested in teaching held these schools in their homes, and parents voluntarily sent their children. Also for pragmatic reasons, schooling in the home continually gave way to organized schools usually of the one-room variety. Organized schools such as the Latin Grammar School, started in 1635, provided a classical education for boys ages 7–14. In 1647, the Massachusetts General Court enacted the "Old Deluder Satan Law," requiring towns of 50 or more families to appoint a teacher of reading and writing (Gutek, 1983). From this historical point, education more and more became the responsibility of the state, and organized schooling increased. The early individualized schooling delivered by parents in the home experienced a paradigm shift to organized schooling in the ''little red schoolhouse.''

The presence of individualism in the school environment has created a powerful paradigm in today's educational environment. Many adults continue to seek a unique education for children that speaks to family values and needs. The return to home schooling is the most pronounced aspect of the paradigm. Many parents feel that education can be individualized in the home, thus avoiding the socialization and pragmatized education that takes place in school. Educators pretend that home schooling has not been successful, but there is reason to think that home schooling has indeed prepared students as well as students housed in the school room.

Individualization has produced a second paradigm. The vast majority of parents who do send their children to the public or private elementary school retain a strong right of parental challenge. Many parents and significant adults believe that the schools should cater to individual beliefs and values. Through the right of parental challenge, adults challenge curriculum, textbooks and other learning materials, teaching methodology, decisions about student behavior, and a myriad of other school decisions. In America, parents challenge the effectiveness of schools and in so doing, challenge another world-class standard – a standard present in many of the world-class countries where parents respect the authority of the school and educators. Authorities have said that when principals report a problem in American schools, the parents go to the school and ask, ''What is wrong with the school?'' In Japan, the parent goes to the school, but the question is, ''What is wrong with my child?'' The difference is profound.

The existence of the individualization paradigm tempers progress toward world-class elementary schooling. Why? Because parental support of education is a strong characteristic of a world-class education system. American adults often undermine this support with negative statements about their own experiences in school or their perceptions that school is not a happy place to be. How many times has one heard an adult say to a child, ''I'll bet you can't wait for summer,'' or ''I hope that you like school better than I did.'' What, therefore, is the ideal paradigm shift? First, elementary school leaders in America must have the slack to develop a generalized, pragmatic educational setting without the constant interference of individuals demanding a personalized agenda. Second, adults must pass positive vibrations to children about school. The transformational elementary school leader must realize the existence of these two paradigms and help educate the populace on the need for a paradigm shift.

Religious Sectarianism

Religion played an important role in colonial schools. Sadker and Sadker (1994) state that the purpose of colonial education was to save souls and teach children to read. The same religious fervor that drove the Puritans to the United States also drove them toward education. The Puritans stressed schooling as a means of establishing and maintaining a society peopled by righteous men and women. As early as 1642, the Massachusetts General Court required parents to see that their children could read and understand religious principles. A few years later the Massachusetts General Court enacted the "Old Deluder Satan Law," requiring towns of 50 or more families to appoint a teacher of reading and writing. The mission was to block Satan's constant attempt to keep individuals from learning the Scriptures. Primary education in the Middle Atlantic colonies followed religious dictates even to the extent of establishing the roots of private and parochial schooling. In the southern colonies, the existence of large isolated plantations retarded the growth of public schooling, but religion played a part in curriculum offered by tutors and the formal public and parochial schools that did develop (Gutek, 1983).

Religion played a key role in the curriculum of colonial primary schools. Bible reading and prayer continued to be a major part of common school practice for years after the formation of the United States in 1789. Sectarian authorities, however, gradually lost control of public education as private individuals and religious groups established schools of their own. In Massachusetts, the state and popularly elected local school committees totally exercised control of education (Binder, 1974). Pulliam (1976) makes the point that the desire for greater religious freedom contributed to the doctrine of separation of church and state in American schools. The various and numerous sects in America could reach no consensus concerning religious principles to be taught in public schools, so they opened and controlled their own schools.

It is a pattern of disagreement about religious teachings that forms the religious paradigm that educational leaders must cope with today. During the past few decades, numerous court cases have ruled that religious practices in public schools are unconstitutional. The major problem on the surface concerns Christmas programs, religious exercises, and the reading of Scripture as part of the school program. The religious sectarian paradigm, however, is more widespread and prevents American elementary schools from teaching values at a time when students are vulnerable to learning right from wrong. Later in the chapter, the reader will see that religious or ethics education is within the educational goals of other successful world-class schools. The American religious sectarian paradigm limits the scope and effectiveness of America's elementary schools.

Universal Education

Universal education is the American dream to educate all youth in the same environment by exercising the concept of equal opportunity. The "Age of the Common School," the name popularly given to the 35 years preceding the end of the Civil War, characterizes the paradigm of universal education. During this period, a largely successful campaign to attain free, universal, public schooling on the elementary level occurred. The importance of this campaign becomes more significant when one realizes that during this period of American history, the population of the United States increased about two and one-half times. Even in a rapidly growing nation, America began its unceasing march toward the urban-industrial nation it has now become. The movement to improve the quality of the free public schools and to extend their influence was one of many ventures in reform (Binder, 1974).

Horace Mann, Henry Bernard, and others espoused the common school as an elementary school (1) supported by public taxation, primarily the property tax; (2) open to all children living within the attendance area it served; and (3) offering a curriculum that consisted in most instances of reading, writing, spelling, arithmetic, health, history, geography, music, and art (Gutek, 1983). Mann believed that the common school could solve all societal problems and even believed that America might see the day when training at the schoolhouse would make law enforcement unnecessary (Spring, 1994).

The paradigm of the graded elementary school started around 1820 and became firmly established as the common school developed (hence the name *grade school*). By the Civil War era, Cremin (1970) reported that a majority of states had established public school systems and half of the nation's children were receiving formal education. Society launched the argument that the rich had an obligation to provide education for the poor and that school should be the right of every child. The payback was to be the development of law-abiding citizens and an educational system that would provide social and economic mobility (Ornstein and Levine, 1985). The negative side of this development, however, was that by 1860, the common elementary school was a crowded, one-room school with poor lighting, bad ventilation, and inadequate furniture. There was no systematic curriculum, and recitation was the norm. Severe discipline stifled creativity. Nevertheless, the paradigm of free, tax-supported, public education had been generally accepted (Pulliam, 1976). The common school paradigm, however, excluded many children of immigrants and slaves who received little or no education, and females who received an education geared only toward homemaking skills.

By the mid to late 19th century, elementary teachers trained for careers in normal schools appeared in the paradigm. The common schools of the 19th century varied from large graded urban schools to the common rural one-room schoolhouse. The McGuffy Reader epitomized literacy, hard work, diligence, patriotism, heroism, and virtuous living. Graded readers that appeared around 1840 paved the way for a totally graded system toward the end of the century (Ornstein and Levine, 1985).

Consolidation marked the evolvement of elementary education during the first decades of the 20th century. Industrialization promoted the need for universal education especially through the elementary level. Rural and urban America featured formal schools emphasizing rote learning. The principles of scientific management affected school management, and bureaucratic ideas permeated school administration. Elementary schooling continued to reach more and more students, but students left schools in large numbers when they became old enough to work in America's new factories.

The Progressive Movement was a reaction to the structured schools of the scientific era. Led by John Dewey, progressives introduced activities, projects, problem solving, field trips, and laboratory learning into elementary schools (Gutek, 1983). Democracy in the classroom became a goal in a society characterized by the Human Relations Era.

During the 1950s, educators stressed academic rigor characterized by drill and seat work. Testing and tracking became common elements of the elementary school populated by almost every youth of elementary school age. A reactionary period followed, however. By 1960, the common school movement moved from the graded school to a nongraded plan. Educators built open classrooms to accommodate the flexible scheduling of students allowed to learn at their own pace. The continuous progress curriculum and individually guided instruction became organized or in some cases, disorganized in the elementary school. Relevancy became the test for the elementary curriculum. In the late 1970s, both educators and parents became disenchanted with the nongraded school, and the "Back to Basics" movement dominated the American elementary school (Gutek, 1983). During the early 1980s, elementary schools were forced to respond to a series of reports crying American education was at-risk. A cry for standards that would increase productivity surfaced and a desire for stronger international competition has became a goal of American schools during the past 10 years.

These paradigms with deep roots in the American common school continue to shape today's elementary school. But the paradigm often shifts so rapidly that the educator wonders if any permanence will come to the schoolhouse door. The elementary educator faces a shifting paradigm that sometimes covets relaxed, individualized instruction and then turns fickle and embraces structured, traditional learning. Classrooms open and close depending on curriculum and pedagogy developed by researchers bent on innovation. The typical state legislature legislates learning one year and changes it the next. But despite this uncertainty, universal education throughout the elementary years is a fact that has been accomplished. The universality of elementary school attendance, however, has not guaranteed the accomplishment of universal literacy. The elementary educator stares at an unstable paradigm that guarantees free public education for all youth but has not produced a model for securing the success of that education. Elementary leaders must manipulate the current paradigm of universal education to incorporate the hopes and dreams of the founders of the American common school.

Social Education

During the colonial period and through the first quarter of the 19th century, elementary education in America was class conscious. Elementary education was for the rich, and the common man struggled to gain an education at home or went without. A rigid class system continued to influence education until comparatively recent times. The role of education to racially integrate society—particularly schools—is well documented throughout the later half of the 20th century. Equal opportunity for females in American education gained attention during the same period of history. Unequal educational opportunity for immigrants, minorities, females, and handicapped persons has been an embarrassment for Americans until recent history; the existence of equal education is still questioned as a result of some current practices such as tracking and ability grouping.

The school, therefore, successfully or unsuccessfully has been a general socializing agent responsible for linking the child to his or her society. The old McGuffy Readers provided heavy doses of Christian morality, and children for centuries have been reminded of local mores and expectations. Selakovich (1984), however, reminded Americans that there is not always complete agreement on this function of the school. Community groups and religious groups have different expectations and, in recent times, have expressed them more vocally. Successful socialization may also be hindered by the competence of the teacher and even more important, by the child's peer group. Peer groups become well defined during the elementary years and form a subculture in the school. It seems to the authors that the peer culture is tolerated more in America's schools than in other countries. The breakdown of the American family as a socializing influence tends to increase the influence of the peer group as a major instrument in socialization. The issues of peer influence and parent influence are subjects covered in later chapters.

Spring (1994) reiterates that the school has been used in a variety of ways in the 20th century to improve social conditions. Before the turn of the century, Horace Mann expressed the belief that education was the key to solving all social problems. Since the turn of the century, the school has become the symbol for the good society and the hope that the social influence of the school would reach out into the homes and neighborhoods of America. The school is the most available social institution and the least controversial for planning social reform. Spring (1994) cites the War on Poverty led by President Lyndon Johnson in the 1960s as an attempt to reduce social tensions caused by economic inequalities. The War on Poverty created several new programs in America's elementary schools including Head Start programs, Title I programs for the economically and culturally disadvantaged, job training programs, bilingual education, and minority education. Spring (1994) says:

> More than a decade later, poverty has not ended in the United States, and serious doubts were expressed about the role of schooling in ending it. Some argued that the War on Poverty's educational program had never really been given a chance because of inadequate funding by the government and mismanagement by federal bureaucrats. Others insisted that better educational programs could be encouraged and that to develop them would require more time and research. Still others felt that the school could accomplish nothing because of community and family influences on the child. (p. 15)

The Education for All Handicapped Children Act, Public Law 94-142, 1975, started a paradigm that has become burdensome for educational leaders today. Public Law 94-142 answered the need for a law that tackled a significant social problem of the 20th century, namely, the exclusion of the handicapped from schools. The same school system targeted as the great social equalizer often ignored handicapped youngsters. Today, the elementary school leader dare not question the solution to a social problem that school leaders created. However, elementary educators today must cope with a system of educating handicapped children that drains money from the school budget and strains the teacher's ability to educate handicapped children in the same environment with all other children. The average population of handicapped children has climbed to over 12 percent of the school-age population, a figure well above that recorded in other world-class education countries. Society must revisit the historical paradigm providing for the education of the handicapped and discover ways of shifting the paradigm to the benefit of all students.

The 1980s and 1990s produced a broad social agenda for elementary educators. Society has asked educators to help solve the problems of teenage pregnancy, sexually transmitted diseases, abortion, automobile safety, gun safety, conservation, crime, and others. An elementary curriculum already stretched to provide basic education and literacy has became bloated with instructional mandates to teach about social problems and solutions. The chore is compounded by the fact that instruction is to take place without teaching values. The controversy surrounding sex education alone wastes time and energy that the elementary educator could use to better the educational climate. Interest groups question the moral content of most social curricula, raising the question of whether the school should be the panacea for the nation's problems.

Economic Education

Since colonial times, citizens have related economic development and growth to education. First, society expects students to learn about the workplace and the marketplace. Educators teach the virtue of capitalism in America's schools as well as the evil of other economic systems. Educators are expected to teach the roles of management and labor and, hopefully, teach the value of economic cooperation. Second, society expects educators to prepare students for the workplace and to sort students according to individual interests and abilities. Economic education is used as one of the best arguments for public support of education (Spring, 1994).

At the elementary level, work competed with schooling until after World War II. Students often had to enter the workplace rather than the classroom door, and scores of students became noncompleters because of work commitments. Dropouts were needed in the workplace, and the business community was comfortable with this source of uneducated labor. Throughout this period of history, however, society considered schooling of the more able student essential to the establishment of a successful economy, and education remained geared to the more able student.

But the market for untrained labor changed to a market for a trained labor force. In the early 1970s, the federal government initiated projects in career education. Elementary students explored various careers as career education became part of the school's formal curriculum. *A Nation at Risk* and other reports of the early 1980s accelerated the influence of the business world into education classrooms. Business leaders blamed schools for the decline of America's economy and looked longingly at the educational systems of other countries where business bloomed. For the last two or three decades, business officials have blamed schools because students report to the workplace ill-prepared. The onset of technology has exacerbated the problem, as society has given schools the task of training graduates to be technologically literate. Curriculum experts have introduced technical education into the later elementary curriculum, and prevocational courses prepare some later elementary students for secondary vocational education.

In the 1990s, one of the primary focuses of national education remains economic. International competition is a national concern, and society is convinced that a trained workforce is the key to successful competition. The major focus of the goals for the year 2000 is economic competitiveness. Business has found ways to influence the educational agenda by promoting school partnerships, taking sides on tax issues that provide public school support, and by influencing state legislators and local school board members (Spring, 1994).

The economic pressure that characterizes the economic paradigm faced by elementary school leaders today signals for a focus on the purpose of elementary schooling. The mission of world-class elementary schools is lifetime literacy. Preparedness for the workplace is but a small part of this agenda. Economic education belongs in the elementary school but only in its place.

Democracy and Politics in American Education

In the educational arena, democracy and politics are strange bedfellows. Democratic principles promise education responsive to the citizenry. Representative democracy ensures decision making by elective bodies including congress, state legislatures, and local school boards. But control by *elected* citizens also ensures the existence of politics in educational decision making. The interaction of democracy and politics has formed an educational paradigm wielding tremendous influence over elementary education in this country. The democracy paradigm has served us well, but politics often makes the paradigm unresponsive to modern demands.

During the revolutionary period, a rising tide of democracy threatened the dual system of education in America formed during the colonial period in which the elite enjoyed good schools and the masses were largely ignored. In the minds of the colonials, philosophers like John Locke and Jean Jacques Rousseau influenced the rationale for this shift. Pulliam (1976) says that Locke contributed a theoretical basis for the Declaration of Independence that included a strong influence on American educational thought. Educational opportunity for all citizens became more prevalent in the minds of Americans.

Citizens in the United States must be more aware of the moves made during the formation of the union that affect education today. Despite the omission of education in the constitution, plans for a national system of education based on the concept of meritocracy persisted among the country's new statesmen. Noah Webster, who believed in free schools and separation of church and state, wrote one of the most successful textbooks in American history. Thomas Jefferson provided the idea for extending educational opportunity to all citizens and put his ideas into action with a proposal to provide 3 years of free education for all nonslave children. In 1975, The Northwest Ordinance provided for educational support in each new Northwest Territory township (Pulliam, 1976). History documents numerous movements toward a more democratic educational system.

Democratic thinking has prevailed throughout the development of America's schools from the National Period to the present modern era. Beyond the goal of basic literacy, schools have provided such democratic functions as (1) Americanizing immigrants, (2) intensifying patriotism, (3) institutionalizing democratic principles, and (4) fostering the nationalistic ideas of service and allegiance to country. America's schools have moved the United States to a leadership position among the world's nations. Democracy has prevailed despite attempts by other ideologies to prove the idea outdated.

The latest player on the educational scene is the federal government. Federal intervention was rare until the postwar period, but national policy and the political agenda of parties caused the federals to intervene in state and local affairs. Federal intervention generally provides for common education and ensures equal access to a system that previously limited opportunity. The Civil Rights Act (1964), Elementary and Secondary Education Act (1965), and The Education for All Handicapped Children Act (1975) contributed a national agenda to the scope of elementary education. National curriculum guidelines and national testing are now on the drawing board. A bipartisan paradigm shift to additional national influence in the control of schools has been in process for a dozen years, but to date, the Republican Party suggests returning curriculum and testing decisions to each state.

The problem is, however, that democratic government encompasses the political activity necessary to make a democracy work. Elected officials become beholden to party platforms and special interest groups. Staying in office is a powerful motivator that often steers decision making. Spring (1994) points out several problems with Mann's vision of a democratic consensus:

LIBRARY
UNIVERSITY OF ST. FRANCIS
JOLIET, ILLINOIS

(1) All races, religions, and social classes have not mingled within a single common school. Racial segregation continues to exist in American schools even after massive efforts at desegregation in the 1960s and 1970s.

(2) A variety of religious groups, including the Amish and Catholics, have maintained a tradition of parochial schools in opposition to the secularism of the public schools.

(3) Children in wealthy suburbs attend private schools or public schools that are quite different from those in poorer school districts.

(4) The involvement of the American public school in the teaching and development of patriotism has created problems for a democratic society with a variety of religious, ethnic, and political groups. (pp. 11 – 12)

When politics impacts the educational agenda, the question becomes, "What individual or group goals should determine the educational agenda?" The legal power of the state to determine educational policy has allowed state legislatures to establish the learning agenda. "Legislated learning" increased during the 1980s after the many national reports labeled America's schools ineffective in many ways. Local elementary teachers and administrators received mandates that sometimes seem to change yearly and that often seem stifling. Even with talk about site-based management, control from the state capital remains well and strong today. The bureaucracy of the state department of public instruction seems overwhelming to many educators; often, interest groups seem to determine educational legislation rather than educators. The authors find it offensive that state governors formulated the America 2000 Goals without the presence of a professional educator. The results of increased legislated learning are clearly debatable.

At the local level, many educators and citizens question the effectiveness of the board of education in many districts primarily because of politics. If school boards cannot positively change their operation, changes should be made by responsible agencies in America's society. Chalker (1992) calls the local school board a dinosaur and proposes the following future orientation for boards:

At the local level, the traditional board of education should be restructured as education enters the twenty-first century. Whether appointed or elected, the board should be advisory and should be composed of teachers, administrators, parents, community leaders, and university educators. Once useful in a less complex society, the current elected lay board of education is becoming a liability. Too often, politics dominate the local board, and individual board members are not student oriented.

Today's superintendent spends far too much time caring for board members who often have little impact on the instructional success of the school. (p. 7)

Teachers and administrators express frustration with the local board of education and turn to their unions for relief. The turf battles between the unions and the school board are often disruptive, and the use of the strike by the union to achieve its means becomes more and more distasteful to the public. In Michigan, one of America's most unionized states, 1994 legislation now penalizes union members who strike. If Michigan is attempting to limit the influence of teacher unions, other states cannot be far behind.

Legislators, board members, and educators themselves are susceptible to the interests of a variety of religious, ethnic, and political groups. The opinions of the various groups are often contradictory, and many groups leave little room for negotiation. Extralegal political action often disrupts the decision-making process as much as legal action. Educational leaders must work in an atmosphere where lawsuits may be initiated not only for negligence but for political reasons. The question becomes, ''Whose political agenda is the educator to follow?'' The elementary leader must deal with that question continually as he or she steers the ship.

COMPARATIVE DEVELOPMENT OF HISTORICAL PARADIGMS IN THE EDUCATIONAL SYSTEMS OF FOUR WORLD-CLASS COUNTRIES

Chapter 1 explains why the authors selected nine foreign countries as world-class education countries. Like the United States, the educational system in each country exists partially because of the historical development of paradigms that define the cultural mores and educational expectations of the citizenry. The elementary educator can learn from the history of others successful in the pursuit of education, as well as from U.S. history. Following is a brief synopsis of events that shaped the educational systems in four of the world-class countries: Canada, Germany, New Zealand, and the Republic of Korea. Every effort is made to compare events with similar happenings in the United States. Brief is a meaningful descriptor. A more extensive historical picture is available by consulting references at the end of the chapter.

During World War II, other countries occupied 5 of the 10 nations named in Chapter 1 as world-class countries: France, Germany, Japan, Korea, and Taiwan. Following World War II, each occupied country had the unique opportunity to reorganize its educational system. In most cases, reorganization meant combining the best of the nation's historical paradigms with fresh ideas from outside. Without the strain of national defense and with restructuring money, these countries built or rebuilt world-class educational systems. Certainly other influences were at work—influences that differed from country to country, but the fresh start seemed to provide a motivational thrust that has resulted in world-class education.

The authors selected Germany as one reorganized country that offers American educators opportunity for comparison. Two paradigms prevalent in the current educational system characterize best the historical development of Germany's educational system: political unity manifested in nationalism and economic education.

Germany

Germany's schools are rooted in church and state. The Reformation had a profound influence on German education, as Martin Luther preached that the function of schools was to give every individual direct access to the Scriptures and to make possible a religious experience. The closeness of the relationship between church and education continued into the 17th century. A more insistent influence on German education came from political sources beginning in the 18th century. Hearnden (1976) notes that, ''An edict in Weimar in 1733 stated that henceforth the *Gymnasium* was to turn out not merely future theologians, physicians and lawyers, but men who wish to serve God and fatherland in other

TABLE 2.2 The Grundschule: *elementary education in Germany, 1990.*

Number of Grundschulen:	14,345
Number of students in Grundschulen:	2,534,600
Grades in Grundschule:	Grades 1–4 (in Berlin and Brandenburg, 1–6)
Length of Grundschule day:	8 A.M. to 12 noon
Length of Grundschule year:	190 days

Source: Report of the Development of Education in the Federal Republic of Germany 1990–1992 (1992).

political offices'' (pp. 10−13). Educators helped foster political unity during the 19th century and helped make Germany a world power in the 20th century. For centuries, German universities spawned the ideals of humanism in Germany's schools, but by the 20th century, an ambitious political agenda caused Germans to reject humanism in favor of politics and nationalism. The goal of political unity and nationalism brought Germany to war during World War I, and the education system gained credit for dissemination of the political agenda. A major educational interest after the defeat of 1918 was the restoration of German cultural pride and the unification of the country.

When the Nazi Party assumed power in 1933, Germans were arguably the best educated populace in the world (Fishman, 1993). The schools became the means for disseminating Nazi ideology, promoting the idea of a gifted class, and convincing students of the need for serious study to advance the government agenda. The near success of that agenda during World War II is well documented.

The occupation of Germany following World War II split the country, but the political paradigm still dominated the schools. The Constitution of 1949 established state control with policy formation vested in the *Länder* of two different Germanies. The German Democratic Republic (GDR), under Communist influence, adopted the goal of a ''universally developed socialist personality.'' Educators taught students the Marxist-Lenin philosophy. In West Germany, leaders stressed education as a civil right with emphasis on self-fulfillment (Führ, 1992). However, the efforts of the British, American, and French authorities to stimulate a desire for change in the system only fortified a German resolve to maintain educational tradition. The two main strands of the tradition were the maintenance of the Gymnasium as preparation for the university and maintenance of the general education of the *Volksschule* as preparation for apprenticeship and a trade (Hearnden, 1976). The historical perspective of the educational development of the two Germanies between the years 1949 and 1990 reveals variations in achievement. East Germany appeared to surge ahead at the beginning of the period, but the Federal Republic closed the gap and gained a reputation for success that increased until the two systems consolidated. In 1990, the GDR dissolved, and the educational system incorporated the objectives of the Federal Republic. Today the national government vests educational control in the 16 Länder, but national purpose prevails in mutual recognition by the Länder of the school-leaving certificate issued by the separate 16 Länder and the continuing objective of the German people to excel. Nationalism continues to drive the German educational system toward excellence.

Economic education is the second historical paradigm responsible for the recognition of Germany's educational system as world-class. Throughout history, Germany remained an industrial giant because of an emphasis on vocational education and cooperation between the schools and the management and labor components of industry. The Federal Republic placed major emphasis on vocational education during the period of the two Germanies, and the German school-to-work program is world-class in today's educational arena. The *Report of the Development of Education in the Federal Republic of Germany 1990–1992* (1992) clearly focuses the importance of united German economic education.

> One of the main aims of the work of the Standing Conference of the Ministers of Education and Cultural Affairs is to ensure the *equal status of general and vocational education*. Vocational education is an important element of the German system. The future social status of vocational education should reflect this fact more strongly. The different levels of vocational education will thus be examined to see whether, through an upgrading of their formal status—as a rule complemented by additional classes in general education subjects or by greater integration of general education subject matter in the vocational subjects—a general education qualification can be acquired through courses alongside the specific vocation qualification. Measures such as these should make vocational education a credible alternative for both parents and young people to the courses offered in general education schools. (p. 19)

Political prowess and economic development work closely together as objectives for German educators. Germany has embraced the two goals for centuries and has today made their accomplishment world-class.

Republic of Korea

Korea has produced one of the most successful educational systems in the world. Korean education today profiles skillful teachers, highly motivated students, and achievement scores that are currently the highest of all developed countries. The historical paradigms forming the roots for this achievement are the family, religious beliefs, and a strong individual desire for education (Smith, 1994).

TABLE 2.3 *Elementary education in Korea, 1992.*

Number of elementary schools:	6400
Number of elementary students:	4,900,000
Elementary grades:	Grades 1–6
Length of elementary school year:	4–6 hours
Length of elementary school day:	220 days

Source: Smith (1994).

The values inherent in the ideas of Confucianism include respect for family and hard work. Sorensen (1994) recognizes the influence of Confucianism but postulates that today Korean children are motivated to work for educational success by prospects for concrete success in the workaday world. Both elements of the Korean culture appear important. Both have historical roots.

The most obvious element, claims Sorensen (1994), is the family structure. A strong family head, a clear division of labor, a defined succession to the male line, and the existence of filial piety (the obligation of children to care for parents during old age) cause effective parental pressure on children to succeed in school. Parents sacrifice to support their children's education. Funding for "cram schools" comes from the top of the family budget, and parents plan their time to monitor student homework and support the child during the school day. Korean children understand that their success is not only for themselves but for the whole family, and they understand early that each has a heavy responsibility to work hard on education.

A strong desire for education also abides in Korea. Most countries reward educational success, but what distinguishes South Korean students from students in other countries is not the condition of education, but rather students' assiduous attention to their studies resulting from a highly motivated social pressure to succeed. South Koreans' educational success seems less a matter of curriculum, class size, and educational technique than a consequence of how education is embedded in the fabric of Korean society (Sorensen, 1994). The degree of social pressure varies in other countries, but none appears greater or more successful than the social pressure prevalent in Korea.

The Korean educational system does deserve credit for using these social educational paradigms wisely. After the Korean War in 1968, the government restructured education by producing the *Charter of National*

Education. Modernization built on the traditions of the past characterizes the Charter's new educational paradigm. Well-trained and respected teachers deliver the curriculum that has two major components: (1) the transmission of knowledge and (2) the transmission of values, morals, and ethical priorities, undoubtedly the most important of the two in terms of success (Smith, 1994). The two components should provide food for thought for American educators, but unfortunately, the second goal dealing with values calls for values, morals, and ethics to be taught outside of the school room. This is unfortunate for the "values in the schoolroom" paradigm is characteristic of world-class schools.

New Zealand

Before British settlers populated New Zealand, the Maori society had its own institutions of learning. The Maori turned to the teachings of missionaries as Europeans penetrated the country, and by the mid-19th century, a considerable proportion of the Maori people could read and write. The British settlers saw primary education as a function of the church, and the first primary school in the Province of Nelson was a Sunday school. New Zealand had a brief period of provincial education from 1852 to 1876; amazingly, in Nelson, 70 percent of the province's children were attending school (Dakin, 1973). It should be of interest to American educators, however, that New Zealand abolished provincial education in 1877 because of slow and unequal progress toward universal education. New Zealand created a national system of education in 1877, and formation of the paradigm of national curriculum and national assessment started. Educators throughout the world recognize the excellence of New Zealand's curriculum. Whole language, reading recovery, and hands-on mathematics are curriculum innovations familiar to most of the world's elementary educators. Educators in the United States have adopted many of these initiatives during the past two decades. Since 1877, New Zealand has required primary teachers to teach subjects listed in national curriculum statements or syllabuses. The subjects are remarkably the same as subjects taught in elementary schools throughout all modern industrialized countries today, but they are standardized for all children. The New Zealand Department of Education requires of all students reading, writing, arithmetic, English grammar and composition, geography, history, elementary science and drawing, object lessons, and vocal music. Girls study sewing and needlework and principles of domestic economy, subjects more necessary to the late 19th century. The government issued a "prescription" of what had to be taught and employed inspectors to visit schools to ensure that teachers taught what was prescribed. Promotion depended on the student's mastery of required standards. The curriculum, therefore, was rigid, and teachers used government-developed syllabuses and textbooks to meet prescriptions. The government exercised firm control over curriculum and teaching methodology (McGee, 1994). The results are hard to argue with, for other countries regard New Zealand as the world's most literate society.

A paradigm shift occurred in the 1920s toward more liberal ideas emerging in other nations. The government in 1929 issued a new syllabus known as the "Red Book" urging teachers to use their own initiative in planning and teaching lessons. Teacher initiatives, however, had to remain within the guidelines of the national curriculum, and inspectors continued to monitor the process. During this period, however, the New Zealand Council of Educational Research was founded for the purpose of providing a background of facts and ideas that could help educators plan for the future (Dakin, 1973). Since the 1940s, a method of revision called "rolling revision" has been used to periodically revise each subject area. Important elements of this plan are the use of subject committees to update curriculum and the development of government-funded resources and teacher handbooks to ensure success (McGee, 1994). With funding from the national government, the Department of Education in Wellington supports curriculum development efforts with a trained staff of specialists in specific subject areas. Nobody expects local teachers to be experts in curriculum development, and each teacher keeps up-to-date through the provision of new ideas and materials from the curriculum development unit. The Department of Education does not use commercially produced curricula, because of cost and programmatic nature. Unit groups provide staff development and take a leadership role in curriculum writing.

Throughout the 1960s and 1970s, the Department of Education recognized the local school staff as the body to identify curriculum needs and plan strategies to meet them. Otherwise, two roles distinctly surfaced: (1) national experts in curriculum development design curricula, and accompanying materials and (2) local educators decide the best method for implementing the curriculum (McGee, 1994).

The New Zealand model has produced world-class results in the area of curriculum and instruction. During the past decade, revised cur-

TABLE 2.4 Primary education in New Zealand, 1990.

Number of primary schools:	2342
Number of primary students:	420,426
Primary grades:	Grades 1–8
Length of primary school year:	200 days
Length of primary school day:	5 hours

Source: Barrington (1994).

riculum flowed from government review teams that included teachers in their membership. Local initiatives featured movements familiar to American educators such as child-centered learning, awareness of cultural differences, and interactive teaching-learning approaches. In 1991, the government produced a national discussion document, *The National Curriculum of New Zealand.* It developed a more cohesive framework for national curriculum and suggested new procedures for the assessment of learning particularly by the classroom teacher. The new framework includes eight essential learning skills and also identifies attitudes and values necessary for all students (McGee, 1994). At the primary level, the education department specifies the time to be spent on each subject. An outside specialist conducts a half-hour religious study course each week (Shuker and Adams, 1988).

The number of 3- and 4-year-old children receiving preschool education is as high as any other country in the world. It is estimated that New Zealand preschools enroll 90 percent of 4-year-old students. This preschool paradigm offers a second important study for American educators.

New Zealand provides preschool education mainly through two kinds of voluntary organizations: the Free Kindergarten Associations and the Play Centres Associations. The state assists both organizations through grants from the state. Both groups adhere to the principle that children learn best through free play, and both structure only simple routines that are absolutely necessary. Parents are heavily involved in their child's education through volunteer activities.

State support is an important component of preschool education in New Zealand. The Department of Education has an officer for preschool education and 12 preschool advisors. The state maintains free kindergartens for 5-year-olds. Kindergartens have their own premises usually designed to accommodate up to 80 children who attend either morning or afternoon sessions (Dakin, 1973).

New Zealand national government has supported and/or developed experiences for children from age 3 and up. The result is a world-class curriculum and method of assessment that works for them.

Canada

The authors selected Canada as a research subject for the study of world-class schools because of its physical and cultural proximity to the United States and because the educational system now in place has historically been respected and admired throughout the world. Chalker and Haynes (1994) found numerous similarities between education in the two countries: (1) both countries are leaders in the provision of funding for education, (2) both countries house a variety of ethnic backgrounds, (3) both countries have chosen local control as a primary means of governing education, and (4) both countries face a substantial populace calling for reform. Both authors recently traveled to Canada covering the provinces of New Brunswick, Nova Scotia, and Ontario. The paradigms that developed in Canada look much like the paradigms of American schools discussed earlier in the chapter, although exciting differences exist. American scholars can learn from the parallel development of Canadian education, a study that hopefully may lead to the development of a North American approach to world-class schools.

During the century and a half of French rule, religious orders started schools in Quebec. French culture spread throughout Canada, and the French influence played a significant role in the shaping of Canadian schools. England seized control of Canada in 1763 and established British parliamentary government between 1763 and 1867. The British North America Act of 1867 established a confederation composed of Nova Scotia, New Brunswick, Quebec, and Ontario and provided for the later entry of other provinces. The confederation did little to provide

TABLE 2.5 Elementary schools in Canada, 1990.

Number of elementary schools:	n/a
Number of elementary students:	2,400,000
Elementary grades:	Grades 1–6 (some include 7 and 8)
Length of elementary school year:	180–200 days
Length of elementary school day:	5 hours

Source: Berg (1994).

education for native Indians who were moved to reservations and Eskimos who were left to pursue their ancient way of life. Under provincial rule, Canada developed from coast to coast during the next decades and gained independence from Britain in 1931. Since gaining recognition as a country, Canada has evolved into a world leader (Johnson, 1961). The educational system received much credit for this success. The historical paradigms presented below that are responsible for this success will look familiar to American educators.

Like Americans, Canadians too have questioned the democratic function of the elementary school. Katz (1974) found Canadian schools very successful in teaching democracy as a social concept. Katz claimed, "That seldom can one find a more democratic, tolerant and classless society than in the Canadian school." But he also called attention to the fact that Canada has no common language, no common economic interest, no common language, and no unifying ideals. The public school must become the laboratory in which to inspire democratic citizenship and to develop free and enlightened Canadians.

The social paradigm also developed in Canadian schools over the past 100 years. Johnson (1961) described the Canadian elementary school in Toronto 100 years ago as follows:

> In organization, the first and most important necessity was to keep the boys and girls separate. This meant several grades combined in one room under one teacher. Such classes often numbered over a hundred children. There were no kindergartens, games or amusements. The teachers were mostly untrained; discipline was rough, with frequent cuffing and caning; of illustrative aids there were none; slates, with the dirty rags they necessitated, were in general use in the lower grades; benches of forms were more common than desks. A good deal of learning was done by chorus repetition. At times pandemonium must have reigned; to many children school meant mostly tedium and sometimes terror; the teacher, under a constant strain, soon developed into a nervous crank. (pp. 3–4)

Johnson (1961) claims that the response of the Canadian elementary school to vast changes in society over the past 100 years has been gradual but thorough. The curriculum broadened in response to social demands including the development of primary courses identical to those offered in the United States. The emphasis upon formality and rote learning gradually changed to a concern for the practical value of subject matter. Child-centered learning, continuous progress, team teaching, discovery learning, and open schools characterized the schools during the 1960s and 1970s (Berg, 1994). The school also assumed many of the instructional functions formerly performed by the family. Canadians called the elementary school "our greatest social experiment." Despite this great social experiment, four purposes of the Canadian school system in the 1960s have drawn criticism: (1) custodial care, (2) sorting of students in social slots, (3) distribution of values, and (4) teaching cognitive skills. During the last two decades, critics have charged that the schools have failed to develop these purposes well.

Despite the fact that all but a handful of countries in the world now have a national system of mass schooling with European origins, a single, national system of education has not developed in Canada. The federal government does assume responsibility for the education of native peoples, and the government has given priority to equalizing the education of Eskimos and native Indians. The federal government assumes responsibility for educating armed forces personnel. But the only semblance of national control is the Council of Ministers of Education, an agency created by the provincial departments of education in 1967 to promote consultation among the provinces about the concerns of education. The council occupies only a single floor at the Ontario Institute for Educational Studies in Toronto, Canada, and completes comparative studies involving the provinces and territories.

Since 1867, the provinces have vested responsibility for education. Provincial education systems differ in organization, policies, and practices. Schools differ in compulsory school attendance ages, the length of the school year, and the years of schooling designated as elementary. Each province has a department of education headed by a minister elected by the provincial legislature. Departments of education have responsibility for supervision and inspection of elementary schools, provision of curricular and school organization guidelines, certification of teachers, and research and support services.

During the 1960s and 1970s, education became even more decentralized with each province giving local school boards more responsibility. The local boards, composed of elected or appointed trustees, became responsible for school management. More generally, they now handle the business aspects, school maintenance, hiring of teachers and negotiation of their salaries, purchase of supplies and equipment, and provision of school transportation. Most provinces authorize local boards to levy taxes and manage grants from provincial departments of education (*Education in Canada*, 1989).

Economic education in Canada also has its roots in the elementary school. By the middle of the 20th century, manual training in the elementary curriculum consisted of training for boys in woodwork, drafting, plastics, sheet metal, and leather work. Girls, to a lesser degree, obtained training in some of these skill areas. The purpose was to give students skill in manipulative devices and to help them acquire a measure of control over materials. Girls received training in home economics (Katz, 1974).

At one time students in the elementary school prepared for high schools that were either predominately academic institutions or vocational schools that were separate institutions. Today, in addition to technical and vocational high schools, most secondary schools are comprehensive and offer both programs (*Education in Canada*, 1989). In Ontario, the Department of Education has eliminated vocational high schools (Connelly, 1995). Pressure to develop a competent and competitive workforce in Canada prevails in Canada as it does in the United States. In fact, Canada's economic welfare throughout its development has been closely linked to the economy of the United States. This has not always been a pleasant situation for Canadians. Schools must deal with the interdependence of the two countries, always stressing the national and economic identity of Canada.

A continuing crisis in Canadian education is the fear that American practices will dictate Canadian education. Canadians have been worrying about U.S. dominance ever since the Revolutionary War created a boundary between the two countries. The Canadians throughout history copied many elements of American education, and the drift of ideas back and forth across the border continues today. Innerd (1995), a Professor of Education at the University of Windsor, claims, however, that education in Ontario is more British in origin and that Ontario classrooms have a distinct flavor.

Americans studying the development of Canadian education will find the development of some paradigms that differ from the United States, but the similarities make comparisons worthwhile. As American educators look for practical ways of making America's elementary schools world-class, they should know that similarities found in Canadian schools offer as much knowledge as the more profound differences found earlier in Germany, Korea, and New Zealand.

WORLD-CLASS IMPLICATIONS OF
HISTORICAL PARADIGMS

Toward the end of the 19th century, legislators in New Zealand abolished provincial education and nationalized the education system.

At about the same time, Canadian leaders established education as the sole responsibility of each provincial government. Two English-speaking nations sharing British traditions took different approaches to educational governance. One century later, those historical decisions impact the educational decisions of each nation. Citizens in New Zealand seem content with a nationalized system, whereas Canadian citizens attempt to make 10 different systems more accountable.

The struggle for control of education continues in the United States with elements of both state and local control and national control. Citizens in the United States struggle to determine the role of the federal government as a complement to education provided by each of the 50 states. State governments have had the most recent impact on elementary school leaders with increased regulatory statutes, curriculum innovations, and additional assessment devices. School leaders now wait for a paradigm shift to national curriculum guidelines and national tests promised by Washington and an attempt to deliver national goals identified by state governors. But wait they will, for the Republican agenda in 1995 has placed national curriculum and testing off the agenda. Although control shifts back to the state, educators seem confused by a

Teacher education majors from Western Carolina University visit Jordanhill School in Glasgow, Scotland to learn about schools in other lands. The school's headmaster joins them, lower left (photo by Loughlin).

decade of legislated learning from the state that often conflicts with a call for site-based management. Decision making is confused by the many directions and direction changes that appear at the schoolhouse door. School leaders deserve a concentrated, directed mission for America's schools that is evident in New Zealand.

The German experience is interesting. The strong national and political paradigm that developed historically in Germany could not be sidetracked by the four powers who occupied divided Germany after World War II. Each of the three Western powers infused their own ideas into the German system, but education in West Germany returned to roots established before 1933, and the integrity of the Gymnasium and the stress on vocational education returned to the educational system. When West and East united in 1990, the educational model of West Germany prevailed. The German educational system performs well today according to international standards, and nationalism continues to motivate those in the system. The historical paradigm was too strong to change.

The resolve to keep American education strong compares weakly with the nationalism present in modern Germany. Many Americans would dismantle the public schools in America rather than make them a national treasure. Americans can learn from the Germans the importance of national strength and the role of the educational system in providing national excellence.

The Republic of Korea historically established schools as institutions to establish personal and societal values. Today Korean elementary schools still identify and teach personal values and societal values. Confucian values cause the Korean family to pressure young members of the family to succeed in school for the sake of their family if not for themselves. Education also legitimizes high social status (Sorensen, 1994), and why not if high social status is a product of education.

It is well documented that the family in the United States is often fragmented and often discourages success in school rather than encouraging success. High social status is often associated with wealth, social class, or talent rather than success in school. The lack of respect for teachers is a classic example of this fact. Korea models for Americans the importance of valuing education or as Chalker and Haynes (1994) report, the establishment of an "education ethic."

The similarities and differences among education in Canada and the United States pose interesting implications. Gaffield (1994) makes several observations based on his studies of achievement in Canada and the United States:

(1) In the United States, many citizens continue to view home and school as quite distinct spheres with respect to the formal curriculum, and the ideal student is one who appears to do well in school without much effort. However, intellectuals have higher status in Canada. Educational policies are more collectivist in their approach, with the goal being to bring all children to the same level of achievement.

(2) Parents in the United States continue to espouse the value of the "self-made man." Otherwise, learning takes place outside the school as well as inside the classroom. In contrast, academic training in schools makes a greater impact on children's test results in Quebec and British Columbia than it does in the United States or Ontario for that matter.

(3) In both countries, recent years have produced new momentum to focus schools on academic achievement, to establish a partnership between parents and teachers in formal education, and to reassess

An old Chinese saying is: "The slow bird starts early." Here a Taiwanese teacher provides out-of-class tutoring to a student who needs extra time to learn (photo courtesy of the Ministry of Education, Republic of China).

the articulation between schooling and the labor market. Citizens in both countries have experienced a decade or more of public criticism of public schooling making changes in mass-schooling inevitable.

Elementary schools in both Canada and the United States seem structured around the agenda of the family. Often, activities in the home and community take precedence over school activities. This factor weakens the elementary school in both countries as an enhancer of academic performance. In recent years, momentum to enhance academics does seem more focused. Both countries, however, must take into account the complex relationship between children's lives and academic performance (Gaffield, 1994).

In summary, Americans can reach world-class status in two different ways:

(1) The United States can continue to compare itself with other successful countries and yearn to adopt their practices. Frustration will continue, however, because our historical paradigms are quite different and difficult to change. Americans might not wish to mirror the practices of other countries. How difficult it would be, for example, to increase the school year in the United States to 220 days. The United States can only borrow those features of world-class education that fit America's cultural past, and leaders should borrow these features with all haste.

(2) The United States can make the uniqueness of American education world-class. We must know where we have been and use that knowledge to shape the future. Education in the United States has produced a country that leads the world in 1996. American educators need not be ashamed. The remaining chapters of this book focus on changes that elementary educators can use to make a world-class difference.

REFERENCES

Barker, J. A. 1993. *Discovering the Future: Paradigm Pioneers.* Burnsville, MN: Charthouse International Learning Corporation.

Barrington, J. M. 1994. "New Zealand: System of Education," in *The International Encyclopedia of Education, Vol. 7.* Second edition. Husen, T., and T. N. Postlethwaite, eds. Great Britain: Pergamon, pp. 4104–4111.

Berg, D. L. 1994. "Canada: System of Education," in *The International Encyclopedia of Education, Vol. 2.* Second edition. Husen, T., and T. N. Postlethwaite, eds. Great Britain: Pergamon, pp. 618–626.

Binder, F. 1974. *The Age of the Common School, 1830–1865.* New York: John Wiley and Sons, Inc.

Chalker, D. 1992. "Refocusing School Leadership for the 21st Century Across the Board," *The Education Digest,* 3(58):4–8 [Condensed from *Thresholds in Education,* (18):26–30].

Chalker, D. M. and R. M. Haynes. 1994. *World Class Schools: New Standards for Education.* Lancaster, PA: Technomic Publishing Company, Inc.

Connelly, G. 1995. Interview (June 12).

Cremin, L. 1970. *American Education: The Colonial Experience, 1607–1783.* New York: Harper and Row.

Dakin, J. C. 1973. *Education in New Zealand.* Hamden, Connecticut: Archon Books, an imprint of The Shoe String Press, Inc.

Education in Canada. 1989. Reference Series N. 39, Ottawa, Canada: External Communications Division, External Affairs and International Trade Canada.

Fishman, S. 1993. "Germany: Education," *Encyclopedia Americana, Vol. 12.* Danbury, Connecticut: Grolier, Inc., pp. 621–625.

Führ, C. 1992. *On the Education System in the Five New Laender of the Federal Republic of Germany.* Cologne, Germany: Inter Nationes Bonn.

Gaffiled, C. 1994. "Children's Lives and Academic Achievement in Canada and the United States," *Comparative Education Review,* 38(1):36–65.

Gutek, G. 1983. *Education and Schooling in America.* Englewood Cliffs, NJ: Prentice-Hall, Inc.

Hearnden, A. 1976. *Education in the Two Germanies.* Boulder, CO: Westview Press.

Innerd, W. 1995. Interview (June 9).

Johnson, F. H. 1961. "The Elementary School as a Social Institution," in *Elementary Education in Canada.* Joseph Katz, ed. Toronto, Canada: McGraw-Hill Company of Canada Limited, pp.1–19.

Katz, J. 1974. *Education in Canada.* World Education Series. Hamden, Connecticut: Archon Books, an imprint of The Shoe String Press, Inc.

McGee, C. 1994. "The Teacher and Curriculum Development," in *The Professional Practice of Teaching.* Clive McGee and Deborah Fraser, eds. Palmerstown, North New Zealand: The Dunsmore Press Limited.

Ornstein, A. C. and D. U. Levine. 1985. *An Introduction to the Foundations of Education.* Third edition. Boston, MA: Houghton Mifflin Company.

Pulliam, J. 1976. *History of Education in America.* Second edition. Columbus, Ohio: Bell and Howell Company, Charles E. Merrill Publishing Company.

Report of the Development of Education in the Federal Republic of Germany 1990–1992. 1992. Report of the Federal Republic of Germany for the 43rd Session of the International Conference on Education. Bonn: Secretariat of the Standing Conference of the Ministers of Education and Cultural Affairs of the Lander in the Federal Republic of Germany.

Sadker, M. P. and D. M. Sadker. 1994. *Teachers, Schools and Society.* Third edition. New York: McGraw-Hill.

Selakovich, D. 1984. *Schooling in America: Social Foundations of Education.* New York: Longman, Inc.

Shuker, R. and R. S. Adams. 1988. "New Zealand," in *World Education Encyclopedia, Vol. 2.* George Kuran, ed. New York: Facts on File Publication, pp. 925–944.

Smith, D. C. 1994. *Elementary Teacher Education in Korea.* Bloomington, Indiana: Phi Delta Kappa Educational Foundation.

Sorensen, C. W. 1994. "Success and Education in South Korea," *Comparative Education Review,* 1(38):10–35.

Spring, J. 1994. *American Education.* Sixth edition. New York: McGraw-Hill Inc.

Valverde, G. A. 1994. "United States: System of Education," in *The International Encyclopedia of Education, Vol. 11.* Second edition. Husen, T., and T. N. Postlethwaite, eds. Great Britain: Pergamon, pp. 6538–6547.

Chapter 3

DEVELOPING A WORLD-CLASS ELEMENTARY SCHOOL CURRICULUM

Learning without thought is useless; thought without learning is dangerous.

— Confucius

This chapter investigates the organization and content of the curriculum in world-class schools. Cartwright's definition of curriculum is simplest and best for this purpose: "The curriculum taught on any given day completes this sentence as the door closes 'All right class, today we are going to . . .'" (Cartwright, circa 1970). Any exploration of the curriculum automatically involves students, teachers, and time on task, all of which are in other chapters in this book. Therefore, this chapter concentrates on: how teachers know *what* to teach, how teachers organize the curriculum, who establishes the curriculum, and unique ideas for American educators who supervise a curriculum.

This chapter is in six major sections: (1) national curriculum standards with New Zealand and Korean examples; (2) preschool programs and the curriculum in Germany and Japan; (3) homework as part of the curriculum, including research and a sample board of education policy; (4) sampling the curriculum in elementary schools, including the French and Japanese structure; (5) samples of policies and research basic to world-class schools; and (6) establishing a world-class curriculum.

The reader should read this, and any other discussion of international curriculum, cautiously. The *names* for the curriculum areas appear to be generic, so at the surface level they may appear to be the same. This invites sophistry—clever but specious reasoning that may be unsound. Deeper investigation into curriculum content and sequence will often

Asian students learn to read multiple alphabets, and to write hundreds of characters. Here Taiwanese students practice "handwriting" by drawing their characters, with subtle additions to characters giving different meaning. Penmanship in these schools is excellent (photo courtesy of the Ministry of Education, Republic of China).

reveal that the unique culture of a society's curriculum greatly affects the organization and delivery of it. For example, studying the aspirations of American mothers of first grade children at the beginning of school revealed the first thing they wanted their child to learn was reading. Similar Japanese mothers rated reading as the last item on their list, ranking ''diligence'' as the lesson they most wanted their child to learn (Hess and Azuma, 1991, p. 3). It may surprise many American educators to learn that the recently revised (1992) Japanese curriculum does not expect Japanese children to become *literate* until the end of lower secondary school (age 15)! This is an example of *why* the reader must be cautious. This example depends on the meaning of the word *literate,* which in Japan, means *fully literate.* Japanese is perhaps the world's most complicated language to learn, involving three distinct forms of writing. First, students learn *hiragana* and *katakana* each of which contains 48 phonetic symbols; English has 26. The third Japanese writing system has more than 2000 symbols! During first grade Japanese children learn to read and write both of the 48 symbol systems, and they learn approximately 200 symbols *annually* during the next 9 years as they master the third system. Small wonder that Japanese mothers want their children to be diligent! A surface reading of the Japanese curriculum reveals language study and reading at grade 1, but a lack of literacy until age 15. Moyer (1995) reported never meeting an illiterate Japanese during 14 years living in Japan. The famous Japanese penchant for order can be seen in Figure 3.1, showing the alphabets to be mastered during first grade.

NATIONAL CURRICULUM STANDARDS

The United States is unlike the others in the way it organizes its curriculum at myriad local levels. Any curriculum is, inherently, a statement of values one generation expects to pass along to the next generation. This is condoned when a nation compels parents to send their children to school (all of the nations studied have compulsory attendance) to learn a certain body of knowledge. The United States and Canada are unique because the other nations follow a nationally prescribed curriculum. One New Zealand educator explained, ''I've never understood *how* American teachers know what to teach or what it means to be an educated American. In my country each teacher knows exactly how their teaching fits what came before and that which follows. You would find New Zealanders have no problem agreeing on the outcomes of education because of our national curriculum'' (Malcolmb, 1993).

Chalker and Haynes (1994, p. 136) concluded that the United States is slowly developing a national curriculum, under the euphemism *frameworks* rather than calling it a national curriculum. The National Council of Teachers of Mathematics has the best developed curriculum, including a course of study, recommended assessment of mastery, suggested methods of teaching, and teacher education standards. At this writing, there are efforts in various stages of development in science, the arts, history, geography, etc. The effort to organize language instruction is difficult with the International Reading Association and the National Council of Teachers of English having feuded over curriculum issues in the past, but now cooperating in a united effort to determine a national framework in language education. Unfortunately, the national effort to assess the outcomes of education, via the National Assessment of Education Progress, is not coordinating with any of the other under-

ワールド・クラス・スクール

HIRAGANA

あ a	か ka	さ sa	た ta	な na	は ha	ま ma	や ya	ら ra	わ wa	
い i	き ki	し shi	ち chi	に ni	ひ hi	み mi		り ri		
う u	く ku	す su	つ tsu	ぬ nu	ふ fu	む mu	ゆ yu	る ru		
え e	け ke	せ se	て te	ね ne	へ he	め me		れ re		
お o	こ ko	そ so	と to	の no	ほ ho	も mo	よ yo	ろ ro	を o	ん n

KATAKANA

ア a	カ ka	サ sa	タ ta	ナ na	ハ ha	マ ma	ヤ ya	ラ ra	ワ wa
イ i	キ ki	シ shi	チ chi	ニ ni	ヒ hi	ミ mi		リ ri	
ウ u	ク ku	ス su	ツ tsu	ヌ nu	フ fu	ム mu	ニ yu	ル ru	
エ e	ケ ke	セ se	テ te	ネ ne	ヘ he	メ me		レ re	
オ o	コ ko	ソ so	ト to	ノ no	ホ ho	モ mo	ヨ yo	ロ ro	ヲ o	ン n

NUMBER	1	2	3	4	5	6	7	8	9	10
PRONUN-CIATION	ICHI	NI	SAN	SHI/ YON	GO	ROKU	SHICHI/ NANA	HACHI	KYU	JU
KANJI	一	二	三	四	五	六	七	八	九	十

Figure 3.1 A copy of hiragana and katakana, the two alphabets Japanese children learn in first grade. The number system is also shown. To the left is a sample of calligraphy, using the third alphabet. Letters are literally drawn, not written. There are subtle variations of basic letters that change the letters meaning. This is read from the top down. The dots separate words. This calligraphy was drawn at the Japan School in Raleigh, North Carolina. Translated roughly, it reads: "world-class schools" (source: unpublished monograph, The Japan School, Raleigh, NC).

48

takings. The authors believe that assessment of mastery should be an integral part of the development of national frameworks, created by the same individuals.

Anyone who is publicly developing a curriculum should expect the process to be controversial and emotional. The first draft of national U.S. history frameworks generated a massive outcry over the question "whose history?" In an effort to be all inclusive, the curriculum failed to mention such major American figures as the Wright Brothers. Despite the denial that a national curriculum is under development, the U.S. Senate voted to reject the draft of the history standards and ordered a redesign. Curriculum, because of the values' statements inherent in detailing learning, is somewhat like art. Frequently, art is outrageous and met with a public outcry. Art evokes strong passions. Curriculum statements evoke a similar form of passion.

Why Have a National Curriculum?

There are national curricula in Great Britain (which first developed theirs in 1988), France, Israel, New Zealand, Taiwan, People's Republic of Korea, Japan, and in many other nations. The latter four nations review and revise their curricula on an established schedule, so the national curriculum exists only for a set period of time. McGee (1994), a New Zealand expert on primary education, explains why a national curriculum makes sense:

> There are several reasons why New Zealand has maintained a national curriculum. [It has had one since 1877.] First, it promoted community acceptance that all children would receive a sound general education. Second, a national curriculum promoted equality of educational opportunity. All had access to the same schooling. Third, geographical mobility had less impact because all schools taught the same curriculum. Fourth, checks could be made on the standard of teaching and learning. Fifth, a government could easily revise the curriculum and disseminate the changes to schools. Sixth, successive governments have had a commitment to fund state education and have supplied essential resources to achieve that goal. At its worst, a national curriculum can produce rigid, conforming classrooms. At its best, a national curriculum can allow innovation and autonomy within a broad framework of suggestions. (p. 4)

American educators frequently cite the 10th amendment to the U.S. Constitution as the basis of state autonomy over the curriculum, reasoning that the word "education" does not even appear in the Constitution.

Nor does the word "democracy." A national curriculum, as McGee explained it, fits within the definition of "general welfare."

There are other advantages with a national curriculum. It allows nationally marketing textbook companies to publish to one content standard rather than a hodgepodge of local standards. A national curriculum allows a population as mobile as that in the United States to move children without academic penalty. In Japan, for example, textbooks conform to standards set by the Ministry of Education, adopted by them, with a list of acceptable books sent to local districts to adopt texts from that list. The American love-hate relationship with textbooks is avoided by Japan in two ways: (1) Japanese texts, which are small by American standards, are given to students, becoming personal property, and (2) teachers teach directly from the books, teaching every page in detail because the book contains the curriculum. This allows the ministry to publish teacher's guides, setting pace and content, and suggesting ways to use effective methods. That frees teachers to use planning time on *how* to teach, not *what* to teach. The national curriculum allows schools to inform parents in advance what the child will be learning and how to support that effort at home. The books are small, in part, to keep the price down, but also to keep them portable so students take them home daily. Many parents buy inexpensive, widely available workbooks to support the child's learning at home, and the nationally marketed workbooks align with the national curriculum. The communication about curriculum content is so clear Scottish inspectors who studied Japanese elementary schools noticed there was great clarity between Japanese teachers and students about teaching and learning (Her Majesty's Inspectorate, 1992, pp. 15 – 16). Such communication can only improve the learning process. Also reduced is the problem of limited instruction, such as in hands-on science, by teachers who are not well versed in a particular area. In the United States, the Mesa, Arizona, schools have an excellent communication vehicle using colorful "learning sequence charts" that fill classroom and workroom walls. Annually, there are booklets about the curriculum sent home for each parent.

A World-Class Idea from Israel

"We think that textbooks in the U.S. are just beautiful. They are written on such nice, expensive paper and they have so many colorful photographs in them. But they are so big, so heavy. In Israel students buy the books and they may keep them at the end of the school year, or they may sell them at a book fair so used textbooks are available for those without enough money to buy new books. They are not printed on such expensive paper, but they are smaller and light weight enough to take the books home every night to do homework. We have a law in Israel that books cannot weigh over a certain amount, so that big books, like Jewish history, are printed in three volumes, but only the volume needed for homework has to go home at night'' (Eldar, 1995).

New Zealand's National Curriculum

Following the development of the national frameworks, aligning with the curriculum allows educators to approach a world-class standard in curriculum. Do not be deceived by the ''frameworks'' versus ''national curriculum'' issue. New Zealand's 125-year-old national curriculum, updated in 1993, became *The New Zealand Curriculum Framework*. The following process guided the curriculum redesign:

(1) During the decade of the 1980s there was a massive education reform movement in New Zealand as there was in most of the developed world.

(2) In 1990 a new conservative government gained control of New Zealand. The core curriculum had been exhaustively reviewed during the 1980s, so the new government launched an ''Achievement Initiative'' with widespread consultation about schools' expectations, what to learn, and how schools and communities could work together. This created momentum for a change.

(3) Both the general public and professional organizations were expected to respond to new curriculum suggestions. McGee (1994, p. 7) reports that in 1987 over 20,000 public responses (roughly 6% of the population!) to questions such as:

• What do you expect of our schools?

• What should young people learn and experience in schools?

• How should schools reflect the many cultures and New Zealand?

• How should all people be given a fair chance in our schools?

• How should people in the schools and community work together?

(4) In 1990 the federal government convened educational experts to draft a new curriculum that reflected the survey's results. In 1991 this draft, along with another questionnaire, got wide circulation for the public's and education's responses.

(5) The refined curriculum framework revision was finished in 1993.

The structure of the New Zealand curriculum reflects principles of learning and teaching, divided into seven essential learning areas: (1) languages, (2) mathematics, (3) science, (4) technology, (5) social studies, (6) the Arts, and (7) health and physical well-being. There are eight essential skills integrated across the entire curriculum: (1) communication skills, (2) numeracy, (3) information, (4) problem solving, (5) self-management and competitive skill (i.e., time management, self-appraisal, enterprise, etc.), (6) social and cooperative skills, (7) physical skills, and (8) work and study skills. Additionally, there is a statement of values and attitudes designed for learning nationally accepted values such as democracy, honesty, reliability, respect for others and the law, tolerance, fairness, compassion, nonsexism and nonracism (McGee, 1994, p. 5). The latter statement is similar to moral education in Japan, patriotism education in Korea, or locally developed religion instruction in the national curriculum in Great Britain. The "character education" movement in the United States is similar to this, and the authors believe an elementary school curriculum should include such education. In Taiwan, it is common for the head to conduct whole school classes on moral education as part of the morning start of school, along with the flag-raising ceremony and the singing of the national anthem (Li, 1995).

New Zealand is unique among the nations with a national curriculum, not suggesting quantities of time teachers should devote to certain subjects.

A National Curriculum from Korea

The national curriculum in the Republic of Korea is redesigned approximately once every 10 years. The Koreans have made great strides during the past decade, lengthening the period of compulsory education from 6 to 9 years, reducing class size from 60 to 48 students per teacher, and revising textbooks as the new curriculum is introduced. There have been six revisions of the curriculum since the end of the

TABLE 3.1 The Korean elementary school curriculum (hours taught per week).

Classification	1st	2nd	3rd	4th	5th	6th
Moral education			2	2	2	2
Korean language	[11	11]	7	6	6	6
Social studies			3	3	4	4
Arithmetic[1]	[6	6]	4	4	5	5
Science			3	4	4	4
Physical education			3	3	3	3
Music	[6	6]	2	2	2	2
Fine arts			2	2	2	2
Crafts			—	2	2	2
Extracurricular	1	1	2	2	2	2
Total	24	25	29	30	32	32

[1] Arithmetic is taught without the use of calculators so students will memorize it.
Note: In grades 1 and 2, 11 hours per week are devoted to moral education, Korean language, and social studies. Six hours per week (7 hours at grade 2) are devoted to physical education, music, fine arts, and crafts.
Source: Ministry of Education, *Education in Korea, 1993–1994*, p. 53.

Korean War. The last revision was in 1992, with the new kindergarten curriculum being introduced first, starting in 1995.

The 1992 curriculum revision was based on four needs:

(1) Decentralization of decision making related to curriculum development
(2) Structural diversity of the curriculum
(3) Relevant content for the curriculum
(4) Efficacy in the operation of the curriculum

The curriculum was designed to produce individuals who were "epitomized by (1) health, (2) independence, (3) creativity and (4) morality" (*Education in Korea, 1993–1994*, 1994, p. 50). Table 3.1 shows the new Korean elementary school curriculum.

With such an organized national curriculum, most people would be surprised to enter a Korean school, where students and teachers could be running around, laughing loudly, and playing games. This is common among eastern Pacific Rim nations, however. The curriculum is designed for a minimum of 34 weeks per year, and 1 teaching hour represents 40 instructional minutes. The other 20 minutes of the hour are spent in very active play sessions, including both students and teachers. As soon as the play period ends, everyone returns to class, assumes a seat, and works for another intense 40 minutes of instruction. The curriculum is taught in individual segments rather than integrating the subject matter. Students often work in cooperative groups with the more academically able students helping slower students. Teachers will provide additional out-of-class assistance for students who need it, but Korean students who need more time to learn the curriculum are simply expected to provide the time.

PRESCHOOL PROGRAMS

Preschool programs are increasingly common in the 10 nations studied. Although the world-class average for years of compulsory education is similar to that of the United States, it is common for students to enroll in school one or more years prior to the compulsory enrollment age. Chalker and Haynes (1994) reported that in North Carolina, for example, the compulsory education age begins at age 7, yet over 90 percent of 5-year-old children enroll in kindergarten or other precompulsory school programs. New Zealand has 50 percent of all children age 2 1/2 enrolled in some form of private preschool program (*New Zealand Official 1994 Yearbook Extracts,* 1994). France reports 97.5 percent of 3- and 4-year-old children attend kindergarten, and 100 percent of students who are 4 years or older attend (Brahm, 1995). Consensus exists among the nations studied that preschool education is important for starting well in school. Yet the state of New Hampshire does not provide publicly funded kindergarten (Linton, 1995). To some extent the international trend toward progressively younger school entering ages may reflect the increasing number of two-earner families.

In Great Britain the National Commission on Education calls for 85 percent of 3-year-old, and 95 percent of 4-year-old children to be enrolled in some form of preschool education program early in the next century. At this writing, Great Britain's Commission on Social Justice wants every 3- and 4-year-old to have access to "nursery" education, linking a good start in school with reduced unemployment and crime (Myers, 1994, p. 11). Another study links quality, early school programs to children's motivation to learn and determination to succeed. Children from low socioeconomic neighborhoods magnify this effect. The British report drew on American studies reporting that money spent in preschool education clearly paid off in the long run, because every $1000 spent for preschooling saved approximately $7160 spent on unemployment, compensatory education, and incarceration of juveniles, not to mention the social costs associated with each of these.

Given the international agreement that quality preschool education is important, two questions remain: (1) what should the preschool curriculum contain and (2) how should preschools and compulsory attendance schools coordinate in the development of a lifelong learner?

German Preschool

Since Friedrich Froebel opened his first preschool program in Germany in 1837, the Germans have been international leaders in the development of preschools and kindergartens. Germany maintains that tradition today with a variety of preschool programs. The *Vorklassen,* preliminary school classes, are voluntary extensions of the Grundschule (primary school) in several Länder. Another form of preschool education is the *Schulkindergärtens* (kindergartens) or other forms of preliminary, school preparation classes in association with the Grundschule. Parents of 6-year-old children have them attend these schools if they are not ready to start school. In either event, the curriculum focuses on learning through play rather than the mastery of subject matter. The objective of these programs is to develop a predisposition to learn, focusing on mental, emotional, and motivational development. The curriculum includes oral expression, movement education, and interest arousal, all individually focused. The curriculum draws on a child's instinct to play and the socialization of the child who learns that school is a neat place to be (Office for Standards in Education, 1993).

The Germans use the term *elementary level* to mean schools organized for children between the third birthday and the day they enter Grundschule (primary school). Führ reported that 75 percent of 3 year olds and over 80 percent of 5 year olds attend kindergarten. German law allows mothers to be away from work during the first year of a child's life, and they view kindergarten as offering "substitute brothers and sisters" for only children. Social development is stressed in the curriculum. During the 1960s and the 1970s there was much debate about kindergarten's role in compensatory education for children from low socioeconomic backgrounds. The emphasis today is on inclusion of children with special needs in "regular" kindergartens. Augmenting the lessons in kindergarten is children's television programming, which provides a German version of "Sesame Street" and a popular program *Augsburger Puppenkiste* among other programs for young children (Führ, 1989, p. 72).

Students with special needs have earlier access to Germany's specialized preschools, called *Sonderkärtens* (special kindergartens) as early as age 2, depending on the diagnosed need. These schools serve selected populations of visually challenged, hearing deficits, mental, physical or emotional challenges, or behavior management disorders. Teachers work in small groups, following an adaptive curriculum. The teachers train for primary school teaching with assistance from special educators. These schools are successful, and experiments with primary school inclusion programs also appear to be succeeding (Office for Standards in Education, 1993, p. 2).

Germany also offers preclasses of kindergarten for developmentally delayed students who are subject to compulsory attendance laws. Unlike kindergartens that are often privately associated with churches, these preclasses are an integral part of the primary school, and they are fully funded by the state. Attendance is voluntary, and the numbers attending have greatly increased in recent years. These schools are also being established at Sonderkärtens (special kindergartens) to meet the needs of challenged children as early as possible. The curriculum in these schools is integrated with the Land's primary schools to assist in the development of the child without stigmatizing the student later on in school (Führ, 1989, p. 71). German Länder are much like U.S. states.

Kindergarten in the Republic of Korea

by Joan Elliot, Ph.D.
Fulbright Scholar of Elementary Korean Education

[Elliot studied early childhood education in the Republic of Korea during 1990. She is a professor at the University of North Carolina at Asheville. Some results of her study are reported here.]

In Korea the home is primarily responsible for preschool education. The mother's role in education may be played by the grandmother or a teacher in a child center. What is apparent is that a child receives vigilant care. The child care center is not necessarily a formal institution. It may use mother volunteers. As opportunities enlarge for mothers to be employed, child centers increase in number.

Children above the age of 5 are exposed to a systematic educational program in kindergarten. The kindergarten program finds its role in laying the foundation for schooling. Children learn in a group; they develop intelligence, curiosity, imagination. Korean kindergarten education aims at providing an appropriate environment for the nursing of preschool children and the promotion of healthy mental and physical growth.

Toward this end, kindergartens in Korea strive to achieve the following objectives:

1. To inculcate habits of joyous daily life and harmonious physical development
2. To develop an ability to understand others and express ideas in correct speed
3. To arouse interest in one's natural and social environment and develop inquisitive habits
4. To develop interest in creative expression in music, dancing, and painting
5. To develop the beginnings of social understanding and cooperation

The kindergarten curriculum is divided into five developmental areas: cognitive, social, emotional, physical, and the development of correct speech. Kindergarten curriculum is developed by the Korean Educational Development Institute (KEDI) and adopted by the Ministry of Education. The Korean curriculum reflects the image of a future-oriented human being—autonomous, creative, moral. While the curriculum is based on curricular objectives at the national level, curricular content can be selected and organized at the local level according to the practical conditions of each community, the characteristics of each program and the developmental level of the children.

Evaluation instruments and methods include five components:

1. Appropriateness of curriculum implementation
2. Suitability of educational environment
3. Efficiency of facilities and equipment
4. Rationality of management and administration
5. Pertinence of the relationship between preschools and local community and family

In the area of curriculum planning and implementation there is much evidence of developmentally appropriate activities and teacher-made materials that reflect current research trends in child development and early childhood education:

- hands-on science centers with vegetables and seeds sprouting, handheld magnifying glasses for children to use
- dramatic play centers with dress-up props, dishes, plastic toy food, sink, telephone
- artwork in abundance displayed throughout the room
- a music center with instruments for children to play in small groups
- children marching around their table, chanting and singing (always accompanied by the teacher on the much-used piano)
- Korean folk stories such as ''The Sister and Brother Who Became the Moon and the Sun'' widely used as learning materials, and the popular foreign stories such as ''Snow White,'' ''Cinderella,'' and ''Pinnochio''
- the main emphasis appears to be on singing and language activities

Kindergarten classrooms are divided into learning centers with small tables and chairs, with the room sectioned off into work or play areas to enable the teacher to work with small groups or individuals.

Classroom size is adequate, and appropriate, colorful manipulatives are in abundance. Kindergarten classrooms, always splashed with multicolors, contain numerous building blocks in varying sizes, inviting rug areas for book sharing, toys, games, and spilling into the hallways, indoor slides, rocking boats, and larger climbing toys.

Public or government kindergartens do not offer academic programs for 5 year olds, preferring a more ideal program according to the developmental philosophy of education, despite parent pressure to make the program academic. A 1987 report to the Ministry of Education warned: ''Mislead zeal for education and overbearing care prompts parents to interfere unjustifiably with school affairs.'' This unusually high degree of enthusiasm for learning is rooted in the Korean cultural heritage. Under Confucian tradition, education was the principal avenue of maintaining social status and success. Much of this subconscious psychology still pervades Korean education today. The result is that children develop a sense of identity that conforms to deeply held beliefs. These beliefs result in the typical Korea kindergarten child who is thoughtful, considerate and who is respectful of parents and teachers. These typical, respectful, and happy children appear to be in abundance in Korean kindergartens.

Japanese Preschool

German preschool programs contrast with those in Japan. The Japanese use day nurseries under the supervision of the Ministry of Health and Welfare as well as kindergartens under the direction of the *Monbusho* (Ministry of Education, 1994, p. 3). Over one-half of the day nurseries, and fewer than one-fourth of the kindergartens have public financing.

The day nurseries exist to accommodate a new trend in Japan—the two-earner family. These schools cater to students of any age up to 6 years, and they operate for 8 hours a day. The kindergartens, however, are open to children between 3 and 6 years of age for 5 hours a day. Low class sizes allow individual attention. They are play centered with a focus on child development. In the kindergartens there is a slight increase in academic focus, but no formal attempt to teach reading exists, although parents often teach it at home and books are readily available for children who want them. The kindergartens follow the national curriculum of Japan with planning around five integrated subjects: health, human relationships, the environment, language, and expression. A study by Scottish school inspectors found surprising variance between the Japanese kindergartens visited. The "quality of work" in one school is reportedly "poor," and inconsistent communications between kindergartens and primary schools exist (The Scottish Office for Education, 1992, p. 19). The type and quality of communication between U.S. programs such as Head Start and the schools could be an area for attention.

A World-Class Idea

From Taiwan

Schools in China were established in 1911 by Dr. Sun Yat-Sen, based on the "Three Principles of the People—namely, Nationalism,

Democracy, and the People's Livelihood. And it was very essential to implement a new education system'' for the new nation to succeed. Following the relocation to Taiwan in 1949, the goals of education were codified in the Constitution of the Republic of China (Taiwan). Part of it is reproduced below and it permeates the curriculum of the Republic of China.

The Goal of Education of the Republic of China

The education of the Republic of China, based on the Three Principles of the People, is to improve national living, support decent existence in the society, pursue economic development, and prolong the life of the nation so as to achieve independence of the nation, implementation of democracy, and advancement of national livelihood. The ultimate goal is to attain to the ideal world of universal brotherhood.

Chapter 13, Section 5, Education and Culture (from the Constitution):

Article 158

Education and culture shall aim at the development of the sense of nationalism, sense of autonomy, national moralities, healthy physique, science knowledge, and earn-a-living ability of the national citizens.

Article 159

All national citizens shall have an equal opportunity to receive education.

Article 160

Those from poor families shall be supplied with textbooks by the Government.

Article 162

All public and private educational and cultural institutions in the country shall, in accordance with law, be subject to supervision of the State.

(Further, in Chapter 10, ''Powers of the Central and Local Governments'' established the cabinet-level Ministry of Education with the requirement that it establish and fund a national school system designed for equal opportunity and achievement of the Three Principles of the People.) *Source:* Ministry of Education, 1994, p. 336.

With such a clear vision for the role and purpose of Chinese education, the establishment of a universal education system and its curriculum was possible. No such system is advocated for U.S. schools, but the impact of this system in Taiwan helps to explain the success of their new school system.

Children with Special Needs

One notable difference between eastern Pacific Rim nations and those in the West, and particularly the United States, is attention to the needs of special students. Eastern Pacific Rim nations generally do not accommodate students' special needs, except for the most severe forms. The Republic of Korea serves less than one-half of 1 percent of its student population with some form of special education (Beauchamp, 1992, p. 16). In Japan, there are no classes for academically gifted students. Although this may sound harsh and surprising to western educators, it springs from Confucian tradition. Japanese parents and educators generally believe in *Gamburo* ("hanging on"), which asserts that student learning comes from hard work, not a gift or the lack of it. Hence, eastern Pacific Rim students sit in heterogeneously grouped classes. Those who finish work quickly may help those who lag behind. Work not completed during school simply becomes homework that slower students finish later. This allows schools to set rigorous standards that the students generally meet (Moyer, 1995).

A Chinese proverb states, ''The slow bird starts early.'' The authors' interviews with numerous eastern Pacific Rim educators, students, and parents reveal a belief that some people simply have to work harder and longer than others to finish a task. The idea of accommodating assignments to meet the special needs of individuals and designing assignments so everyone spends equal learning time is a foreign concept in which there is little interest.

HOMEWORK AS PART OF THE CURRICULUM

Homework is the easiest and least expensive means of extending school learning time. It has a proven impact on student mastery, particularly for slower students or those from lower socioeconomic backgrounds. It is an excellent means for involving parents in the education of their child. Yet the overall quantity of homework given to American students is insufficient and haphazard.

Why is homework so uncommon? It has become traditional and unfashionable to give homework, and both teachers and administrators frequently lack training in the proper use of homework. Additionally, students will not willingly do extra work, particularly if homework is not common. With uneven philosophies of homework, sibling rivalries and social group tension can be heightened if uneven homework expectations occur. Also, parents are not generally given information about the value of homework. Therefore, it lacks support by parents, except among those who have the highest expectations for their children and the highest education themselves.

Homework expectations vary widely internationally. MacBeath and Turner (1990, p. 2) reported that in Belgium homework is not allowed below age 10. Spain prohibits it by law. Luxembourg limits homework to 30 minutes a night during the first year of education. France, with its 27-hour school week and relatively short (currently 180 day) school year, relies on homework to extend learning time. The French report over 50 percent of 13 year olds spend in excess of 2 hours on homework daily (Chalker and Haynes, 1994, p. 105). A group of French middle school children laughed about homework in the United States, expressing amazement that American youth do homework in bed, in front of a TV, or not at all. Children at age 11 often do more than 12 hours of homework each week. Additionally, they are expected to have a desk at home as part of their workstation (Newsam, 1994, p. 16).

The use of homework was studied by the Scottish Department of Education (McBeath and Turner, 1990, p. 9). The following suggestions will help to avoid problms with homework:

- Do not allow for inconsistent use of homework between schools, grades, or teachers. That confuses parents.
- The amount of homework assigned should be consistent.
- Parents need to be informed of the importance of homework and how they can support assignments at home.
- A copy of the policy on homework should be given to parents.

McBeath and Turner (pp. 7 – 10) reported from the research that:

- There is a correlation between the level of home support of student success and the quality of student work.
- Students who struggle in school can out-perform others if they do homework regularly. The Asian idea that ''the slow bird starts early'' is related to this finding.

- Homework should be started when students start school so it is part of the routine.
- Students are going to complain about homework, yet most will continue to like school.
- Both educators and parents find that consistent use of homework develops responsibility and a feeling that students are responsible for their own success. That is an important development.
- Giving clear instructions about an assignment is important if it is to be completed successfully.
- The education of the parents is directly related to the understanding (and completion) of homework by the student.
- Males are less likely to complete homework.

MacBeath and Turner (pp. 11 − 32) recommend the following:

- Learning should occur in the classroom with homework providing further practice.
- Any elementary reading assignment should include comprehension questions. This is an area where parents can assist easily. The second area most commonly used for homework should be math.
- Homework needn't be assigned for one night only. Projects and other activities make good homework assignments, but the deadlines need to be carefully explained to parents, as should the criteria on which it will be graded. Having a means for parents to call with questions is helpful.
- As students mature, they should be expected to assume the responsibility of homework, and parents should encourage that independence.
- Homework should always be directly related to the taught curriculum. It must be graded efficiently, and returned as classwork is. This reinforces the role of homework in the teaching-learning scheme.
- Before starting a homework pattern, the administration needs support from a board of education policy which sanctions homework as part of education. The policy (see proposed sample, Figure 3.2) should provide guidance to teachers and parents. A copy should be sent home.

The authors recommend this study for further reading.

The board of education recognizes that homework is a necessary part of the learning process, teaching students to be responsible, independent learners. Because the United States has one of the shortest school years among developed nations, homework is a means of extending learning time at no expense to taxpayers. It fosters parents' involvement in their child's learning while monitoring their child's progress.

Therefore, the board of education endorses the regular use of homework. Both parents and teachers should discuss this policy with their children.

There will be homework assigned 4 days a week, Monday through Thursday, reflecting the grade level of the child. The length of assignments shown are averages as individual assignments and student learning rates will vary. Parents should confer with teachers if homework is either lacking or excessive.

Kindergarten: 15 minutes per night, limited to reading with the parent
Grades 1 and 2: 30 minutes per night
Grades 3 and 4: 45 minutes per night
Grades 5 and 6: 90 minutes per night
Grades 7 and over: 2 hours per night

Homework should include a reading activity, and the parent should check the child's understanding by discussing it with the child. Beginning at grade 1, mathematics homework will occur at least two nights a week, with additional assignments if needed. On the remaining nights there will be science or social studies homework, or time spent on a project assigned by the teacher. Time spent in school rehearsals or learning activities such as studying for a test, count as homework. Sports-related activities do not count as time spent on homework. Any student regularly failing to do assigned homework may be ineligible for school sports.

Teachers are responsible for assigning and clearly explaining homework. Teachers will monitor the time spent on it to avoid conflicts such as two teachers assigning heavy homework loads the same evening. Homework will directly relate to current classroom instruction. Every teacher will have staff development on the role and purpose of homework. Teachers will assess homework expeditiously and confer with parents about the quality of homework their child does. Homework is to be part of assigning academic grades. It is not be used as punishment. With rare exceptions, all students in the same class will do the same homework assignment. Teachers will keep a portfolio of student homework throughout the year.

Parents should discuss homework with their child, reviewing reading activities nightly. Parents should keep a log of time spent on homework

Figure 3.2 Sample school board policy on elementary school homework.

and discuss it with the teacher regularly. Parents should provide a quiet work environment for the child, away from television and family noise if possible. The school will offer regular parent information sessions on helping the child learn through homework. Homework missed as a result of student absence is to be made up following the policy on makeup work. Students should do their homework. Students will take books home that are part of their homework. If there is confusion about an assignment, students are to ask the teacher for an explanation. Students are to bring books and homework back to school daily.

The board of education recognizes that some family situations may make homework more difficult for some students. In such cases the board encourages the home and school to work together, finding a significant adult to assist with homework or a quiet place to work, based on the needs of the child.

Figure 3.2 (continued) *Sample school board policy on elementary school homework.*

This suggested policy will require adaptation to the community a particular school serves. By having a school board policy an individual school will avoid the problem of inconsistency with others, and so will teachers. Teacher in-service education on homework informs parents that teachers have training in it. Homework needs mention in curriculum guides and parent communications. The impact on time on task may amaze some. Ninety minutes of homework is below the world-class standard for 13-year-old students (2 hours is the standard). Yet it adds 270 hours to the instructional year. On the basis of a 5 1/2 hour day of school, that is the equivalent of almost 10 weeks of additional time on task. It costs nothing.

SAMPLING THE CURRICULUM IN ELEMENTARY SCHOOLS

The structure of world-class school curricula varies by nation. The national elementary school curricula for France and Japan follow. A brief introduction proceeds each.

The Elementary School Curriculum in France

The French education system is the most widely copied in the world.

It has been in flux for the past several decades, and a blend between a national curriculum and local control has emerged which may be of interest to American educators.

Virtually all 3-year-old children attend *écoles maternelles* (nursery schools) which they attend until age 6. Over 99 percent of children by age 4 are in school (Brahm, 1995). The French view the purpose of nursery schools as twofold: they provide a safe place for children away from home, and they stimulate a child's social and intellectual development. Since 12 percent of students in France are the children of immigrants, the importance of the latter role has increased (Anderson-Levitt et al., 1991, p. 80).

They enter *école élémentaire* (elementary school) at age 6 where they spend 5 years at that level prior to moving on to middle school. There is no official tracking in elementary school, although the system has a long history of early grade retentions with as much as one-third of a grade's students retained. There is a strong relationship between retention and social class, with immigrant children disproportionately retained (Anderson-Levitt et al., 1991, p. 81). All students attend school until they reach age 16.

The French elementary school offers 27 hours of instruction weekly. The system is arranged around the concept of "school rhythms" (by day, week, and year) to maximize learning time ("time on task"). According to French research, young children cannot learn for more than 4 hours a day, and learning increases when periods of academic engagement are broken by periods of physical exercise. Although regions vary the way in which they organize an instructional week, Fowler reports: "The school week consists of nine three-hour sessions . . . a typical week would be six hours on Monday and Tuesday; Wednesday off; six hours on Thursday and Friday; three hours on Saturday; Sunday off." On days when there are 6 hours of instruction, they break the routine with a 2-hour lunch so children can go home. The curriculum includes 5 hours a week of physical education, which helps to break the academic routine as well (Fowler, 1988, p. 9).

Most French children, following 3 years of nursery school, arrive at elementary school with some sight-reading skills, knowing their colors, able to recite the alphabet, and counting. As in the United States there is a debate about phonics versus whole language instruction, and most teachers use a blend of the two. Those who cannot decode proficiently usually repeat the grade with disastrous results. Ninety-three percent of students who repeat first grade never make it to *lycée* (Anderson-Levitt et al., 1991, p. 81). French elementary education divides into three parts or courses:

- *Cours préparatoire,* or preparatory course, is grade 1. Students begin to learn to read at this level. Essay testing also begins at this age (Pierre, 1993). The children have basal textbooks to learn reading skills. Within the 27-hour teaching week, at least one-third of the time is used on reading and writing lessons. Mathematics is stressed 6 hours a week. By the end of the grade students can count to 100 and add two-digit numbers vertically (Anderson-Levitt et al., 1991, p. 84). Science education is "science and technology" with computers commonly used. Social studies education has lagged as have test scores in that area.
- *Cours élémentaire,* the elementary course, is grades 2 and 3. The second grade includes grammar and more writing with the same curriculum balance as first grade. The third grade level is largely an expanded repetition of the second grade curriculum. Language and mathematics instruction continues to be emphasized, receiving nearly half of the instructional time each week.
- *Cours moyen,* or the intermediate course, is when the fifth grade curriculum expands on and repeats the fourth grade curriculum. Starting at grade 4 students must receive 50 hours of computer education annually; that is continued in fifth grade. Most elementary schools are equipped with computer labs. Second language instruction is started in grade 4. By fifth grade students use decimals, fractions, and simple geometry, and they solve measurement problems. They read silently with comprehension and write with grammar properly used. Teachers continue to use dictation for spelling.

The curriculum is closely defined, but teaching methods are left up to the teacher. Homework is an integral part of the learning process. Since 1993 the school year grew by 8 additional days, to 180 days (Brahm, 1995).

The Elementary School Curriculum in Japan

Japan underwent a scheduled curriculum renovation in 1992. The new curriculum stressed the development of lifelong learning. The fabled

Japanese textbooks are written to a single national curriculum so they automatically align. Several books for early elementary school make a light, portable stack to go home every night. The book bag (background) is made to official size standards for the books to fit in. A space inside the book bag is designed for teacher or parent to send a note; parents and teachers check that space daily (photo by Haynes).

Japanese school year underwent changes. The 1990 school year had been 240 days. Saturday classes are one-half day long. The Monbusho reduced the school year by one Saturday a month in 1992. Parents complained loudly, not knowing what to do with children who had a Saturday off. As a result the Monbusho issued a lengthy guide of educational activities for parents to use with their children. In 1994 the Monbusho reduced the school year by another Saturday a month. There was again a loud outcry. This time the outcry came from students who complained the curriculum was as demanding as ever while the time for learning it was too short. The Monbusho requires 210 days of instruction. Other days were for festivals and other nonacademic activities. Table 3.2 displays the Japanese elementary school curriculum as redesigned in 1992. The number of instructional hours are shown for each area. The Monbusho provides something akin to a course syllabus or curriculum guide so that teachers know what to teach and the pace to follow. Teacher planning concentrates on how to best teach what the Monbusho expects to have taught.

The Japanese curriculum considers each teaching hour to be 45 minutes for elementary schools. The other 15 minutes are used the same way the Koreans do—for vigorous play before settling back down for the next work session. Stevenson reports that Japanese educators think of American schools as sweatshops because of the preoccupation with time on task. Japanese children also appear to be happier in school than American children, and they are sick about one-half as much (Stevenson, p. 73).

A review of the curriculum reveals some interesting features. In grades 1 and 2, students learn basic Japanese social skills of self-reliance (called ''Life Environment'') rather than taking social studies that starts at grade 3. In grades 1 and 2 there is more time spent on Japanese language (including reading, writing, and learning two Japanese alphabets) than at higher grades. In first grade students must master a total of 96 characters. The curriculum in grades 5 and 6 includes ''homemaking,'' which is not the equivalent of American home economics. It is a course for both sexes stressing the need to adapt to change and basic consumer skills. The time devoted to learning science is the same as the time for social studies, but arithmetic instruction receives considerably more time each year. Overall, nearly 26 percent of elementary school

TABLE 3.2 Elementary school curriculum in Japan.

	Annual Teaching Hours (per grade)						
Subject	1	2	3	4	5	6	Total per Subject
Japanese language	306	315	280	280	210	210	1601
Social studies	—	—	105	105	105	105	420
Arithmetic	136	175	175	175	175	175	1011
Science	—	—	105	105	105	105	420
Life environment	102	105	—	—	—	—	207
Music	68	70	70	70	70	70	418
Arts and handicrafts	68	70	70	70	70	70	418
Homemaking	—	—	—	—	70	70	140
Physical education	102	105	105	105	105	105	627
Moral education	102	105	105	105	105	105	627
Special activities	34	35	35	70	70	70	314
Total teaching hours	850	910	980	1015	1015	1015	6203

Source: Unpublished monograph, Japanese Consulate, Atlanta, GA, 1994.

teaching times goes to Japanese language, and over 16 percent of the time goes to teaching arithmetic.

Reflections on Research

The knowledge base for American education is extensive and often cited by educators in other nations. The reader is urged to read the full studies that are reported below. Among the research findings are:

1. What helps students learn? Direct influences such as classroom management, time spent learning, metacognative processes, parental support and teacher-child interactions were more important than policies, organization schemes such as site-based management, and demographic factors (Wang et al., 1994, pp. 74–78).

2. Homework makes a difference in student learning, but it should be tied to the taught curriculum, differentiated by grade (Cooper, 1989, pp. 85–91).

3. The impact of grade retention is negative over the long run. It costs approximately ten billion dollars annually to reteach students who tend to do worse than if they had not been retained. Grade retention appears linked to dropping out. Better alternatives are afterschool and summer programs and the use of teacher assistants with targeted students. Grade retention is extremely stressful for the student. Contrary to popular belief, retaining students in kindergarten appears to be as negative as any other grade (Shepard and Smith, 1990, pp. 84–88).

4. Character education (i.e., ethics, moral, religious education in other nations) is part of world-class education, and it can exist in a multicultural society such as the United States. Parents expect the schools to impart universal values such as right and wrong, fairness, and respect for others (Nucci, 1987, pp. 86–92).

5. Integral to a well-designed curriculum is the motivation for students to learn. That motivation should start in the home, but it can be taught and designed into a curriculum if teachers know how to motivate students to learn. Specific tasks and activities that assist students in seeing the relationship between classroom

events and success out of school should be part of the curriculum design (Brophy, 1987, pp. 40–48).

AN AGENDA FOR ACTION: ELEMENTARY SCHOOL CURRICULUM

This section outlines a broad cross section of world-class curriculum and instruction in five parts: (1) establishing a world-class curriculum, (2) role of the teacher with the curriculum, (3) role of the school administrator with the curriculum, (4) role of the student and community with the curriculum, and (5) distinct American needs to support the curriculum.

Create a World-Class Curriculum

- *The world-class standard for curriculum is a single, nationally designed curriculum.* This allows textbooks to have full curriculum alignment. Instead of a national curriculum, American educators should become familiar with the emerging national curriculum frameworks and align with them. In states and districts that use textbook adoptions, calls for adoption should specifically state the need for national framework alignment.
- *The curriculum is specifically designed based on community input.* The questions used in New Zealand need replication. A world-class curriculum is known and understood by the community it serves. A school charter can include references to regular curriculum redesign and a means for the community to be involved in that effort.
- *There is coherence between the purpose of school and the developed curriculum.* An excellent example of a clear statement of purpose exists in the Republic of Korea. The constitution guarantees a free, compulsory education for each citizen. In 1968 the constitution goes further with a 1968 Charter of National Education and by Korea's Education Law that states the purpose of education succinctly: ''Education shall, under the great ideal of *hongik-ingan* [benefits for

mankind], aim to assist all people in perfecting their individual character, developing the ability for independent life, and acquiring the qualifications of citizens capable of participating in the building of a democratic state and promoting the prosperity of all human mankind'' (Smith, 1994, p. 17). A similar statement of purpose could be the introduction to the curriculum.

- *The curriculum is widely disseminated* among various constituencies, including educators, parents, students, and the community. This curriculum can be clearly understood and articulated by group members.

- *The curriculum accomplishes three functions* for teachers as it establishes a view of a child's education from beginning to end.

  (1) It determines what content is to be taught at each grade level.

  (2) It sets a pace of instruction, setting minutes per day to hours per week to each academic area, giving priority to language instruction and mathematics instruction for time spent during the elementary school years.

  (3) It articulates the academic areas that comprise the whole body of education, including some assessment of student mastery within each area. Most commonly, the academic disciplines include:

    A. Language (reading, writing, grammar, spelling, etc., with a single national language, but allowing for additional minority or indigenous language instruction) is given teaching priority and the most teaching time.

    B. Mathematics (or arithmetic or numeration) instruction has second priority for teaching time.

    C. Science instruction is sometimes not formally started until third year of compulsory education.

    D. Social studies (some form of geography, culture, history instruction to establish a sense of nationhood)

    E. Arts education, including aspects of art, music, calligraphy, dance, etc., is often taught by a specially trained teacher.

    F. Physical and health education

    G. Ethics or character education (various religions, morals, behavior, patriotism, etc.)

   H. Social education is specifically absent in Asian curriculums (i.e., sex education, AIDS education, etc.) for
home use or by other aencies, leaving more time for
academics.

   I. Preschool curriculum, if there is one defined, is play-
centered, nonacademic, and designed for social development of the child.

- *Learning out of school (i.e., homework) is considered a vital
part* of the curriculum. France overcomes a short 22-hour
classroom teaching week and a short year (only in this decade
expanding to 180 days) with several hours of homework
nightly.

Best Practice

The most inexpensive and effective way to increase the outcomes
of education is for American school administrators to establish a
well-defined, well-explained homework policy for use districtwide.
The French make excellent use of homework to make up for a very
short school day. The British are working hard on nationalizing the
routine use of homework, or learning out of school. Given a very
short school year and tight budgets the no-cost action can pay major
dividends. Perhaps a gradual, phased-in homework policy could be
tied to the staff development teachers need in this area.

Teachers Are Assigned Specific Responsibilities for Teaching the Curriculum

With a nationally defined curriculum, teachers do not have to decide
what to teach, the fundamental sequence of it, or the time allotments for
it. This allows teachers to focus on methods and student mastery. With
a national assessment of student mastery, the teacher is accountable to
the test. With a national curriculum and textbooks written to teach it, the
teacher may focus more on teaching from the book. The teacher's role
includes the following:

- *Teachers must have knowledge of the national curriculum* to
explain it to students and parents. Most world-class elementary

school teachers are generalists who teach most, if not all, of the curriculum.

- *Teachers plan lessons together* (as in eastern Pacific Rim nations). This process carefully refines and polishes teacher lesson plans.
- *Teachers collectively reflect* on the success of the common lesson and expected student mastery. This process helps to maintain a common pace among teachers.
- *Teachers often design common assessment instruments* for the curriculum; results of these tests are shared.
- *Teachers make themselves available to students out of class,* especially for students who are lagging behind the whole class pace.
- *Teachers communicate frequently with the home,* explaining individual student progress. Part of this communication includes suggestions for parents to assist students with homework.
- *Head teachers* provide leadership with the curriculum. This may be grade level or academic content leadership of a specific discipline. The head teacher assumes leadership in common planning meetings.

Best Practice

The idea of a national curriculum allows test manufacturers, textbook publishers, and school personnel to align with a single curriculum that would give credence to the term *an educated American.* New Zealand follows a public, open process that invites the population to be involved in determining what is taught while allowing understanding of what an educated New Zealander is. Given the multicultural population of New Zealand the concept could work in the United States as well.

The School Administrator Assumes Specific Responsibilities Concerning the Curriculum

Internationally, the school administrator is called the head. There may also be deputy heads in larger schools. In elementary schools, the head typically maintains some teaching responsibility providing for more collegiality among teachers and administrators. U.S. administrators can be the instructional leaders of their schools by acting in the role of head teacher. The heads have several responsibilities:

- *The head retains some teaching responsibility.* In Taiwan, for example, the head is the person who teaches moral education to the entire student body. This allows students and parents to regard the head as an educator rather than a business manager. It is a powerful statement of what is most valued in the school.
- *The head is a conduit of information about the national curriculum* to the school. The head typically works with school inspectors who represent the Ministry of Education and make routine school visits. Heads realize that an intelligent inspector can be a good source of ideas for improving instruction as inspectors see so many different settings.
- *The head is expected to be knowledgeable about the curriculum,* assessment, and to organize the school to function effectively.
- *The head is expected to provide common planning time* for teachers, usually with staff work space clustered around the planning area.
- *The head communicates with parents and the community* about student learning in the school and is largely responsible for public accountability about student mastery.
- *The head appoints lead teachers,* provides mentors for novices, and organizes the school for teaching.

Best Practice

Most of the developed nations of the world are greatly increasing participation in preschool programs for children as young as age 2. With the increase in both single-parent and two-earner families, preschool education fits the United States needs well. The Germans have a well-conceived program that can be adopted elsewhere. There is a common, agreed upon preschool curriculum allowing for a smooth transition for children moving from preschool to public school. It is an idea worthy of study in the United States for schools that are church or otherwise affiliated. Students with special needs may have the early intervention needed, and the German model provides for single-child's needs as well. There is coordination among programs and shared training of staffs.

The Students and the Community Assume Specific Responsibilities to the Curriculum

Given community information about the purpose and content of the curriculum, it seems reasonable for the community to be aware of the curriculum. That means parents and students may focus on learning and how accountability affects the student. Their roles in the curriculum include:

- *The student is responsible for understanding* that learning takes work:
  (1) Being serious about the work involved in learning and accepting the responsibility to learn
  (2) Using time out of school to further learning by doing homework as assigned and seeking adult support in that endeavor
  (3) Maximizing learning time in school by attending regularly and reducing absences
  (4) Using and treating school learning resources with respect
- *The parent is responsible for motivating the student to learn* and for assisting the learning process by:
  (1) Communicating with the school to understand the curriculum and the role of learning at home; actively overseeing their child's learning at home
  (2) Cooperating with the teacher's reports of student progress and needs
  (3) Becoming actively involved in the child's school governance and social activities
  (4) When an Asian child is having trouble in school, the parent expects to be told what is wrong with the student—and then to fix it.
  (5) The statement of parents' rights and responsibilities from

Scotland, page 210, relates directly to this as does the sample school charter (Chalker and Haynes, 1994, p. 170).

- *The community is responsible for assisting the learning process* by:
  (1) Cooperating with parent efforts to make children's learning most important
  (2) Not distracting students while studying. The American emphasis on sports as a function of education is not commonly found in the other countries studied. Heads may want to inquire how much time is spent in practice for various sports. The administrator could recommend that no more time be spent on practice than is spent on homework.
  (3) Supporting students who excel academically
  (4) Developing a positive attitude toward school and learning
  (5) The community can encourage the media to cover school successes, and it can lobby with local governments when television cable company contracts are negotiated. An emphasis on programming such as that found on *The Learning Channel* could be emphasized in basic program packages and provided gratis to the schools.

The World-Class Curriculum Must Recognize Unique U.S. Needs Which Should Be Addressed

(1) *Students must be serious* and industrious about the work involved in learning. That will start when students accept the responsibility to learn.

(2) *Teachers need to expect time out of school to be used for learning* by assigning meaningful homework and seeking adult home support for it.

(3) *Maximize the time in school for learning without interruption.* Stigler and Stevenson (1991, p. 16) found far fewer interruptions of learning time in Asian schools. They found examples of lunch counts, announcements of various activities, calling students to the office or to resource rooms provided a constant disruption to teaching continuity in U.S. schools. Twenty percent of all first grade lessons and 47 percent of all fifth grade lessons in American classrooms encountered interruptions by some nonrelated event,

yet in less than 10 percent of the time in Asian classrooms were such interruptions allowed.

(4) *The organization of instruction needs to be coherent* and designed to maximize learning. Stigler and Stevenson (1991, p. 16) noted: in "American classrooms . . . students spend more time in transition and less in academic activities, more time working on their own and less being instructed by the teacher; . . . teachers spend much of their time working with individual students and attending to matters of discipline, and . . . the shape of coherent lessons is often hard to discern."

(5) *School learning resources use and treatment will be respectful.* Li (1994), a visiting scholar from the People's Republic of China, reported that children in China get rewards for working hard just as they are in American classrooms. The difference is the reward — in America it is likely sugar-based, in China it is some small item to support learning.

(6) *There should be a clearly understood policy about homework.* Students should expect to have homework assigned nightly and to have a review by the parent. In elementary school that should include a reading assignment and comprehension check at the least. A board of education policy should support that effort, and parents should know about the policy.

(7) *Students should accept responsibility for learning out of school.* They need to organize a study area for this purpose and to have it away from television, radios, and telephones. Great Britain controls telephone use by charging for every local call. The authors were told by one father of three students in Scotland that he installed a pay telephone in the hall! In New Zealand each television is subject to an annual tax.

(8) *Parents must accept their role and function of homework.* Caplan et al. (1992, p. 42) cited it as the reason Indo-Chinese students succeeded in American schools, and research in Great Britain concluded that homework raises student achievement, but only when it has the support of parents (MacBeath and Turner, 1990).

(9) *Out-of-school social functions, including sports, need to be put in balance* with homework. In 1994 a school board member from Half Moon Bay, California, was given national publicity for recom-

mending that homework be abolished because it interfered with students' social lives! A good start for American educators would be an assurance that as much publicity is given for academic excellence as for sports.

(10) *Motivating students to learn.* Asian students do not typically need motivating to learn. It is part of their culture. Because such motivation is not common in the United States, teachers must learn how to motivate students.

(11) *Principals can provide leadership* by starting every faculty meeting with curriculum and instruction items and by checking to see if at least one-half of every faculty meeting addresses curriculum and instruction. Sharply reducing the number of teaching interruptions will facilitate the learning process.

(12) *Review the curriculum to see how much time social education* takes from time for developing academic skills. Beauchamp (1992, p. 16) estimates that 38 percent of American teaching time goes to nonacademic learning. Coupled with a short school year and a lack of homework, students from the United States cannot compete successfully.

(13) *Stress student attendance.* Asian students are typically absent from school roughly half as much as American students, and they are happier in school. Historically, when a child is absent in Japan, the mother goes to school, sits in the student's desk, and takes notes so the student will not fall behind. With the growth of two-earner families in Japan, this is becoming less frequent, however.

REFERENCES

Anderson-Levitt, K. M., R. Sirota, and M. Mazurier. 1991. "Elementary Education in France," *The Elementary School Journal*, 92:79−95.

Beauchamp, E. 1992. *Japanese and U.S. Education Compared*. Phi Delta Kappa Fastback # 338.

Brahm, Bernard. 1995. Interview (May 14), French Embassy, Washington.

Brophy, Jere. November 1987. "Synthesis of Research on Strategies for Motivating Students to Learn," *Educational Leadership*, 45(2):40−48.

Caplan, Nathan, Marcella H. Choy, and John K. Whitmore. February 1992. "Indochinese Refugee Families and Academic Achievement," *Scientific American*, 266(2):36−42.

Cartwright, William. Circa 1970, class lecture.

Chalker, D. and R. Haynes. 1994. *World Class Schools: New Standards for Education.* Lancaster, Pennsylvania: Technomic Publishing Company, Inc.

Cooper, Harris. November 1989. "Synthesis of Research on Homework," *Educational Leadership,* 47(3):85−91.

Education in Korea, 1993−1994. 1994. Seoul, Korea: National Institute of Educational Research and Training, Ministry of Education.

Education in New Zealand. 1991 Yearbook. Ministry of Education, Wellington.

Eldar, D. 1995. Interview (May 15).

Fowler, F. 1988. "In Search of Egality and Competitiveness: French Education After 58 Reforms," *International Education Journal,* 18(1):5−14.

Führ, C. 1989. *Schools and Institutions of Higher Education in the Federal Republic of Germany.* Bonn: Inter Nations.

Her Majesty's Inspectorate. 1992. *Teaching and Learning in Japanese Elementary Schools.* Edinburgh: The Scottish Office, Education Department.

Hess, R. D. and H. Azuma. 1991. "Cultural Support for Schooling−Contrasts Between Japan and the United States," *Educational Researcher,* 2(9):2−12.

Li, C. C. 1995. Interview (May 14).

Li, G. L. 1994. Interview(March 15).

Linton, R. T., Sr. 1995. Interview (November 24).

MacBeath, John and Mary Turner. 1990. *Learning Out of School.* Scottish Education Department, Her Majesty's Inspectorate, Edinburgh.

Malcolmb, P. M. 1993. Interview (June 14).

McGee, C. 1994. *New Zealand's National Curriculum,* monograph.

Ministry of Education. 1994. *Education Statistics of the Republic of China.* Taipei.

Moyer, F. 1995. Interview (April 27).

Myers, Kate. 1994. "Plain Truth about High Flyers," *Times Education Supplement.* Nov. 4.

Nelson, A. ed. *The Modern Reader's Japanese-English Character Dictionary.* Rutland, Vermont: Charles E. Tuttle Company. Second edition.

New Zealand Official 1994 Yearbook Extracts. 1994. Washington, D.C. Monograph provided by the New Zealand Embassy.

Newsam, P. 1994. "They Do Things So Differently There," *Times Education Supplement.* London, November 4, p. 11.

Nucci, Larry. February 1987. "Synthesis of Research on Moral Development," Educational Leadership.

Office for Standards in Education. 1993. *The Initial Training of Teachers in Two German Länder: Hessen and Rheinland-Pfalz.* Her Majestey's Inspectorate, Edinburgh.

Pierre, Bridgette. 1993. Interview (May 12).

The Scottish Office for Education. 1992. *Teaching and Learning in Japanese Elementary Schools.* Edinburgh: Department for Education.

Shepard, Lorrie A. and Mary Lee Smith. November 1990. "Synthesis of Research on School Readiness and Kindergarten Retention," *Educational Leadership.*

Smith, Douglas C. 1994. *Elementary Teacher Education in Korea.* Bloomington, IN: Phi Delta Kappa.

Stevenson, H. 1992. "Learning from Asian Schools," *Scientific American*, December.

Stigler, J. and H. Stevenson. 1991. "How Asian Teachers Polish Each Lesson to Perfection," *American Educator*, 15(2):12−47.

Wang, M., G. Haertal, and H. Walberg. December−January 1994. "What Helps Students Learn," *Educational Leadership*, 51(4):74−79.

Chapter 4

WORLD-CLASS ELEMENTARY SCHOOL TEACHERS

Modern cynics and skeptics . . . see no harm in paying those to whom they entrust the minds of their children a smaller wage than is paid to those to whom they entrust the care of their plumbing.

—John F. Kennedy

This chapter examines world-class teachers—where they come from, what they do, and how they are rewarded. The developed nations of the world all have some form of teacher certification, teacher education, and a system of induction. Teachers around the world hold various levels of status, however. The rewards for teaching are generally slim financially, but other forms of status are lavished on some teachers. Worldwide, it is common for the buildings in which they teach to be in poor repair as well. But the teaching profession is three times larger than that of the world's militaries. For every one soldier there are three teachers.

World-class teachers are examined four ways in this chapter:

- teacher education programs
- teacher mentoring and certification
- teacher's workloads and salary
- teaching methods and organizing instruction

The chapter ends with an agenda for creating world-class teaching.

WORLD-CLASS TEACHING

Imagine a school like this. There are no school buses, children arrive at school two ways. Either mothers walk them to school and chat easily with teachers, or students arrive on public transportation not separate school busses. The children are happy and ready to work. Parents expect first graders to learn how to work hard, get along with others, and to find a way to learn from the teacher. These children all arrive with every textbook having been home each night. The books are given to the children to own, and children are expected to revere the books, make notes in them, and keep them as a personal library. Parents expect homework, which they oversee once the child is home. These parents buy extra workbooks and provide tutors if the children are not learning enough.

The school administrator strolls the halls, thankful that there is no janitorial staff. After all, the children and the staff clean the rooms by washing desks, windows, doors, and chalkboards every day. Of course the days go by quickly because the students leave by 1 P.M. to go home for lunch so there is no cafeteria. They do not come back until the next day!

The halls are always quiet because class changes involve teachers changing rooms while the students obediently stay in their room. When the teacher enters the room an elected class leader greets the teacher with a grin, shouting, ''We are eagerly looking forward to a most interesting lecture!'' The whole class bows to the teacher and immediately sits down to work.

The children love school. So the schools need no truant officers. Students are seldom sick, and when they are the mother may come to school, sit in the child's desk, and take notes to take home to the child. Of course, when the child has a problem in school the parents (there are two parents in almost every home, and they stay married to each other) get very upset, fire down to the school, and demand to know, ''What is wrong—*with my child?*'' They work diligently to fix the problem and work with the teacher.

Teachers take their jobs seriously, working together to polish lesson plans to perfection, and they reflect on each lesson as a group, trying to find out how to teach it better next time. The teachers have orderly classes of well-behaved students. They respect the chief school administrator who teaches a daily lesson to the whole school, which usually focuses on morals, hard work, and good behavior. The children listen attentively.

Not every day at school is all work. Teachers love Confucius's birthday (he is called the Foremost Teacher), which is nationally recognized as Teacher's Day. Teachers are thanked for being so important to

A major national holiday is "Teacher's Day" on September 28 the date of Confucius's birth. Teachers are honored and showered with gifts from a grateful community (photo courtesy of the Ministry of Education, Republic of China).

the nation! There are other ways that teachers are thanked: they pay no income tax, and homes are easy to buy because the school district finances teachers' homes at a very low rate of interest, in part to keep the honored teachers in that district. At any public event, teachers are expected to sit at the head table due to their revered position.

That certainly describes a world-class teaching setting, and it really exists. But not all of it exists in any one nation. In Taiwan teachers do not pay income taxes. In Japan the school district provides low-cost home loans, in the Republic of Korea teachers are the ones who change class and the students greet the teacher with a slogan and a bow. In Germany the children go home at 1 P.M., and there usually are no cafeterias, thus no breakfast or lunch programs. In England small, centrally located schools serve a community that is often within walking distance, and mothers stroll to school with their children.

But not all is well in this world-class setting. A Japanese widow sued her prefecture for working her teacher husband to death—and won (*Asheville Citizen Times*, 1994). In Taiwan students have been punished for not working hard enough, and the punishment for top students may require kneeling on a concrete floor, back straight, with a chair on the head, for hours. Not all children in this world-class school are well treated, by U.S. standards. As few as one-half of 1 percent of a nation's students might be identified for special education. No programs exist for the gifted in Japan. Teaching is primarily lecture, even at primary grades. Class sizes can be huge, as many as 55 – 60 students in Korean classes. In extreme cases children commit suicide due to the pressure of "exam hell." In other cases parents will bankrupt themselves to provide cram school education. If the child fails to work hard enough in the cram school, they fire the student! No tuition is refunded to the parents when that happens (Chalker and Haynes, 1994, p. 133).

The teaching world is full of variables, and only the best practices should be adopted for U.S. schools that wish to become world-class. The teachers' world is examined below.

TEACHER EDUCATION

Teacher education provides a continuous flow of intellectually pre-pared individuals to become teachers who fit into the school system smoothly, with as little disruption as possible. The process of preparing new teachers involves an apprenticeship during which the transition from student to teacher occurs. This is overseen by individuals who are already socialized into the profession. New teachers are expected to maintain the school system as it is rather than changing it.

Each nation studied had a process of teacher education, appren-ticeship, and a form of certification, but there is wide variation in the process. Student teaching varied from a period of 2 weeks in Japan (Her Majesty's Inspectorate, 1991, p. 22) to as much as 2 years in some German Länder (OFSTED, 1993, p. 15). Each nation professes to honor teachers, yet they commonly report teacher shortages in areas such as science, technology, and second language teaching. These nations make exceptions for certification of teachers in areas of shortage, thus weaken-ing teacher preparation. Globally, the trend in teacher preparation has moved from normal schools and 2-year college preparation programs to university-based, bachelor of education degrees for all new teachers. Both Taiwan and South Korea, for example, have changed their programs from 2-year normal schools to 4-year university-based programs. The trend for longer periods of teacher preparation continues with several nations offering postgraduate programs for those with academic degrees who wish to become teachers. The University of New Brunswick in Canada reported over 800 applicants for 200 vacancies in their program of teacher preparation, which takes 6 years to complete (Smith, 1995). The lengthiest program is found in Germany where secondary academic teachers may take 7 or 8 years to complete their training program (Führ, 1989, p. 164).

Each nation's teacher training program is designed to produce teachers who will primarily maintain the schools as they currently exist in that country. In the United States teachers frequently complain about isolation, long hours, and heavy loads all of which are commonly reported in comparative studies of teachers around the world (Chalker and Haynes, 1994, p. 95). Yet teacher education programs frequently terminate with an isolated cadet teaching experience in one classroom with assistance from a limited number of people.

There is an international trend for more academic rigor in teacher education programs. Japanese elementary teachers are prepared in Monbusho-approved university programs where they complete a university degree with nearly two-thirds of their course work in a specific academic area (Her Majesty's Inspectorate, 1991, p. 22). In Germany admission to teacher education accentuates rigor stemming from Germany's long history of full university training for its teachers (Führ, 1989, pp. 164–167). Any high school graduate who can pass the rigorous *Arbitur* may be admitted to a primary school teacher training program, which lasts for 3 or 4 years of university study. There is no interviewing or other form of screening candidates at this stage. At this point there is a limited amount of public school experience included. Students take a Land-created examination (German Länder are not dissimilar from U.S. states, and there is as much variance between their programs as there is between U.S. states, but Länder accept the teacher certification from each other). This examination, the *Erstes Staatsexamen*, is a professional qualification examination that professionals, including doctors, lawyers, pharmacists (among others), and teachers must pass to move into the profession. There is a single passing grade for everyone taking the exam, holding teachers to the same academic standard of other professionals (OFSTED, 1993, p. 13). Given such standards German teachers are not subjected to the ridicule U.S. teachers faced from *A Nation at Risk*'s reference to "a rising tide of mediocrity," which largely focused on the quality of teacher education majors as academic scholars, using international comparisons (notably with Japan and Germany) to focus attention on the quality of U.S. schools (Clabaugh and Razycki, 1990, pp. 113−114).

Unfortunately, the low esteem with which education is regarded may have a genesis in teacher education. Lanier and Little (1986) researched the low esteem of teachers, concluding:

> The institution of public schooling in America remains conservative and relatively slow to accommodate a responsible, intellectual role for professional teachers. . . . The maintenance of teacher education as a nonprofession is comparable to the maintenance of teaching as a non-career. . . . Change is particularly difficult in teacher education because the occupation serves two groups traditionally weak in institutional influence: women and children. While legend has it that emergency situations provoke a ''save the women and children'' attitude, such does not seem to be the case in the more mundane activities of life, such as those encountered in teaching children and teaching teachers. (p. 558)

Lanier and Little reason that teachers' clients are children with whom they cannot intellectually connect, and they cannot select the group of children to whom they are assigned. Coupled with this is the way in which university and college faculty view teacher educators whose roots come from normal schools not pure academia. The authors do not wholly support this view, but it does provide an insight into an important area for developing world-class teachers.

Student Teaching

Beyond the length and quality of scholastic preparation of teachers, the cadet (or student) teaching experience varies widely among the nations studied. All cadet teachers are expected to have an adequate grasp of the curriculum they teach, and those nations with a national curriculum and a national ministry of education that oversees both public school and higher education have an easier time ensuring such mastery exists. The teacher training institutions are expected to provide the basics of child psychology, learning theory, and methods (addressed separately, below) which are expected in their schools. But the field-based experience and the dynamics between a university student and a public school guest vary significantly, which greatly affects the socialization of the new professional. Examples from Japan and Germany follow.

Teaching in Japan

In Japan teaching is not conducted in isolation because of the expectations teachers have of each other. Stigler and Stevenson (1991, p. 45) report that the Japanese like most Asian teachers are provided with a large teachers' room centrally located where all teachers are given a desk at which to work. In the U.S. teachers generally do such work in their own isolated rooms, avoiding a smoke-filled group of "lounge lizards" who frequently make a workroom anything but that. Asian elementary teachers teach classes only 60 percent of the time they are at school. The remaining time is spent in groups to plan lessons jointly, discussing what methods to use, even what questions to ask and how to assess student understanding. The same team of teachers repeat the process after the lesson, reflecting on the relative success of the lesson and how to improve it the next time (Stigler and Stevenson, 1991, p. 45). The void between teaching success or failure is team based, not an individual matter of skill. In the United States where the entire process of planning, teaching, and reflection is limited to one adult, the overall quality is also assessed by a single individual.

Because Japanese teachers work collectively to improve the school's teaching, the cadet teacher is introduced to team planning during a few weeks of student teaching. The real induction occurs during the first year of actual teaching. By law, the novice teacher receives 30 days of additional teacher training during the first year. They are not certified to teach until the end of the first year (Her Majesty's Inspectorate, 1991, p. 15). The novice is assigned to a mentor who is a recognized master teacher who wants to assist a beginning teacher. The master teacher is given a year's leave of absence to work continuously with the novice (Stigler and Stephenson, 1991, p. 46). Given the observations and feedback from the master teacher, the collective approach to planning and executing instruction, and the extensive in-service days, the novice matures quickly. After a full year of public teaching only those novices who meet a high standard are awarded certification which is a lifetime teaching credential in Japan. Although a teaching certificate is permanent, teachers are under continuous pressure to succeed. Schools in the Asian Pacific Rim nations are publically ranked from good to bad. The public is aware of each school's reputation, and "famous" teachers are assigned to "star schools." Teachers held in lower esteem may be assigned to "cow schools."

Teaching in Germany

Student teaching in Germany follows a route that varies by Land, but which is quite different from the Japanese or U.S. experience. The university-based teacher education program includes a theory of education component with four parts: (1) politics of education, (2) educational psychology, (3) sociology of education, and (4) general theories of teaching and learning (pedagogy). Student teachers are expected to be prepared to teach all content areas with a specialization in one of them. The teacher education program takes advantage of the time, sometimes several weeks, when the university is out of session but public schools are still in session. During this time the teacher education majors are placed in public school settings to observe, to actually teach, and to write journals about their experiences (OFSTED, 1993, p. 15).

Novice teachers pass from university study to actual teaching experiences for a period of 18−24 months. During this time the cadet teacher is not yet credentialed and support includes study seminars and in-service opportunities to develop competence in the beginning teacher. The novice has not graduated at this point (Führ, 1989, p. 167). A university tutor (supervisor) is expected to visit and critique the cadet teacher, but the primary responsibility for assistance and feedback falls on a mentor who is in and out of the novice teacher's room as much as time permits. The mentor's pay is limited to a small honorarium and a salary for involvement in planning and teaching the extraschool seminars for the new teachers. There is no reduction in the mentor's teaching load. As is the case in U.S. teacher education, there tends to be a shortage of such supervising teachers in Germany.

Mentoring

Mentoring novice teachers is world-class. All 10 nations have some form of program reminiscent of the old craft guilds. Mentoring depends on using seasoned veterans to continue the professional development of novices. The primary difference among the mentoring programs is the quality of investment made in mentoring. The United States, Canada, and Great Britain, for instance, support the concept of mentoring but normally with no financial investment in the process beyond some form of training package. Providing extra pay for mentors is sometimes tried, as the state of California does with its new teacher program (Gless,

1995), but release time such as Japan provides is a scarce commodity. Normally, an already overburdened teacher (see teacher work and pay conditions below) has an additional responsibility with no real provision for making it possible to accomplish. The result is increased isolation for the novice who was promised help, and a sense of guilt for a good, seasoned professional. Table 4.1 displays, for the United States, the percentage of teachers, by state, who plan to stay in their position for as long as possible. The ramifications of these data are obvious in terms of attrition and the need for mentoring. Similar data were not available from other nations.

The problems of inadequately supported mentoring occur in Great Britain just as they do in the United States. Although the benefits of mentoring accrue to both the novice teacher and the mentor (Barrs, 1994, p. vii), most elementary school teachers lack the time to be effective mentors because so much time is demanded by children in the classroom (Hofkins, 1994, p. 16).

Stress

Teachers commonly complain about stress and "burnout." This is not unique to U.S. teachers. The excessive demands of the job are reflected in a growing number of marital problems among English teachers (Dean, 1995, p. 5). The reader may be surprised to learn that 16,000 teacher assaults are reported annually on school grounds in England. In Japan the death of a teacher was officially blamed on "overwork" (*Asheville Citizen Times,* 1994). The stress of teaching in Asia's Pacific Rim countries is concurrent with the "exam hell" students endure. Teachers in these nations believe in the concept of Gamburo (literally, "hanging on"), so they expect students to succeed based on hard work, not because of an innate intellectual difference. But the same holds true of teachers; if the student fails to learn, then part of the cause is the teacher's failure to teach. Teachers often spend long hours after school, working with students who need special attention they cannot get in class.

Stress among the world's teachers could be highest in the United States. A 1993 Metropolitan Life Insurance Company nationwide poll of teachers revealed that 11 percent of teachers reported being victims of assault within the past year. Among that number, 95 percent of the assaults were from students. Worse yet, during the same year the U.S.

TABLE 4.1 Percentage of public school teachers who plan to stay in their position as long as they are able (by state: 1990–1991).

Rank Order of States[1]	Percentage Planning to Stay	Rank Order of States[1]	Percentage Planning to Stay
New Hampshire	45	Tennessee	34
California	43	Texas	34
New Jersey	43	Mississippi	33
New York	43	North Dakota	34
Connecticut	42	District of Columbia	33
Maine	42	Georgia	33
Massachusetts	42	Idaoho	33
Wyoming	42	Missouri	33
Florida	40	Oregon	33
Rhode Island	40	South Dakota	33
Vermont	40	Wisconsin	33
Nevada	38	Kentucky	31
Pennsylvania	38	South Carolina	31
Indiana	37	West Virginia	31
Michigan	37	Alabama	30
Alaska	36	Arkansas	30
Arizona	36	Iowa	30
Colorado	36	Minnesota	30
Kansas	36	Hawaii	29
Montana	36	Louisiana	29
Nebraska	36	Oklahoma	29
Illinois	35	Utah	29
National average	35	Virginia	29
New Mexico	35	Delaware	25
Maryland	34	Washington	25
Ohio	34	North Carolina	23

[1]States with the same percentage are listed in alphabetical order within that percentage.
Source: United States Department of Education, 1993, p. 43.

Labor Department reported that 29 teachers died at work, with six of the deaths resulting from assault (U.S. Department of Labor, 1994). Add the long teaching days and nonteaching duties along with the survey (see Table 4.1) showing that fully 65 percent of the teachers in the United States do not intend to work in their current jobs as long as they are able. The result is a statistical picture of a stressful profession.

Certification

Once the teacher education sequence is completed, it is common in the nations studied for the graduate to complete an examination that leads to teacher certification. In Germany, for example, each Land has its own test, and certification is honored by the other Länder, allowing teachers to move within the country. In the United States it seems almost illegal to take a teacher across state lines, making the teacher a hostage within each state. Worldwide, once certificates are granted, they are generally given for life. That does not mean continued teacher development is over. For example, in Taiwan, Wednesday is one-half of a day for students, and teachers use the other half of the day for weekly in-service training (Lin, 1994, p. 3).

TEACHER WORKLOADS AND PAY

Perhaps the most commonly asked comparative education questions about teachers involve workload and pay. Many Americans have heard stories about Asian children bowing when the teacher enters the room and about the high esteem with which teachers are held, but how does the United States compare when it comes to the actual work of teaching? There are many variables to consider when answering these questions. The length of the school year, teaching hours per week, noninstructional duties and planning time, teacher pay schedules, and incentives for staying in teaching all shed light on the workload and pay issues. Teacher esteem in the community is also a factor. Each is addressed below.

Teaching Days per School Year

The number of teaching days per school year is one significant variable that sheds light on teachers' workloads. Table 4.2 displays the length of the instructional school year for each of the 10 nations' studied. The United States ties for the shortest school year, which, taken alone, indicates that teachers in the United States appear to work less than other teachers each year. That is not the case, however. These data actually mean that U.S. elementary school students have significantly less time to learn than do students in several other nations.

As the reader studies Table 4.2, the column on the far right may be

TABLE 4.2 *A comparison of the length of the school in 10 nations showing number of days per year and total days in 7 years of elementary education.*

Nation	Instructional Days in 1 School Year	Net Over 7 Years
Canada	188 days[1]	1316 days
France	180 days (Wednesday is 1/2 day)[2]	1260 days
Federal Republic of Germany	190 days[3]	1330 days
Great Britain	192 days[4]	1344 days
New Zealand	200 days primary grades[4]	1400 days
Taiwan	222 days[4]	1554 days
Israel	215 days (Friday is 1/2 day)[4]	1505 days
Japan	216 days (Saturday is 1/2 day)[5]	1512 days
Republic of Korea	220 days[6]	1540 days
United States	180 days (or less in some states)	1260 days
World-class average	200 + days per year	1400 days

[1]Donald J. Weeren, interview at St. Mary's University, Nova Scotia, 6/12/95.
[2]Bernard Brahm, interview, French Embassy, Washington, May 4, 1995.
[3]Brickman, 1994, p. 2472.
[4]Chalker, D. and R. Haynes, 1994.
[5]Moyer, Francis A., interview at The Japan Center, Raleigh, North Carolina, 3/2/96.
[6]Ministry of Education, 1994. p. 48.

most revealing. Internationally, it is common for elementary schools to include 1 year of kindergarten and 6 years of elementary grades. When compared with the world-class average, the aggregate lost number of days in school for U.S. children amounts to 28 *weeks* of schooling over 7 years. When compared with the world-class leader (Taiwan) the difference is almost 59 *weeks*, equivalent to about 1 1/2 extra years spent in school! The U.S. school year has been mired at 180 days since the end of World War II, whereas other nations have adjusted the length of their school years. It is interesting to note the various ways that the school year fluctuates internationally. France lengthened its school year from 174 to 180 days per year in 1993. Japan has scaled back the length of its fabled long school year from 240 days a year by dropping Saturday classes from each Saturday to two Saturdays a month. The first time Saturday classes were dropped the parents complained bitterly, and the Monbusho produced a book of educational activities for parents to engage children in while they were not in Saturday classes. The second time they dropped a Saturday class a month, it was the students who complained because they were still accountable for the full curriculum and they felt they were cheated by a shorter school year! New Zealand provides a longer school year for elementary schools than secondary schools (190 days for high school), which is an interesting statement about the value of elementary education. Overall, during the last 5 years the world-class average for number of days in the school year has actually dropped from 204 to barely over 200 (Chalker and Haynes, 1994, p. 53).

Length of the School Day

Another way to view the teacher's workload is to examine the length of the school day. Table 4.3 displays the length of the school day, an area in which the United States gains ground with its short school year.

The reader should approach this table with caution. In Japan, Republic of Korea, and Taiwan an hour is, in reality, 40−45 minutes of instruction with a break for the balance of the hour during which rigorous play occurs before settling in for another period of intense instruction. As was shown in Table 4.2, three nations afford half-days during their week of instruction, thus instructional time is reduced during that day. Table 4.3 only displays the actual time involved in teaching per se. France, which has increased the number of days in the school year is actually *reducing* the length of instruction per day and attempting to outlaw homework at the elementary level (Brahm, 1995).

To understand the workload of a teacher, one must examine the amount of teaching time and the amount of time devoted to teaching outside of the classroom, including all noninstructional duties of the teacher. The teacher's day varies substantially among the nations studied when non-classroom time is examined. For U.S. teachers, two major duties include cafeteria and transportation supervision. Most U.S. school systems operate the largest restaurant and taxi service in the community. That is not common in the other nations. Nations like Great Britain cut transportation costs by utilizing small, accessible schools within walking distances so children walk to school with a parent. Avoiding transportation expense means a higher percentage of education funds can be invested in classrooms. It also frees teachers from supervising busloads and ''double loaders,'' which engage the teacher in nonacademic activity before and after school. In densely populated countries such as Japan,

TABLE 4.3 *A comparison of the instructional hours of teaching per day in 10 nations.*

Nation	Length of Instructional Day in Hours
Canada	5 hours[1]
France	5 hours, 20 minutes[2]
Federal Republic of Germany	3 hours at lower grades to 4.5 hours upper elementary[3]
Great Britain	4 hours, 30 minutes[4]
New Zealand	5 hours[5]
Taiwan	5 hours, 20 minutes[6]
Israel	4 hours, 40 minutes[7]
Japan	5 hours, 30 minutes[8]
Republic of Korea	4–4.5 hours, based on student age[9]
United States	5 hours, 30 minutes[10]
World-class standard	5 hours[11]

[1]Hanley, Ministry of Education, New Brunswick, interview 6/14/95.
[2]Anderson-Levitt et al, 1995, p. 85.
[3]Führ, 1989, p. 70.
[4]McAdams, 1993, p. 134.
[5]Barrington, 1994, p. 4106.
[6]Liao Chwan-Huey, interview 2/13/93.
[7]Eldar, interview 5/15/95.
[8]Monbusho, 1992.
[9]Ministry of Education, 1994, p. 53.
[10]North Carolina Department of Public Instruction.
[11]Note: This figure was reached by calculating the mean for the 10 nations. In those nations where the length of the day varies based on the age of the child, the median length for the grade span was used. This is rounded off to the nearest quarter hour.

Taiwan, and Republic of Korea students use public transportation, either for free or at a discount, but the schools are free from running a taxi service.

Reflections on Research—Class Size

Perhaps the most common demand from teachers is reduced class size. They argue that smaller classes allow for more individual student-teacher interactions, improve classroom atmosphere, and improve student achievement. Is that the case?

Glass (1994, p. 165) reported on a survey of hundreds of international studies that were conducted to determine what linkage exists between smaller classes and higher student achievement. The data are based on a student who scores at the 50th percentile in a class with 40 students. That student's achievement would raise to the 65th percentile if class size was reduced to 1:15. The cost-benefit ratio raised costs nearly three times to generate a 15 percentile increase in measured achievement. The expectation that lower class size has the greatest effect on young children was not supported in the literature.

The issue of increased cost versus lower class size is at the crux of the issue. Computer-assisted instruction is liable to be more cost-effective as computer costs drop and teacher salaries increase. The costs of lengthening the school year offset the cost of lower class size, and the academic results are likely to be better. Based on gains in achievement versus cost, the use of a tutor or classroom assistant is superior to either a longer year or smaller classes, particularly if the tutor is paid less than a teacher salary but is under the direction of a teacher. The use of teacher assistants is perhaps the most cost-effective means of lowering class size, with the added savings that additional classrooms are not needed in this situation.

The debate about class size will continue, with taxpayers feeling it is not worth the cost and teachers continuing to demand a smaller class load.

The reader should note that the greatest gains in smaller classes are associated with teacher satisfaction rather than student achievement. Nothing can take the place, however, of a really gifted teacher, regardless of class size. Those who insist that American students cannot learn effectively in a classroom of 40 students might be interested to know that Orville Wright attended a kindergarten class with 45 students in it (Haynes, 1991, p. 18). His education did not appear to suffer.

The practice of feeding schoolchildren eats into a school's workday and budget. Offering breakfast appears to be a practice primarily unique to U.S. schools. In Germany, for example, the short instructional day is over by 1 P.M., so students leave for the day to go home to lunch. In Korea cafeterias are not common, but those that exist are staffed by parents (usually by women) who provide all of the services of cleaning, supervising, etc., as a civic duty. These cafeterias generally do not include cooking facilities, but trays, utensils, etc., are provided (Elliot, 1995). In Taiwan children are expected to bring a lunch from home, which meets the standards set by the school. Although there is time to eat, it is done in classrooms the children will clean at the end of the day. It behooves the students not to make a mess because they must clean it up. Precious funding is saved by not building single-purpose areas to cook and serve, and the teachers do not perform cafeteria duty.

Class Size

Perhaps the most common demand from U.S. teachers is the reduction of class size. Table 4.4 displays the class sizes or student-teacher ratios reported among those nations for which reliable data could be found. New Zealand and the United Kingdom did not report comparative data. The reader is cautioned not to treat the term class size as synonymous with student-teacher ratio because they are not the same. Class size should provide an understanding of the average number of students per teacher in a typical elementary class. That data were judged preferable to student-teacher ratio. The latter provides an insight into

TABLE 4.4 Class size or student-teacher ratios for elementary schools.

Nation	Class Size or Student-Teacher Ratio
Israel	30 students/class all grade levels[1]
France	24 on average, varies, by law, limit is 25 at first grade; 35 all others[2]
Taiwan	41 students/class[3]
Republic of Korea	55–60 students/class[4]
Japan	22.2:1 student-teacher ratio[5]
Canada	17.5:1 student-teacher ratio[6]
United States	18.6:1 student-teacher ratio[7]
Germany	15:1 student-teacher ratio[8]

[1] Shumueli, 1995, p. 3025.
[2] Anderson-Levitt et al., 1991, p. 82.
[3] *Education Statistics of The Republic of China*, 1994, p. xix.
[4] Elliot, interview, 6/27/95.
[5] Tobin et al., 1989, p. 60.
[6] Hanley, 1995.
[7] Chambers, 1996.
[8] Führ, 1989.

how many professionals a school provides for a given number of students, but nonteaching personnel, such as principals, bursars, and guidance staff, are included in the ratio, which does not provide an idea of the size of a typical classroom. No world-class standard is calculated in this area, although there is wide variance among the nations studied.

Are teachers in the United States worked harder than their counterparts internationally? They are. McAdams (1993) studied six school systems around the world using Fulbright teacher interviews as a research base. He reported (p. 4):

- American teachers must complete a burdensome amount of paperwork.
- The American teacher works a very long day with few breaks or other opportunities to interact with colleagues.
- Students in American schools are more closely supervised than are students in foreign schools. Most exchange teachers were unfamiliar with hall passes, bathroom patrol, and cafeteria supervision.
- The exchange teachers considered American students to be too concerned with grades and to expect higher grades than they had earned.
- The exchange teachers seemed to be accustomed to a lighter teaching load than they were assigned in the United States.
- Exchange teachers missed having teaching aides to help them with setting up labs or with the supervision of students.

The term *exchange teachers* refers to teachers from the other countries who came to the United States to teach while a Fulbright Teacher taught in another country.

Stigler and Stevenson (1991) conducted an exhaustive study of elementary schools in the United States, Taiwan, and Japan, focusing on the work teachers do. Like other researchers, they concluded that U.S. teachers are, simply, ''overworked'' which should come as no surprise to the reader. Expecting such teachers to develop outstanding lessons on a daily basis isn't reasonable. Asian teachers are not expected to teach every hour of every day that school is open but U.S. teachers are. Good lesson plans take time to create, and teaching them dynamically is hard work. They concluded that time and energy ''. . . are in very short supply for most American teachers'' (pp. 45–46). The researchers concluded that Japanese elementary schoolteachers are actually in classes teaching 60 percent of the time they are at school. Although teachers in Taiwan and Japan spend longer days at school than do U.S. teachers (9.5, 9.1, and 7.3 hours, respectively), that does not mean a lighter workload for the U.S. teachers who take work home to do in isolation rather than resting and enjoying family time.

A World-Class Idea
for Increasing Teacher Professionalism
from the United States, Japan, and Korea

Teachers in Japan and many other Eastern Pacific Rim countries have a large area set aside as the teachers' room. Each teacher typically has a desk in the teachers' room, not in the classroom. The teachers' room is used for teacher planning groups, not for sipping coffee, smoking, and complaining. This cuts down on the isolation faced by U.S. teachers who typically plan alone in their classroom or at home. A teachers' group is formed among those teaching similar subjects, and because the Ministry of Education provides the curriculum and pace of instruction, teachers planning focuses on how to most effectively teach. The same groups reconvene after instruction to discuss how effective the joint plan had been. In these planning sessions teachers focus on framing questions and how they expect students to respond to them. The entire lesson often uses a single well-designed question.

An American educator, Harry Wong (n.d.), suggests that teachers need to *look* professional to be regarded as professional. Because other professionals from plumbers to brain surgeons frame their degrees and licenses for display in a business office, he recommends that teachers do the same thing. A display of degrees and certifications in a teacher's room is impressive.

In Korea teachers wear suits to work (Elliot, 1995), looking the part of the professional a world-class teacher should be. One other means of creating a professional atmosphere occurs in several Asian nations. The school sends home a teachers' directory, including a photograph of each staff member, their areas of academic expertise, and a brief educational biography. In the United States simple black and white photos could be provided, but it would help parents to understand who is teaching their child, linking a name, face, and credentials.

Asian teachers have desks located in a centralized teacher's room. These Republic of Korea teachers may plan together or work by themselves. Such a room keeps teacher planning and evaluation from the isolated chore it is in the United States (photo by Elliott).

Salary

One of the most commonly asked questions about world-class schools focuses on teacher pay. Because of the difference among currencies and standards of living, it is not feasible to list the starting and ending salaries of teachers in 10 nations, with the pay translated into constant U.S. dollars. The cost of living varies greatly among the 10 nations, as do taxation structures and incentives some teachers get, which do not actually appear on a paycheck. For example, teachers in Taiwan do not pay income taxes (Li, 1995). Teachers in many prefectures in Japan are given very low interest mortgage loans as incentives to buy a home and settle. Having a teacher move into a neighborhood is considered a privilege, and such an incentive greatly affects purchasing power without increasing the paycheck (Moyer, 1995). In Taiwan the celebration of Confucius' birth is a major national holiday called Teacher's Day; it is common for students to give gifts to the teacher as part of the celebration. These gifts are often in the form of cash, and they can total a substantial sum, particularly for the most "famous" teachers who may have hundreds of students (Huang, 1995). A meaningful comparison of teacher salaries, therefore, must be made some other way.

Unfortunately, primary schoolteachers in other nations are frequently paid on a lower scale than are lower secondary teachers. The latter often have a lower pay scale than upper secondary teachers. In one area of Canada where kindergartens are a recent addition, those teachers are paid on a scale akin to the pay of a teacher assistant in the United States, despite having university degrees and full certification. These teachers are offered the promise of future pay raises, as funding becomes available, equal to other elementary schoolteachers once funds are available. Despite the low pay, there are many applicants, and the kindergarten classrooms the authors judged to be of excellent quality. Perhaps the reason that primary schoolteachers are paid on a lower scale reflects the lingering vestige of the normal school and the 2 years of training some nations had required of such teachers.

The American Federation of Teachers (AFT) conducted an interesting study of teacher salaries that included six of the countries in this study. Nelson and O'Brien (1993) derived a comparative index that allows salaries to be compared using the gross domestic product (GDP) for each nation, using a baseline year of 1992. The GDP is the total worth produced in a nation during a particular year. By dividing the GDP by the workforce, a per capita figure may be calculated. The mean per capita GDP is indexed at 100 for that nation. Therefore, 100 represents the average pay per worker per capita for that country. If the teacher's salary is lower than 100 it falls below the average. Subsequently, a figure over 100 indicates a greater salary. The further from 100, the greater the pay gap.

Table 4.5 shows the pay scales for teachers in six nations. It also shows the pay ranges for those just starting (minimum), midcareer or midsalary range (middle), and the highest salary range (maximum). All six countries reward teachers for longevity.

A review of Table 4.5 reveals that U.S. teacher salaries appear to be lower than those in other countries, and the potential for salary increases across a career is lower than the average among the other nations. Japan is notable for the lowest starting salary and the largest range of increases. Given the workload of American teachers there does appear to be an unreasonable gap in teacher pay versus teacher work.

TABLE 4.5 Primary teacher salaries for 1992 indexed to per capita GDP (100 = average per capita GDP).

Nation	Minimum	Middle	Maximum	Range[1]
United States	97	150	165	68
France	90	148	172	82
Germany	135	165	178	38
Canada	108	186	197	89
England	106	192	200	94
Japan	93	168	228	135
Average[2]	105	168	190	84.3
U.S. deviation[2]	−8	−18	−25	−16.3

[1]Range was calculated by the authors. It is the difference between lowest and highest pay, showing the potential for salary increases across a teaching career.
[2]Devised by the authors.
Source: Nelson and O'Brien (1993).

Reflections on Research

Wang et al. (1993–1994) conducted a massive investigation into which factors are most important when organizing instruction. Using 300 studies and 11,000 findings, they concluded which variables appear to be most directly related to improving student learning. They organized their findings into 28 categories, which ranged from direct influences to indirect ones. They found the direct influences were more closely related to increased student learning than were the indirect ones. The 28 categories were grouped into six broad types, from most direct to most indirect:

1. Student attitude
2. Classroom instruction and climate
3. Context
4. Program design
5. School organization
6. State and district characteristics

Teachers can have the greatest effect on areas two and four. Classroom instruction and climate includes factors such as classroom management, student-teacher interactions, the quality and organization of instruction, assessment, and classroom routines. Program design includes issues such as advance organizers, alignment, and size of instructional groups.

Factors such as school leadership and school improvement relying on reform and organizational variables did not appear to greatly affect student learning.

The authors regard this as a very significant study. A synthesis is reported in *Educational Leadership,* and a more complete report appears in *Review of Educational Research,* 63:3. This is recommended reading for developing world-class schools.

TEACHING METHODS AND ORGANIZING INSTRUCTION

Teaching methods vary among the nation's studied, and it is believed that cultural variables account for different ways in which teachers organize a lesson. The most notable differences occurred between Asian and European approaches to the teaching-learning process. Particularly at the elementary level the expectations that originate in the home affect the way in which the teacher approaches the organization of the learning process. Hess and Azuma (1991) provided an unusual insight into the role of parent expectations by surveying 500 mothers of children starting first grade in both the United States and Japan. The results of the survey are startling. Basically, they concluded that Japanese mothers expect their children to adapt to school, whereas U.S. mothers expect the school to be an attractive place to learn, stressing the child's independence. When the 500 mothers in both countries were provided with a list of 13 attributes of students they were asked to rank the three most important in order. The Japanese mothers rated as most important: "basic habits," "compliance," and "patience" (34.1%, 37.8%, and 31.9%, respectively). Mothers in the United States had different values, rating "independence," "basic habits," and "tolerance of difference of opinions" most important (41.7%, 34.1%, and 31.1%, respectively). U.S. respondents rated "compliance" 9.5%, and "patience" 19.7%. It would be interesting to see how the latter would be rated by U.S. teachers. They concluded: "The Japanese mothers stressed diligence; American mothers were more concerned with independence and acceptance of diversity" (p. 3).

Hess and Azuma (1991, p. 3) reported on another study (Tobin and

Davidson) in which 300 Japanese and 210 American administrators and parents were asked what should be taught in preschool. A real dichotomy is noted (J = Japan):

- perseverance (J = 16%; U.S. = 5%)
- sympathy/empathy/concern for others (J = 80%; U.S. = 39%)
- beginning reading and math skills (J = 1%; U.S. = 39%)
- self-reliance/self-confidence (J = 44%; U.S. = 73%)
- communication skills (J = 5%; U.S. = 38%)
- good health/hygiene/grooming habits (J = 49%; U.S. = 7%)
- creativity (J = 30%; U.S. = 37%)

Parents in different cultures responded differently when their child failed to do well in school. Japanese mothers were more willing to blame the child for a lack of effort, whereas U.S. mothers were more likely to blame the school for failing to teach the child. Rowell and Gehlhar (1990) reported another facet of the power of home expectations when they analyzed a group of Japanese teachers who studied schools in the United States. Among the U.S. practices that surprised them was the use of substitute teachers. She explained, "Having substitute teachers when regular teachers are ill was also a surprise expressed about U.S. schools. Japanese students," the visitors state, "study on their own when teachers are ill" (p. 18). When school is approached with that attitude, different teaching methods can be used when teaching. This same approach to school as "work" rather than as a place to "dump the kids" probably explains why the Republic of Korea has no truancy officers. They are not needed (Duck, 1993). Dr. Park Sun-young explained the Korean approach to school: "The Confucian educational tradition has provided Koreans with a reasonable way of thinking, a strong moral sense, and a zeal for education of stressing that man can be a man only through education" (Smith, 1994, p. 9). What zeal is needed for American youth to follow for "man to become man" in the United States?

European Methods

There is considerable similarity in the way that teachers in European-tradition schools approach teaching and learning. The term *European tradition* refers to schools in the United States, Canada, England, France, Germany, Israel, and New Zealand. Particularly among the English-speaking nations the ease of exchanging teaching methods and culture appear to account for many of the similarities. However, the idea of whole language instruction and reading recovery, both of which originated in New Zealand, is reported to be commonly used in Germany (Krug, 1995).

In such classrooms, there is an effort to make classrooms inviting, with walls and ceilings lavishly covered with student work and visual stimulation from the teacher. Although grouping (the international term is *streaming*) is not common from class to class, grouping within the classroom is. The amount of time devoted to a subject varies greatly when the national curriculum does not assign a time for teaching certain subjects. A British study found that the time spent teaching mathematics varied from 2 to over 7 hours per week prior to the 1988 development of a national curriculum. Within the variation of teaching time was similar fluctuation of student engaged time, averaging about two-thirds of the teaching time provided in the class. The actual amount of engaged time fluctuated from 50 to 90 percent of the teaching time provided (Bennett and Desforges, 1991, p. 65). The students' lost time was spent in social interaction, paper shuffling, and other nonengaged activities.

In France, where there is a prescriptive national curriculum, the content is specified, but the teaching methods are not. Teachers, therefore, use whatever variety of methods will be successful. In the teaching of reading there is great variance from wholly phonics-based instruction to wholly whole language instruction. Most teachers appear to offer a hybrid of the two, combining elements of each approach when needed (Pierre, 1993).

The Germans approach to instruction is practical. The ministry defines the curriculum and its pace, providing teachers with a course syllabus to follow, along with sample lesson plans, which indicate methods that could be successful. It is up to the teacher to determine which methods to actually use. Accountability, however, ultimately assesses the learning that takes place (Führ, 1989, p. 77).

Classrooms in both Great Britain and Canada resemble those in the United States. Teachers use extensive grouping, cooperative learning, and individualized instruction in the daily routine. The use of textbooks, classroom libraries, ''ditto sheets,'' and workbooks is similar to classrooms in the United States. The stress between the efficiency of whole class teaching and tailored precision of individualized instruction is obvious to the observer. Time is lost with classroom interruptions over noninstructional issues such as lunch counts, office reports, and intercom calls for one student, which disrupt the entire school. That sends the message that teaching/learning is not as important as an issue in the main office.

Israeli education follows a similar pattern with two notable differences. Teachers in Israel are regarded as close friends who are called by their first name. That is a big departure from the formality of other classroom teachers in European-based schools. The Israelis also use field trips extensively as part of their teaching-learning arsenal. The authors found a belief that school is a very artificial structure if students are not continuously taken into the real world to see the links between what is being learned and the utility of it in the working world. Israeli field trips are a simpler form, not elaborate, daylong sojourns common to U.S. field trips. Parent permission slips are not needed because learning from the community is so common. Students visit stores, government agencies such as hospitals and fire stations, and use public transportation to see the adult world at work (Eldar, 1995).

A World-Class Quote from Taiwan Book Fairs

Dr. Huang is a university professor in the United States who is a product of Taiwanese education. When his elementary school-age son told him the school in the United States was having a book fair, he was excited. He told his son to buy as many books as he wanted, which the son did. The youngster came home after the book fair excited about the day and what he had purchased. Father and son looked at the result, and the father said, "What is this? It is not a book fair, this is the Disney Store! You already own all of these things—videotapes and computer games—you brought home comics and meaningless materials! Where are the *books*? I expected you to bring home books about Abraham Lincoln, George Washington, Martin Luther King! Why does the school give you such things? Where is good literature, history, or art?"

In Taiwan there are book fairs, but they are designed to give lower cost books to children to encourage reading, not to entertain and raise money for the school. Book fairs are designed to stimulate an understanding of the culture and history of the Chinese people and to transmit an appreciation of culture while reading out of school (Huang, 1995).

Asian Methods

Because students approach work (not school) in a business-like manner, the role of the teacher is quite different in classrooms in the Republic of Korea, Japan, and Taiwan. Confucius permeates the teaching-learning process. Students arrive motivated and ready to learn. Parents associate hard work with academic success. U.S. parents normally express satisfaction with their students' academic performance, whereas Asian parents tend to push students to do better. Elementary students in the United States, Japan, Taiwan, and China were asked what they would wish for if a wizard could grant any wish. The responses fell into four basic categories: money, material items, fantasy, or educational growth. The latter was selected by 10 percent of U.S. children and 70 percent of Chinese children (Stevenson, 1992, p. 72).

Teachers in Asian schools have the advantage of a national curriculum, the Confucian approach to the value of learning, and teachers who are regarded as top professionals. The key is in the planning and group approach to the teacher's craft. Carefully honed lessons are presented to students who start classes with a bow to the teacher. Lessons typically begin with a statement of purpose, phrased in student terms. This is frequently followed by a carefully planned question, often using concrete materials (manipulative) to accentuate the issue. In a mathematics class, for example, the teacher may pose a realistic question about how to accomplish something that requires mathematics skills. Stigler and Stevenson (1991) reported how a third grade mathematics lesson was taught in one Japanese classroom they observed. The purpose of the lesson was to demonstrate fractions in use. The teacher had a large glass container displayed. Asking how many liters it would hold, students began to guess. The teacher asked how they could be sure, and produced a one liter container. The teacher drew lines on the beaker, dividing it in thirds. Then colored water was poured into the larger container, with one filling leaving one-third in the liter container. The teacher followed this activity with a similar demonstration using another set of fractions. But fractions were not mentioned, simply observed by the students. Then the teacher repeated the findings of the two experiments to reinforce it with the class. At that point the mathematical representation was printed on the blackboard. Following this, the teacher asked how other fractions could be used, returning to the liter measurements again. The students were able to respond to other concepts like fifths and quarters. ''Near the end of the period he mentioned the term *fraction* for the first time and attached names to the numerator and denominator'' (p. 20). The lesson ended as a U.S. lesson would, with a summary. Such lessons take time to develop and are of use to any teacher teaching this concept, so why should planning a lesson be done in isolation? Stigler and Stevenson were struck by the amount of time the teacher directed lessons in Japan, Taiwan, and the United States, concluding that instruction was not being led by someone 9 percent of the time in Taiwan, 26 percent of the time in Japan, and over half of the time in U.S. classrooms.

Japanese students are expected to be actively engaged in solving whatever problem the teacher presents. This may involve a student coming to the board to work out an answer. Everyone else is engaged in critiquing the solution, because the teacher may ask others to pose different solutions or to explain why the first solution is correct. Such lessons create high student-engaged time on task. Stevenson (1992, p. 75) reports Asian students actively listen to the teacher 80 percent of the time and U.S. students about 60 percent of the time. Periods of intense play and social interaction are sprinkled throughout the day, breaking the routine of heavy engaged time. U.S. students typically get one period of recess and a supervised lunch with the expectation that the entire rest of the day will be spent heavily engaged in the learning process, often without teacher direction.

There is less seat work assigned in Asian classrooms than in U.S. schools. During seat work there is limited interaction with the teacher or other students. Given the grueling day American teachers experience, seat work can give the teacher a well-deserved respite, but at the expense of student learning. Asian teachers use seat work to quickly monitor student understanding, to correct errors, and then they move on. Stevenson (1992, p. 75) reported his study of 160 classrooms in the United States revealed that nearly half of the time teachers failed to evaluate student seat work or to provide seat work. That was never observed in China and seldom in Taiwan. When teachers in China were asked the characteristics of a good teacher, the most common answers were clarity and enthusiasm. U.S. teachers in the same study stressed sensitivity and patience.

Teaching in the Asian classrooms is regimented. Desks tend to be in rows, rooms are not normally as visually stimulating as are classrooms in the United States. The learning climate is traditional, with less teacher interest in innovation (Elliott, 1995). But the enthusiasm for learning extends beyond the classroom; Asian students spend more time on homework and leisure reading. Surprisingly, Japanese children may attend a cram school after school hours, do homework and read, yet they also watch more television than their American counterparts (Moyer, 1995).

Detractors of Asian Schools and Teaching

Any time an entire nation's schools are characterized, there must be a degree of stereotyping for obvious reasons. No discussion of Asian teaching methods would be complete without some reference to the negative views of their methods. Japanese education is criticized as sterile, with children not being encouraged to be creative (Moyer, 1996). Korean teachers, among others, use corporal punishment, and students have no recourse if they are hurt. In fact, the issue of bullying often starts in the classroom, spilling over into the schoolyard where students sometimes viciously assault the student who was criticized by the teacher. Elliot (1995) reported that rare cases of gang rape and broken bones are rumored to occur. She also said that there are physical barriers at many schools, which are designed to keep parents out. New Zealand educators who studied Japanese schools reported hearing about teachers who would not call on a student if the student's hand was not raised in just the right manner, about boring classes, and cases of student abuse (Henshall, 1992).

Among the critics of Japanese public education, Goya (1993) was particularly negative. She taught English for 15 years in Japan. She reported that testing was designed to keep students out of classes, not to assess mastery. She indicated that the aim of education is admission to the University of Tokyo (Japan's number one ranked university) and that all textbooks and teaching were aimed at that goal. Goya termed the quality of education in Japan ''pathetic.'' Further stating that: ''Virtually 100% of public school graduates would fail college entrance exams if they depend on the public schools alone to prepare them.'' She reported that a diploma from a Japanese high school was meaningless (p. 128).

The reader should not be surprised to learn there are critics of Asian education. An exhaustive review of the literature found far more advocates of Asian education than it did critics. Complaining about the public schools is an international pastime as is the older generation complaining about the younger one or griping about airline meals.

Organizing Instruction

One of the most important determinants of world-class education is the atmosphere that exists behind the classroom door. The Scottish Office calls the essential relationship that develops among teachers and students *Ethos*. In Israel, the most important operating principle of the elementary school is the establishment of a social and educational atmosphere that makes the classroom a more enjoyable and efficient place to learn. Educators expect a relaxed, informal, yet productive Israeli classroom (Eldar, 1995). Proper classroom atmosphere in any country depends on many factors: (1) what the children bring to school from his or her own background, (2) resources, and (3) the characteristics of the school itself. But the primary factor is the teacher. The school expects the teacher to be the leader and to do whatever it takes to get children to learn. The teacher determines the rules, routines, and groups with which the students function. Every world-class school has teachers who establish a productive learning climate. The best schools have an abundance of these teachers.

A World-Class Quote
about Teacher Esteem

Huang (1995) describes the esteem of the teacher in Taiwan as follows:

> In Taiwan, the teacher is a very respected person. The position is so respectable, you just want to be in that position. We trust the teachers so much that we believe they make the right decisions. We have a Teacher's Day in China. It is a holiday. We have a banquet for distinguished teachers on September 28. Any time a teacher attends a function in the community, they are always seated at the head table out of respect.

> We do not praise students very much. We appreciate and admire people, but we do not say it. Teachers tell students that they are good but there is always somebody better. This keeps them working hard. Teachers give students a false impression when teachers praise their work too much. That way students do not get into drugs, because they can't face reality.

World-class teachers deliberately organize the learning environment for optimum learning to occur. Large classes in Korea, Taiwan, and Japan meet the expectation that students learn the curricula by rote memory. Teachers prepare students for national exams given at the end of the elementary experience, and an added advantage is that students in Asian Pacific Rim nations have scored well on international tests of students mathematics and science knowledge. In the United States, educational leaders discourage teaching by rote memory (Rowell and Gehlhar, 1990). Japanese teachers with teaching experience in America cited the practice of teaching individual differences in American class-rooms as a plus. That is an interesting insight given the often cited proverb, "The nail sticking up gets pounded down," meaning that students who are different in Japan are pounded until the difference disappears.

Tracking or "Streaming" Students

Tracking, grouping, and/or streaming (the latter is the international term) students are practically nonexistent in world-class elementary schools. Other nations identify fewer students for special education by not recognizing categories such as learning disabled, gifted, or attention deficit-disordered. When asked about grouping in the German Grundschule, Krug (1995) emphatically stated, "Everybody is treated equally. When you put people in a lower group, they don't think they can do it." A Chinese proverb carries the same message, "The slow bird starts early." When the authors queried Asian educators about the length of time students were expected to do homework, the answer routinely was, "Until the student was done." Although it took "the slow bird" longer, that was not the concern. The quality of the learning was what mattered.

Although elementary educators in many other nations frown on the practice of streaming, elementary educators in the United States have practiced grouping in the classroom since the turn of the century. Austin-Huling (1995) reported that, by Christmas break, kindergarten students in the high group had focused on the way the teacher responded to students in the low group. The high students then began to treat the low students the same way.

Reflections on Research—Streaming Students

Streaming in *not* world-class. The area of streaming (i.e., grouping) is widely studied internationally. Gamoran (1992) provides a synthesis of the research in this area, finding that grouping does little, if anything, to improve the achievement of a school. It does promote student stratifications, which condemns the slower students to learn alone, rather than having student models to learn with. The research in England supports this conclusion. Myers (1994) reported on the research of David Hargreaves who studied student achievement in Great Britain. To raise school achievement, grouping was not effective. Higher expectations and student work made the difference between high achieving and low achieving students. The authors recommend that education leaders become well versed with the research (rather than conventional wisdom) in this area.

Alternatives exist for organizing elementary schools with cooperative learning; the most frequently mentioned alternative calls for grouping students effectively. A comparative study of world-class education yields one clearly dominant alternative – high expectations for all students. From the time students enter school, world-class teachers expect them to work hard regardless of their ability. In such schools grades reflect the reality of these standards; therefore, a grade of C is perfectly acceptable. In the United States many students and parents expect nothing less than an A even if it does not reflect top work. That is one result of the lack of national standards. Where there is no common performance criterion against which all students are measured, each teacher sets individual standards. Because no one ever complains when students receive high grades, grade inflation is a safe alternative.

Elliot (1995) describes the climate in Korean schools that one typically finds in countries with superior educational systems: "Teachers have high standards for all students and don't lower standards for slower students. They must work hard to catch up. Those who can't catch up might have to stay another year. However, students who work hard are standard in Korean schools."

In the United States, educators have yet to identify high expectations nationally. The task will be easier with a national curriculum or at least common state curricula that are measured against nationally normed achievement tests.

AN ELEMENTARY SCHOOL AGENDA FOR MAKING TEACHERS WORLD-CLASS

1. *Become actively involved in teacher preparation programs.* Most schools recruit and hire students from a small group of teacher-training institutions. There should be (but often is not) open dialogue between the teacher preparation programs and the school systems for which new teachers are prepared. Summer is a good time to get public school personnel together with teacher educators to explore common needs. Ask what the teacher preparation program requires for prestudent teaching field experience and how to cooperate with it. Ask about accreditation (including NCATE, a national accrediting agency) status. Then present your agenda. How can cooperating teachers who work with student teachers be prepared for their role? What areas of teacher shortage exist and how can those areas be aided? How are professional development schools funded? Collectively, how can teachers be better prepared in the future?

2. *Do not accept teacher isolation and low prestige as a fact of life.* Establish a teachers' room with the teachers' desks in one place. Create the expectation that planning will be done jointly. Teacher in-service about this process is *strongly* recommended because teacher cooperation is not automatic. Have teachers work on sharing resources, setting teaching calendars with a common pace. Tie this effort to test score improvement. If lesson plans are required, encourage a single lesson plan from several teachers as an incentive. Try common test questions for teachers with a common curriculum, common testing accountability, etc. To induce such cooperation, offer to have the office staff run off tests and student handouts to save the teachers' time. Have an extra copy run for the administrator's file, with common test questions marked. Have the teachers inform the administrators how students did on those questions. Encourage the development of a test item bank for use in future years. A peer coaching program requires volunteers to start, and it will go a long way toward breaking down teacher isolation.

Teacher prestige starts with the way the boss treats the teacher.

Compliment teachers who dress professionally, and expect student teachers and those new to the system to dress appropriately. Examine the dress code for the district, if there is one. Encourage teachers to frame and display diplomas and certifications. Does the school have an area where pictures of the staff can be displayed? Could a directory of the staff be published, with pictures, teaching assignments, and credentials listed? Does the district office have a public display area where teachers of the year have their photos? Is the board of education informed when new degrees are earned by teachers. Is the press informed?

3. *Make the mentoring program a priority.* The literature on the success of mentoring is replete with evidence of its value in both teacher retention and teacher maturation. What is provided to ensure mentoring can work? Is the mentor's nonclass workload reduced to provide time for mentoring? Can the mentor and the novice observe each other's teaching? Can room assignments be arranged to place the mentor and novice near each other, with a common planning time? Is mentor training provided? Is it possible to have mentor and novice start the year (for pay) a few days before other teachers report? What criteria are used to select mentors? How can the administration demonstrate that mentoring is a priority?

4. *Support efforts to increase reciprocity of teacher certification among states.* This is largely a political issue, but action begins with awareness. Use the press, school board meetings, and political contacts to make people aware of the problems teachers face when moving from state to state. Unfortunately, the current effort to create national certification appears to be too cumbersome, expensive, and nearly void of financial incentives to be practical. That does not mean a national teacher's license is not a good idea.

5. *Support a longer school year.* The more people are aware of the shortcomings of a 180-day school year, the more likely they are to realize the need for more time in school. The best way to increase teacher pay is to increase the length of the teaching year with salaries raised proportionately. Given the expense of such a move and the political backlash from some constituents, the best route may be adding a week to the school year annually until at least 200 days are provided. At the same time, examine the school day to see what breaks in high engaged time are provided for the students. One message the school needs to send is that school is fun, and that means some time invested in play. Long-term, that message will probably help with potential dropouts.

6. *Examine the routine of the school day for two items: (1) what additional noninstructional duties can be handled by nonteaching staff and (2) what noninstructional interruptions of teaching send the message that teaching is not important?* What can be accomplished by volunteers (Koreans, after all, run cafeterias with volunteers)? Can nonteaching staff assume more responsibilities for routine operations? Study the school for antiteaching activities such as guidance pulling students from academic classrooms when other time could be used. Are coaches leaving classes and taking students to away games by leaving early? That sends the message that sports are more important. Does someone use the intercom on all-call to have one student report to the office? How could it be made more inconvenient to have students leave early? Make interruptions to teaching time taboo.

7. *Are calls for reducing class size supported by the research in this area?* If teacher satisfaction is the reason for calling for smaller classes, then alternatives may need to be examined. The authors' experience has been that teachers will teach more students if disruptive students are removed. Investigate the alternative schools research by Christopher Chalker (1996). Alternatives to class size reduction may be more cost-effective and a morale boost at the same time.

8. *Are teachers and students expected to be dependable?* Schools can be replete with routines, rules, and activities that send messages that teachers and students are not to be trusted. The phenomenon of "learned helplessness" results when teachers are not "allowed" to leave campus during nonteaching times to tend to personal business, when unnecessary paperwork is required, etc. If students constantly are under the watchful eye of an overseer, how will they learn independence? Teachers need breaks, professional dialogue with other teachers, and time to reflect on their teaching. Audit the school for unnecessary routines and ways to free teachers to be professionals.

9. *Focus school improvement efforts on areas the literature clearly indicates is most related to organizing effective learning.* The most significant area is student attitude, and the school can focus students on the academic purpose of school in several ways. Is there a trophy case for academic awards? Does the school award academic trophies (in a number comparable with athletic trophies)? Are parents invited to the school regularly, at times they can attend? As a rule of thumb, faculty meeting agendas should begin with teaching-learning items, and at least 50 percent of the meeting should focus on such issues. Classroom instruction and climate should get considerable attention. The principal

can circulate journals with stimulating ideas, and the media center could dedicate a percentage of funds for a professional collection housed in the teachers' room.

10. *Teaching methods should be a topic of constant discussion.* The Asian concept of group planning and group reflection has considerable merit. Investigating a peer coaching program is an excellent way both to start and to polish new methods. Whole class teaching with heavy student involvement and the expectation that students will reason through a problem is one effective teaching method to develop. Although whole language and reading recovery methods appear to have long-term success, the development of some phonetic skills should not be dismissed out of hand. Teacher evaluations and observations should be designed to support new methodologies and to provide teachers with an insight into the quality of their teaching, not to fill out a form which rewards only one method of teaching. This means administrators will need to develop new skills just as the teachers will be doing.

REFERENCES

Anderson-Levitt, Kathryn., Régine Sirota, and Martine Mazurier. 1991. "Elementary Education in France," *The Elementary School Journal*, 92(1):79–95.

Asheville Citizen Times. 1994. *Overwork Death Suit Settled.* December 21, p. 17.

Austin-Huling. 1995. Interview, May.

Barrington, J. M. 1994. "New Zealand: System of Education," in *The International Encyclopedia of Education, Vol. 7.* Second edition. T. Huser and T. N. Postlethwaite, eds. Great Britain: Pergamon, pp. 4104–4111.

Barrs, Angela. 1994. "Enter the Mentor," *Times Education Supplement,* September 23, p. vii.

Bennett, Neville and Charles Desforges. 1991. "Primary Education in England: A System in Transition," *The Elementary School Journal*, 92(1):61–77.

Brahm, Bernard. 1995. Interview, May 14, French Embassy, Washington, D.C.

Brickman, William. 1994. "Education in Germany," *Encyclopedia Americana, Vol. 12.* Danbury, CT: Grolier, Incorporated.

Chalker, C. S. 1996. *Effective Alternative Education Programs: Best Practices from Planning through Evaluating.* Lancaster, PA: Technomic Publishing Company, Inc.

Chalker, Donald M. and Richard M. Haynes. 1994. *World Class Schools: New Standards for Education.* Lancaster, PA: Technomic Publishing Company, Inc.

Chambers, Gurnery. 1996. Interview, June 2.

Clabaugh, Gary K. and Edward G. Rozycki. 1990. *Understanding Schools.* Grand Rapids, MI: Harper and Row.

Dean, Clare. 1995. "At Last, a Few Words about Class Size," *Times Education Supplement.* September 28, p. 6.

Duck, H. 1993. Interview with the General Council of the Republic of Korea Consulate in Atlanta.

Education Statistics of The Republic of China. 1994. Taipei: Ministry of Education,

Eldar, Dorit. 1995. Interview, Embassy of the State of Israel, May 15.

Elliot, Joan. 1995. Interview, June 27.

Führ, Christoph. 1989. *Schools and Institutions of Higher Education in the Federal Republic of Germany.* Bonn: Inter Nations.

Gamoran, Adam. 1992. "Is Ability Grouping Equitable?" *Educational Leadership,* 50(2):11–17.

Glass, Gene V. 1994. "Class Size," *Encyclopedia of Educational Research, Vol. 1.* Sixth edition. New York: Macmillan Publishing Company.

Gless, Janet. 1995. Interview, May 4.

Goya, Susan. 1993. "The Secret of Japanese Education," *Phi Delta Kappan,* 75(2):126–132.

Hanley, Thomas. 1995. Interview, Fredicton, New Brunswick, June 14.

Haynes, Richard M. 1991. *The Wright Brothers.* Englewood Cliffs, NJ: Silver Burdett Press.

Henshall, Kenneth G. 1992. "Education in Japanese Society: Lessons for New Zealand?" *Delta,* Palmerston North, New Zealand, May.

Her Majesty's Inspectorate. 1991. *Aspects of Upper Secondary and Higher Education in Japan.* London: Department of Education and Science.

Hess, R. D. and H. Azuma. 1991. "Cultural Support for Schooling–Contrasts Between Japan and the United States," *Educational Researcher,* 2(9):2–12.

Hofkins, Diane. 1994. "Mentors 'Ignored' Trainees," *Times Education Supplement,* September 23, p. 16.

Huang, Alex. 1995. Interview, February 2.

Krug, John. 1995. Interview, German Embassy, Washington, D.C., May 17.

Lanier, Judith E. and Judith W. Little. 1986. "Research on Teacher Education," *Handbook of Research on Teaching,* third edition. New York: Macmillan Publishing Company.

Li, Dr. Chen-Ching. 1995. Interview, Taipei Economic and Cultural Office, Washington, D.C., May 17.

Liao, Chwan-Huey. 1993. Interview. February 13.

Lin, Ching-Dar. 1994. "A Day in a Public Elementary School in Taiwan," *AASA Professor,* 16(4):1–3.

McAdams, Richard P. 1993. *Lessons from Abroad.* Lancaster, PA: Technomic Publishing Company, Inc.

Ministry of Education. 1994. *Education in Korea, 1993–1994.* Seoul.

Moyer, Francis. 1996. Interview, The Japan School, Raleigh, North Carolina, March 2.

Myers, Kate. 1994. "Plain Truth about High Flyers," *Times Education Supplement,* November 4, pp. n-4.

Nelson, F. Howard and O'Brien. 1993. *AFT Local Union PSRP Salary Survey, 1991.* Washington, D.C.

OFSTED (Office for Standards in Education). 1993. *The Initial Training of Teachers in Two German Länder: Hessen and Rheinland-Pfalz.* London: Her Majesty's Scottish Office.

Pierre, Bridgette. 1993. Interview, French Embassy, Washington, D.C., Nov. 3.

Rowell, C. Glennon and James N. Gehlhar. 1990. "Comparing U.S. and Japanese School Systems: Some Observations from Japanese Teachers," *International Education*, 20(1):16−20.

Shmueli, E. 1995. "Israel: System of Education," *Encyclopedia Americana*. Danbury, CT: Grolier, Incorporated.

Smith, Dean LaVerne. 1995. Interview, University of New Brunswick, June 6.

Smith, Douglas C. 1994. *Elementary Teacher Education in Korea*. Bloomington, IN: Phi Delta Kappa Educational Foundation.

Stevenson, Harold. 1992. "Learning from Asian Schools," *Scientific American*, 266(12):70−76.

Stigler, James W. and Harold Stevenson. 1991. "How Asian Teachers Polish Each Lesson to Perfection," *American Educator*, 15(2):12−47.

Tobin, Joseph Jay, David Y. H. Wu, and Dana H. Davidson. 1989. "Class Size and Student/Teacher Ratios in the Japanese Preschool," *Japanese Schooling: Patterns of Socialization, Equality, and Political Control*. James J. Shields, Jr., ed. University Park, PA: The Pennsylvania State University Press.

United States Department of Education. 1993. *School and Staffing Survey*, Washington, D.C.: National Center for Education Statistics.

United States Department of Labor. 1994. *U.S. Labor Department, Worker Safety Report, 1994.*

U.S. Labor Department, Worker Safety Report, 1994.

Wang, Margaret C., Geneva D. Haertel, and Herbert J. Walberg. 1993-1994. " What Helps Students Learn?" *Educational Leadership*, (December-January):74−79.

Weeren, Donald. 1995. Interview, St. Mary's University, Halifax, Nova Scotia, June 12.

Wong, Harry. n/d. *You Can Be a Super Successful Teacher*. Cassette program. Sunnyvale, CA: Harry K. Wong Tapes.

Zhiming, Hou. 1988. "Chinese Culture Encounters the Western Classroom," *International Education*, 18(1):27−31.

Chapter 5

GOVERNING WORLD-CLASS SCHOOLS

If we practiced medicine like we practice education, we'd look for the liver on the right side and the left side in alternate years.
— William Bennett quoting Alfred Kazin

World-class school governance is quite different from that found in the United States. U.S. school boards are not world-class, but individual school governing boards are. School-accrediting agencies are not world-class, but the use of school inspectors is. World-class school leaders are head teachers who continue some teaching responsibilities. This chapter examines:

- ministries of education and the funding of education
- school boards versus school governors
- the era of school downsizing
- local education agencies (LEAs) and regional offices of the ministry
- strategic planning and site-based management
- school vouchers versus school choice and the role of parents
- head teachers and the training of school administrators
- school inspectors and assessing standards
- teacher assignments and beaucracy
- school charters
- setting an agenda for world-class school governance

World-class school governance is not the adversarial form found in so many U.S. school systems. Although schools around the world are easily identifiable as schools, the manner in which they are led is quite different. In a world-class school, the instructional leader is not called a principal (the name evolved from the term *principal teacher*), rather the

121

leader is called a head teacher or, simply, the head. School leaders come from the ranks of outstanding teachers. The head teaches on a daily basis, albeit for only a portion of the day. The school is not burdened with the piles of paperwork that accompany Chapter 1 or special education programs in the United States. If the school has students who have learning needs, then a trained special educator is assigned to teach and assist classroom teachers. There are no IEPs and no unannounced audits, which can result in money being taken away if a set of initials is found missing in a folder. The focus is on helping the student and the teacher. The school's mission is teaching and learning. Interruptions of teaching are nearly nonexistent.

In a world-class school if enough students come from low socioeconomic status homes, the school automatically qualifies for preschool education programs and for 130 percent of funding levels for other schools. Think of the impact that would have on inner city schools or rural areas of the United States where greater resources are needed.

There is no board of education. Although there is a district office to serve LEAs with ministry of education services, the school is run largely as its own entity. Community involvement comes from a board of governors whose interests focus on a single school. Governing a world-class school involves many issues familiar to U.S. educators such as controversy over vouchers and school choice, downsizing, the power of the ministry of education and its inspectors, etc. All 10 nations in this study underwent a cathartic reform movement in the decade between the early 1980s and 1990s. No nation reforms something that is in satisfactory condition. Concern about the quality of world-class schools is normally the focus of world-class school governance.

GOVERNING SCHOOLS FROM THE NATIONAL LEVEL

The locus of control is commonly at the national level in world-class schools. The United States, Canada, and Germany do not have a single agency that crafts the national meaning of being educated. The Canadians have a small, titular national office of education that makes no pretense of overseeing education in the provinces. Therefore, each province has its own ministry that sets standards for Canadian schools. There is much intercourse among the provinces, however, so a teacher who is certified in Nova Scotia has no problem teaching in Alberta.

Decisions about curriculum and assessment are provincial matters. The maritime provinces (Nova Scotia, New Brunswick, Prince Edward Island, and Newfoundland) frequently work in a consortia, unlike U.S. states, which often work alone. In Germany, each Land has its own autonomous ministry of education, but the Länder are generally cooperative, and wide variance among them is less common than U.S. states.

The United States, with its Rube Goldberg-like concoction of local school districts, state agencies, and the national education system in Washington seems hopelessly confusing in comparison with the world-class model. This morass invites turf battles, conflicting agendas, and funding issues, causing the system to be ineffective at best, and moribund at worst. The authors doubt anyone can define what it means to be an educated American. Such is not the case in a world-class school. For instance, teachers in New Zealand have no problem indicating what it means to be an educated New Zealander (Malcolm, 1993).

National Ministries of Education

The concept of a national ministry of education with real power is an anathema to many U.S. educators. But the concept is world-class.

A national ministry of education is an agency with significant political power and esteem. In Japan, for example, the Monbusho is run by one of the most respected political figures in the nation. The Monbusho controls the curriculum, assessment, oversees teacher licensure, inspects schools, accredits teacher preparation programs, while overseeing the funding of education. Moyer (1995) reported never having met an illiterate Japanese, despite the fact that their language is among the most difficult to master worldwide.

In Israel the education system is centrally directed. Given Israel's flood of refugees and polyglot population, the Ministry can declare a school district to be in need of compensatory education. Although there are strict guidelines for designating these areas, the result is significant. A designated area is provided with state-paid preschool programs and 130 percent of state funding. The Israelis use a kinder term for students who need compensatory education, calling them "those in need of nurturing" (Eldar, 1995). Perhaps most remarkable is the lack of paperwork required. Youngblood (1995) reported, "The purpose of the Israeli school system is to educate, not to regulate." He examined a school district in North Carolina and found, in addition to federal regulations, 400 pages of state statutes, 60 pages from the State Department of Public Instruction, and in excess of 500 pages of board of education regulations. In contrast, the Israeli Ministry of Education, Culture, and Sport oversees the management of schools with *seven pages* of regulations! Site-based management is alive and well in Israel within a federally structured school system.

Funding of Education

The funding of a national system of education does not mean that all moneys must come from the national level. Taiwan, for example, includes funding statements in the Republic of China constitution. Figure 5.1 provides quotes from the constitution which regulates the funding of education.

The funding of education is a major political issue in each nation studied. With worldwide recession and many nations electing conservative governments in the 1990s, the issue of adequate funding for schools is a hot item. In many Canadian provinces, for example, the government is ordering mergers among several agencies. Nova Scotia education faces a 5 percent reduction in funding between 1995 and 1997. To accommodate the funding loss, the number of LEAs is being greatly reduced, and even government-funded universities are being merged. The result of these mergers is that redundant programs are being phased out, resulting in an overall loss of jobs (Rich, 1995).

The ROC Constitution states that:

- All national citizens shall have an equal opportunity to an education.
- No less than 15 percent of the national budget, 25 percent of provincial budgets, and 35 percent of county and municipal budgets shall be appropriated for education.
- Free textbooks shall be provided to children from low-income families.
- Special grants shall be awarded by the national government to aid poorer areas, particularly rural mountain communities, in developing educational programs.

Source: Government Information Office, 1995, p. 336.

Figure 5.1 *The legal framework for funding the Republic of China's schools.*

As the funding for education is scaled back, there is an effort to "cut the fat." In Great Britain one means of making such cuts fell on the LEA district offices. They were staffed with specialists in various curriculum and specialty areas who provided consulting and staff development services for the district LEAs. These offices served as conduits of information about the radical reform movement during which Great Britain moved from locally designed curriculum and assessment to national forms of both. Parliament divided the funding for the district offices proportionately among the LEAs, sending the funds to the districts that could spend the funds as they saw fit. There was a similar move in Canada, which embraced the Kentucky reform movement for the accountability that follows the decentralization of funds. Such moves sound familiar to U.S. readers because the total amount of money divided into block grants is smaller than the total amount previously spent.

When comparing international funding of education, focus on two issues:

(1) What the funding is spent on. Using Taiwan as an example, more money is spent on education than any other expenditure except defense. Of that funding, over 40 percent is spent on compulsory education (grades 1−9), 6.4 percent on senior secondary schools (high schools), 7 percent on both vocational education and community colleges, and 15.8 percent on university education. Within that budget, 8.7 percent is spent on administration, none on transportation, and very little on lunchroom programs (Government Information Office, 1995, p. 336). Students from low-income homes are given their textbooks, whereas others buy them. Funds for most optional preschools and cram schools are paid by parents with no government support. U.S. schools spend vast sums on transportation, special education, feeding and health programs, and sports activities. This is not to infer the United States is wrong, but it reflects a value system based on different cultural expectations of the schools.

(2) Concern for those of limited means. Israel spends more money on those "in need of nurturing," and Canada's special educators spend their time on teaching rather than mind-numbing paperwork. Internationally, there is an effort to provide extra funding for students with compensatory needs, but at levels far below those found in the United States.

GOVERNING THE SCHOOL DISTRICT

School districts exist in all of the world-class schools studied. The ways in which districts are governed is more similar than diverse.

School Boards versus School Governors

The U.S. concept of a single school board to oversee a single district made sense when the nation's school districts were small and included few schools. Since the 1880s, when consolidating districts began, school boards faced enlarged school districts. Today, megasystems, such as those found in the nation's urban areas, use school boards to oversee thousands of employees and hundreds of schools. But with what insight at the school-based level? World-class school governance varies from this concept.

In nations such as Japan there are school boards at the prefecture (not dissimilar from a state) level, which are involved in issues like the licensure of teachers and the assignment of key personnel. But daily school governance rests on the shoulders of parents who work with a single school.

Great Britain's school governors are an example of an alternative form of school governance. The governors are community representatives who live in immediate proximity to the school. The authors visited many British schools while researching this book. In several cases the school governors met with them. The interview setting was usually a principal's office or a staff workroom. There was a relaxed climate among individuals who knew each other well. Members of the board were often parents, a local constable, area business persons, and others involved with the school's community. The meetings started with coffee served in china cups and, between sips, the head and the governors discussed issues in the school, asked about new programs, and the like. The formality of a U.S. school board meeting is out of place in such a setting. The head serves as a member of the board, and the climate is informational with consensus formed around the needs of students. Such boards may be akin to the early form of school boards in the United States 100 years ago.

The Era of Downsizing

The United States has plenty of company when the issue of downsizing

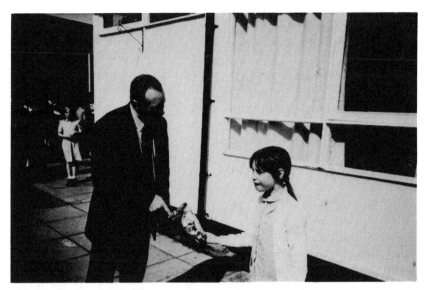

Headmaster John Fisher greets a student at the beginning of the day at Rush Common Elementary School in England. While the authors were interviewing him, the "head" excused himself, picked up a guitar and joined a large roomful of children during pastoral time. He led the children in singing a hymn (photo by Loughlin).

administrative staffs is examined. Given the worldwide economic downturn of the early 1990s, questions about the amount of money spent on education are common. In many nations there have been cuts in funding, followed by bellicose educators bemoaning the cuts. Canada, with its long history of social spending, has not been spared the budget ax. Cuts generally occur in ministry offices, in district ministry offices, and in nonteaching positions. Curiously, at the same time positions are being eliminated, calls for reducing class size sometimes succeed. In Taiwan there has been a steady reduction of class size since 1950. The student-teacher ratio fell from 36 students per class to 23 in 1994 (Government Information Office, 1995, p. 336).

A significant factor in questions about school budgets is the ratio of families with children in school to the population as a whole. Those nations, such as the United States at this writing, with a declining percentage of the families with children in school face an aging population who does not have children in school. The social value of school is questioned by the majority. The cost of education continues to rise, and aging generations generally look with disdain at younger generations.

Schools in Taiwan often open with children in formation for the flag raising ceremony. The head will lead the group in saluting the flag, and singing the national anthem. The head then addresses the student assembly, encouraging such activities as patriotism or hard work for success in school. Notice the school uniforms (photo courtesy of the Ministry of Education, Republic of China).

Questions about the outcomes of education and the cost of the system are hard to answer in such a setting.

LEAs and Regional Offices of the Ministry

The term *local education agency* (LEA) is common to many nations, with the focus more on individual schools than school districts. In England and Japan, a superintendent and board of education oversee the individual schools. National ministries of education provide regional offices of the ministry that serve the needs of local school districts. Such structures are often targets of budget cutters, however.

STRATEGIC PLANNING AND SITE-BASED MANAGEMENT

World-class schools use both strategic planning and site-based management to direct the reform of education. Malcolm (1993) credited both ideas to New Zealand, which uses them in conjunction with a national ministry of education.

One good example of strategic planning can be found in the Canadian Maritimes. In *Restructuring Nova Scotia's Education System* the Nova Scotia Department of Education (1994) outlined a vision of education in which all students are prepared for a lifetime of learning. Then it reported the goals of education.

Education should:

(1) Inspire students to learn and help them to achieve their personal best.

(2) Ensure individual mastery of appropriate knowledge.

(3) Promote development of skills for implementing knowledge.

(4) Cultivate positive attitudes, behaviors, and values.

(5) Equip every student for entry to the workplace.

(6) Prepare and motivate students for lifelong learning.

The concept of lifelong learning is familiar to U.S. educators, and it is a primary objective in Japan's 1992 restructuring efforts as well.

The *Restructuring* document drew on previous works such as *What Work Requires of Schools: A SCANS Report for Canada 2000* (Department of Education for Nova Scotia, 1994), which outlined the competencies, skills, and personal attributes needed to become a productive worker. Figure 5.2 displays how simply, and usefully, those skills were explained. A sensitivity to the needs of the business community was clear in their planning documents.

With a clear vision, goals, and a simple statement about the outcomes of education, Nova Scotia designed a strategic plan. A similar process was used in another Maritime province, New Brunswick. Their approach to designing the strategic plan for New Brunswick included a considerable amount of discussion among the provinces as this process unfolded. The authors believe that similar discussions among U.S. states could be beneficial.

New Brunswick approaches strategic planning in a unique and interesting way. The Minister for Education hired a deputy minister, Bryon James, who prepared the ministry for strategic planning by organizing an "Innovation and Development Team" under the direction of Tom Hanley, a visionary who was uniquely suited for the job. Tom insisted that his title would not be czar, director, or anything with an authoritarian sound. He is simply called "Leader of the Innovation and Development

SCANS Report:
Foundations and Competencies
Secretary's Commission on Achieving Necessary Skills (1991)

Competencies
Effective workers can productively use:

Resources
Allocating time, money, materials, space, and staff.

Interpersonal Skills
Working on teams, teaching others, serving customers, leading, negotiating, and working well with people from culturally diverse backgrounds.

Information
Acquiring and evaluating data, organizing and maintaining files, interpreting and communicating, and using computers to process information.

Systems
Understanding social, organizational, and technological systems, monitoring and correcting performance, and designing or improving systems.

Technology
Selecting equipment and tools, applying technology to specific tasks, and maintaining and trouble-shooting technologies.

The Foundation
Competence requires:

Basic Skills
Reading, writing, arithmetic and mathematics, speaking and listening.

Thinking Skills
Thinking creatively, making decisions, solving problems, seeing things in the mind's eye, knowing how to learn, and reasoning.

Personal Qualities
Individual responsibility, self-esteem, sociability, self-management, and integrity.

Source: *Restructuring Nova Scotia's Education System*, Appendix B (1994).

Figure 5.2 *Nova Scotia's list of skills, attitudes, and competencies needed to be a productive Canadian worker.*

Team." With an able and energetic staff around him, the team functions as the name implies (Hanley, 1995).

New Brunswick might appear an improbable place to find world-class school governance ideas. It borders northern Maine and only has two cities of significant size. The rest of the area is rural and not affluent. That is what makes world-class management all the more important. The New Brunswick Ministry organized a Commission on Excellence in Education, similar to the Commission on School Excellence in California. There is one notable difference. Although both the province and the state faced stringent budget cutters, the work in New Brunswick continued, whereas the California commission, regrettably, was not funded to continue. New Brunswick's commission authored *Schools for a New Century,* providing the vision for New Brunswick schools. The commission also issued *Education 2000: Preparing Students for the New Century.* Unlike Goals 2000 in the United States, this document defined specific, *achievable* objectives to prepare students for the new century. It issues annual updates divided into three parts: "we said we would" with specific notes about promises, then "since [last year] we have . . ." with achievements listed, and third "our future plans include" with the next year's activities explained. This makes the strategic plan dynamic. An example of the 1994 document is:

2. Teachers and Teacher Preparation

We Said We Would:
- explore the possibilities of a beginning teacher induction program.
  [there are four other similar actions listed]

Since September 1993 We Have:
- established a "Beginning Teacher Induction Year" pilot program. The pilot involves the schools in Districts 12 and 17 and is now in its second year.
  [five additional specific actions are listed as accomplishments]

Our Future Plans Include:
- continuing the "Beginning Teacher Induction Year" pilot program and beginning to develop recommendations for a provincial program. (p. 4)

This effort continues, with the province developing a mentor teacher-training program at this writing.

Sited-based management is world-class. True site-based management with the oversight of a national ministry of education may sound like an oxymoron, but it is not. New Zealand provides a good example. The nation stretches across hundreds of miles of ocean, with much of the population living along the meandering coastline. But there are numerous sheep farms and other rural, isolated areas where New Zealand's schools thrive. Radio schools and teachers who fly in and out of isolated areas require much local control. Although New Zealand has had a national curriculum for over 100 years, community involvement in local schools continues to be a common parent expectation.

In New Brunswick, Canada, Keswick Ridge School sits at the end of a winding road on which signs warning of bus stops and moose crossings appear. The school is shopworn and unpretentious from the exterior. But the interior radiates children's enthusiasm. Its principal, David Nielson, runs the school with gusto, which the staff clearly mirrors. Keswick Ridge School is accountable to the provincial ministry for education for achievement test scores. But it is free to prepare students in the manner that fits the community needs. The school is filled with computers because the local staff invests much instructional time and money in technology. The school performs well while being filled with happy children and happy educators.

SCHOOL CHOICE

Where students attend school and the *quality* of schools are concerns common to caring parents worldwide. Answering those questions are common duties for school administrators.

Because schools are such a large business, each of the 10 nations studied had some form of attendance district in which students were assigned to schools. During the compulsory school years, prior to standardized tests determining what specialty school students attend, ministries of education tend to assign students to the nearest schools. The physical condition of school buildings, normally poor, is a problem common to each nation studied.

Nations in the Asian Pacific Rim rank schools publicly based on quality. Each nation has something akin to states or Länder in which regional authority over schools is vested. Within those regions, municipalities or other political artifacts are used as local school attendance zones. Usually, students are assigned to the school nearest to them. But in Taiwan, for example, with huge extended families, parents may send students to a family member who lives near a ''star school'' so the child attends that school if its reputation is better than the closer local school (Liao, 1993).

Germany employs a unique means of assigning students to schools. Through age 10, children are sent to the nearest available school. At age 10 parents may begin to think about their child's talents, and they are free to send their child to another school with a program they believe is in the best interests for their child. They may also change their minds and send the child elsewhere if the selected school does not perform as expected (Führ, 1989, p. 79).

Interest in school vouchers occurs in several nations, with the United States taking the lead. Church schools in England, France, and Canada have long received education funds, so the question of vouchers for religious freedom is largely mute. In Israel, parents may send children to Hebrew or Arab schools. In rare cases, an Arab child may attend a Hebrew school, which is taught in Hebrew. The ministry also funds Hebrew religious schools for increased religious instruction. In these instances, parents have choice, but not vouchers. Vouchers do not appear to be world-class.

QUALITY CONTROL

Each nation is concerned about the quality of education their students receive. Two ways in which quality is ensured are the caliber of administrator running the school and the use of school inspectors.

Head Teachers and the Training of School Administrators

In the United States and Canada the idea of a principal teacher has evolved into full-time administrator with little or no teaching responsibilities. The training of the head teacher varies greatly among world class schools.

In many European and Asian schools, the head teacher comes from the ranks of those who are recognized as excellent teachers. Those individuals may respond to an advertisement for a head teacher. The expectation in Japanese schools, for instance, is that the individual applying for a head teacher position will accept the most distant, most needy assignment in the region. The individual who is appointed as head will move, often leaving the family behind, to devote 100 percent to the job (McAdams, 1993, p. 217). That parallels the Japanese administrator in industry. The new head assumes a responsibility without any prior training.

The United States and Canada are largely alone in ensuring the new principal is trained in meeting school responsibilities prior to assuming them. In British schools, those with ultimate local autonomy (called "grant-maintained" schools) have nearly total control of the school budget. These schools are granted an additional 5 percent budget for becoming grant maintained. The authors visited several grant-maintained schools in England and Scotland. Most reported their first independent move was the hiring of a bursar to oversee the books, often at an expense exceeding the extra funding accompanying grant-maintained status. Principals in the United States and Canada have such skills prior to arrival on the job, but they may lack the teaching reputation of their world-class counterparts.

Worldwide, elementary schools are gaining more responsibility for the rearing of children than they have had in the past, and that affects the principal's role. Among the nations, the common denominator is the increasing percentage of two-earner families, eclipsing families in which one parent is responsible for child rearing. Schools in the developed nations increasingly fill the roles of breakfast provider, doctor overseeing immunizations, and postschool day care provider. The distinct roles between schools and families blur, putting more responsibility on the school administrators.

World-class school heads are dependent on the quality of training they experience. The United States and Canada may prepare the best trained leaders, but the world-class expectation that the head will teach is largely absent for them. David Nielson at Keswick Ridge School in New Brunswick personifies a world-class school administrator. There was one large classroom with 120 students, grades 6 to 8. Two teachers worked purposefully with groups of students while other students engaged themselves independently. Nielson (1995) moved easily to a table where the students had a chair waiting for him. Immediately he became engrossed in a math lesson. Later he explained that he taught math 2 hours a day in that room. "If I couldn't do that then I'd only be a paper pusher. I'd quit the principalship if I couldn't teach."

School Inspectors

One of the favorite targets of downsizers are central office supervisors. In an attempt to "cut the fat," school improvement suffers. In world-class schools, from France and Germany to New Zealand and Japan, supervisors are called school inspectors. The name has an unfortunate connotation to U.S. educators who think in terms of meat-packing houses and feckless inspectors. In world-class schools the inspector is a crucial part of the school improvement team.

Inspectors are gleaned from the ranks of established, high achieving teachers who are known for the quality of their craft. Advertisements appear in British trade journals, for instance, asking for applications. The successful candidate works for the Ministry of Education at the district level. From country to country the inspector's role varies somewhat, but they generally appear at a given school site at a predictable time, spending a week or more on an inspection team. The purpose of the inspection is to determine if the school meets the standards set by the ministry. After several weeks a report is sent to the school. In Britain, there is a week's grace period to digest the findings from the inspectors before the report is made public via the press.

The role of inspectors is not adversarial. Because the inspectors are respected teachers first, they are sources of knowledge who pass along tips for improving achievement. Because they see a variety of good practices in schools teaching a common curriculum they are walking sources of "best practices" information. A New Zealand principal explained that one of the reasons for the success of his school came from inspectors who shared the best ideas from school to school (Malcolm, 1993). He lamented that inspection has become so rigorously tied to accountability, that the sharing of ideas is being replaced with directives and guidelines. Glickman (1990, p. 434) noted the riptide of school reform in the United States has two currents flowing in opposite directions. One current supports site-based management and the professionalism of teachers. The use of processes such as action research flow in this tide. The opposing current distrusts local control and teacher authority. Processes such as accountability based solely on test scores and the concept of education bankruptcy flow in this tide. Caught swimming in this sea are the teachers and administrators who are raising the next generation of U.S. citizens.

Assessment Standards

The use of national testing standards as measures of student learning are world-class, and U.S. educators should expect to spend the remainder of their careers with them. Accountability will not go away.

Using school inspectors to assess a core of standards is not unlike the school accreditation process found in the United States. During an interview with Her Majesty's Chief Inspector of Schools in Scotland, the authors reviewed the standards used by the school inspectors. The standards are published in *Standards and Quality in Scottish Schools, 1991 – 1992* (The Scottish Office of Education, 1992) updated routinely to keep the standards aligned with the school reform movement. Similar publications are found elsewhere, in England and New Zealand, for example. Among the standards the inspectors look for are:

- continuous assessment, emphasizing classwork, writing, and a sample of student work in individual folios
- time on task in specific areas such as writing instruction, writing across the curriculum, and writing in a variety of contexts
- a sense of school pride, including school uniforms that identify students as part of a particular school (the uniforms are well known in the community), a school climate of expectation and purpose
- the use of learning out of school (i.e., homework) which is evaluated, linked to learning in school, and based on a clear rationale that links parent involvement to school learning
- a review of school policies and procedures, focused on the support of student learning
- involvement by the school governors in the work of the school, its curriculum, standards, quality, and resources

A full list of the standards is too long to fully report here. The standards are widely available to the public as well as to educators. The purpose of school inspection is to locate evidence that national standards are adhered to and to point out both strengths and weaknesses in each school. The head and the governors are responsible for leading the effort to improve on weaknesses and to maintain strengths.

In Great Britain the work of Peter Mortimer (1992) guides the standards that are assessed. He identifed 12 ethos indicators of an effective school. They are:

- pupil morale
- teacher morale
- teacher's job satisfaction
- the physical environment
- the learning context
- teacher-pupil relationships
- equality and justice
- extracurricular activities
- school leadership
- discipline
- information to parents
- parent-teacher consultation

Mortimer's ethos list emphasizes parent involvement and school climate. His work mirrors the effective schools research in the United States. The focus on ethos (distinguishing characteristics and beliefs of a group) are much like the school climate movement started by Manatt and Sweeney in the early 1960s. The school effectiveness research from the United States is well respected and is widely used internationally.

TEACHERS AND CHARTERS

The success of any school ultimately depends on the quality of each teacher's work. The ability of world-class teachers to change jobs depends on the agency controlling them.

Teacher Assignment

Like any other professional, teachers need to be able to change worksites for a variety of reasons. In the United States teachers can move between states with some difficulty. It almost appears that it is illegal to spirit teachers across state lines. Do world-class teachers face the same certification boundaries as U.S. teachers? The answer is no.

Canada's national ministry of education is small. Most education decisions are left to the 10 provinces and 2 territories in the confederation. The origin of the name Canada is likely from the Huron-Iroquois word "kanata" meaning "village" or "community" (Young, 1985). The sense of villages is seen through the provincial ministries of education cooperating and planning together, although the federal government does not require it. Based on that cooperation, teachers trained in New Brunswick have a relatively easy time moving to Alberta to teach (Ott, 1995). Conversely, a U.S. teacher in one state who wishes to move to another may find no reciprocity exists between the states. Relicensure may involve additional testing and perhaps college work as well. This indicates a lack of trust among the states while colleges of education routinely seek national accreditation for their programs. The concept of national certification is in its infancy in the United States, and it is cumbersome and tedious while offering uncertain rewards.

Teachers in Great Britain do not face such artificial barriers. The universities that train teachers must be accredited and certified by the Department for Education from London. Once certified, their graduates are free to move within the four areas (England, Wales, Northern Ireland, and Scotland) to practice their craft.

In Japan the licensure-granting body is the individual prefecture. There are 8 basic regions in Japan and 46 prefectures, which rather closely parallel the 50 states in the United States. Traditionally, Japanese workers begin with, and retire from, the same employer, so Japanese teachers are less likely to move among prefectures. Within them, however, teachers move from school to school about every eight years (White, 1987). Once licensed in one prefecture, the likelihood of being certified to teach in another one is easier than in the United States. More emphasis is put on teaching quality than on the licensure issue. Teachers in areas of shortage (such as science or math) find movement easier than teachers in areas of teacher surplus (such as elementary education).

The world-class standard for teacher certification is national just as curriculum, governance, accountability, and funding are. The current effort to combine the U.S. national teacher education association standards with state department of education standards (Florida is a good example) offers a better chance of having universal reciprocity among states. Once that exists, teachers will be able to move among states and be assigned based on existing need.

School Charters

The concept of school charters is world-class. Although they take

---

The Children's Charter

Inasmuch as children are new citizens who shall determine the future of the nation, their minds and bodies shall be treasured. All efforts should be made to see that children grow with justice, beauty and courage.

1. Children should be valued as human beings and raised properly as members of society.
2. Children should be born healthy and educated with genuine affection at home and in society.
3. Children should be provided with proper facilities and an environment in which they can study and play as they please.
4. Children should not be burdened with excessive study or other duties.
5. Children should be rescued first in time of danger.
6. Children should not be made the object of exploitation under any circumstances.
7. Hungry children must be fed, sick children treated, physically and mentally handicapped children assisted, delinquent children reformed, and orphans and juvenile vagrants cared for.
8. Children should be brought up to love nature, the arts and sciences. They should develop an inquisitive nature and moral character.
9. Children should be brought up as good citizens to contribute to the freedom and peace of mankind and to the development of culture.

Source: *Education in Korea, 1993–1994* (1994).

Figure 5.3 *The children's charter (May 5, 1957).*

various forms, these charters are statements of belief and purpose for a school. Unlike mission statements, the charters are a form of contract between a particular school and the community it serves. The process of writing a charter can be valuable for a faculty and community when done cooperatively. It causes the writers to wrestle with fundamental issues such as the purpose and limitations of school. The school charter referred to here should not be confused with the charter school movement found in parts of the United States.

The constitution from the Republic of Korea establishes the education laws that govern it. In 1957 a children's charter was written into law. It is reproduced in Figure 5.3. Those who think of Korean schools as grueling factories for children may be surprised to read it.

A second form of charter exists in Scotland. It is called "the parents' charter," and it is reproduced in Chapter 8. A similar charter exists in England, but the authors prefer the Scottish version because it lists parents rights *and responsibilities,* whereas the English version is limited to the rights of parents.

The authors have not been able to find another form of charter that fits with the idea of a children's charter and a parents' charter: an educators' charter of rights and responsibilities. Glickman (1994) provides a school charter that could also be of use in developing a world-class school.

AN AGENDA FOR ACTION: SCHOOL GOVERNANCE

1. *World-class schools utilize a national ministry of education and funding comes from the national level so that equity of funding is ensured. This is not likely to occur given the U.S. form of education.* Although a powerful national ministry of education will not occur in the United States, elementary school leaders can affect the same type of governance by following the developing national frameworks and aligning local school curriculums to the frameworks that are being developed nationally. As consumers of educational products, school leaders can make publishers aware of the need to have textbooks, computer programs, etc., aligned to the national frameworks. By creating a demand for national assessment instruments that align with the national frameworks, a market can be created for such materials. Additionally, where states are centrally establishing curriculum and assessment, school leaders can be proactive by making the state curriculum and assessment responsive to the national frameworks. The issue of inequity in funding schools is more difficult to rectify. In some areas, low-wealth school districts have combined efforts and addressed the funding inequity in the courts. If enough such cases are won within states, then the issue of state-to-state equity could be addressed.

2. *World-class schools have a governing board for the individual school. This does not supplant the LEA board of education, but it could augment it.* Elementary school leaders can approach this concept as part of site-based management. A school should begin the process by inviting a group of active community participants to help forge a school board of governors. The title given to the group may need adjustment, but there should be an election process, bylaws, and some formality during the meetings. The principal should serve as the head of the board, with a parent or other nonschool member serving as the assistant head. The membership should reflect the key constituencies from the community:

teachers, school staff, business and industry, local government, etc. Using existing organizations, such as chambers of commerce, county commissioners, would make a representative group possible, and inviting support from such groups will help to ensure support. The board would not "run" the school but would become familiar with the curriculum, the school improvement efforts, the strategic plan, etc. The board could have a member attend LEA school board meetings, and students could report their activities to them. Members should be asked to serve as a conduit of information between the school and their constituent groups, alerting the school to perceived needs and explaining the school to those groups.

3. *Downsizing is common in the world's schools. Elementary school leaders can become proactive during the era of downsizing. This will require that old paradigms are broken when costs are increased by redundancy and that needed personnel, such as those who improve instruction, are explained to the community. One effort in this area will be to explain to the community what is, in fact, fat and what is necessary but not understood.* This is not an easy area to deal with because the livelihoods of certain individuals may be involved, and that is an emotional issue. Because schools are so paradigm-bound it is not easy to realize where efficiency and expense are wasted. Creative thinking will highlight this effort. For example, is there redundancy between the public library and the school library? Could Head Start, or similar groups, share resources such as busses, staff development, and facilities? In rural areas where specialty staff such as special education coemploy personnel and share that person's services or does each system really need its own individuals? To reduce class size efficiently, can teacher assistants be used rather than more expensive teachers (the latter, in addition, need individual rooms which assistants do not need). One approach to this process could be to study the school's history, determining what was added over time and then investigating the educational efficiency of the addition.

4. *World-class elementary schools use strategic planning and site-based management. The strategic plan provides the long-term road map for getting to world-class status. World-class schools are staffed by world-class teachers, so site-based management takes advantage of their expertise.* One feature of world-class elementary schools is the open involvement of the community in the work of school. This includes parents, business, and others with a vested interest in the future. Such

schools are deliberately crafted, and the process of becoming world-class begins with a vision of what a world-class school is, an in-depth study of the common values held by the school's stakeholders, and a review of the literature on school improvement. Studying the world's schools is an excellent way to glean best practices for local school improvement. But each school head must remember the unique character of his or her school and community. The school is expected to develop students with specific characteristics. What is a best practice in one culture may not be best in another. Remember one of the two rules for developing a world-class elementary school is, "Just because it is world-class does not mean Americans will want it." The use of strategic planning is an excellent means of establishing a vision, common beliefs, and goals that the school will achieve. It is also an excellent way of involving the community in the work of the school and of informing the public about the school's purpose and direction.

Site-based management is world-class. It also recognizes the expertise of a faculty. The use of grade level chairpersons is one way to start such management. The chair should be selected because of expertise rather than by election or rotation. Another means of organizing a lead teacher concept among a faculty is by curriculum expertise (one person leading in language arts, another in mathematics, etc.). Using curriculum councils and curriculum audits also assists the site-based management process. For site-based management to succeed, however, the principal must be secure enough to share real decision making with the faculty as well as with the community served.

5. *World-class elementary schools are organized into larger units at the district and national level. The term* LEA *is common to world's schools, and school districts are the norm. The ministry of education typically has district level offices, so access to national authorities is available locally.* In some states the downsizing craze is reducing or eliminating district offices from the state department of education. In other states, such district offices are being developed. These offices are necessary as long as they are staffed with hardworking experts who serve the schools as conduits of information and expertise.

The era of downsizing continues the trend of ever-larger school districts in the name of efficiency. In states where school districts are organized in K−6, and separate 9−12 situations, such mergers might be in order. However, school systems can become too large and impersonal. Although the LEA assists with curriculum, assessment, and funding, the use of a single school board of governors is world-class.

6. *World-class elementary schools are led by true teacher leaders. The head should be selected from the ranks of the best teachers who have expertise at the school level that they will lead. Although not the world-class norm, the United States and Canada do well by preparing the qualities of school leadership prior to electing a school head. The head maintains a teaching connection with both teachers and students by retaining regular teaching responsibilities.* An elementary school principal should have been recognized as an excellent teacher prior to becoming a principal. Ideally, that person's experience and skill should have been at the elementary school level. The principal would then have the teacher's wisdom about developmental and learning theory for that age group. One superb elementary principal came from the high school level where he was recognized as a superior teacher. Once appointed to an elementary school principalship, he enrolled in a course on the development of an elementary school curriculum at a nearby university. That validated him with the elementary staff who wondered if he could effectively lead an elementary school.

Maintaining a regular teaching load is difficult for a principal. But it is the ultimate statement of value, putting teaching and learning ahead of paperwork, meetings, and accountability. Time is never found; it is made. Making time to teach is the mark of a world-class head teacher. The time can be limited to an hour a day or several regular times a week, but it must be inviolate. The principal should select the teaching area in which he or she has greatest expertise and then add it to the faculty. Staff meetings should always start with curriculum and instruction issues first as another statement of priority.

7. *Vouchers are not world-class, but elements of choice and parent involvement are. The issue of vouchers is hard to study internationally because of unique historical and cultural alignments that are found in the United States. Choice within LEAs and availability restrictions are found in the international world of schools. Parent involvement is essential to developing a world-class elementary school.* Vouchers are an emotional and potentially divisive issue for world-class school leaders to discuss. On the one hand, the use of state funding to support religiously based schools are found in places such as England and Israel. That support, however, comes from historical ties between the church and state. For instance, in England the churches were among the first to use their buildings for schools when the British education system was being developed. Ownership of the building and early development of the local school curriculum began with the churches and passed from there to the

state. Over time, such concepts as compulsory attendance and multicul-
turalism were added to that base; thus the relationship between church
and state continues today and funding church-based schools continues.
Such a history is not paralleled in the United States.

The isolation of church and state in the world of school is largely unique
to the United States. One of the authors stood in Brookhaven School in
Dartmouth, Nova Scotia, talking to the principal, Jean Llewellyn, and
several staff members, while visiting in the fifth and sixth grade hall. At
9 A.M. the intercom crackled on and, with no announcement, the children
stood up. ''Oh, Canada'' played softly as several students joined in
singing their national anthem. When it ended, they sat down to work.
The next sound the author heard was the strings section of the elementary
school band rehearsing for a performance. The strings played ''How
Great Thou Art.'' Both teachers and principal were surprised that that
was not common in U.S. schools.

Some form of school choice is common in world-class schools. That
is not wholesale choice, however. Based on availability, parents in places
such as Germany and England may choose a particular school if it is
within the LEA in which they live. Transportation is provided to the
local school but not to another one the parents may select, making parents
responsible for providing it. In the United States the concept of magnet
schools is somewhat akin to such choice. When the school system
provides both choice and transportation, however, the costs can be
prohibitive. Kansas City, Missouri, is an example of such a system, and
transportation costs reportedly run at $1000 per child annually.

Parent involvement is discussed in detail in Chapter 8. When governing a world-class elementary school, the availability of parents is a factor
to be considered. Schools generally run on a banker's mentality (open
after two parents go to work and closed before they get out of work).
Banks, however, are extending their hours, and some are even opening
on Saturdays. Supermarkets and discount stores have gone further with
''Open 24 Hours'' increasingly the norm. One elementary school principal, Toni Hill of Forest View School in Durham, North Carolina, has
broken the banker mentality, allowing teachers to work nights and
weekends, developing '' comp time'' to be taken on days when the school
is closed. The result is an involved staff that is far more accessible to the
public it serves.

8. *School inspectors and the use of national assessment standards are
world-class. The term* inspector *has a vastly different connotation else-*

where than it does in the United States. The British have an affinity for
the inspector of Scotland Yard lore, for example. An inspector in the
United States is liable to conger up visions of meat and poultry inspec-
tors. The concept might be of use, but the name needs changing for U.S.
schools. Assessment and accreditation at the national level exist in some
forms in the United States, and that area is expected to increase. That
growth will continue to be suspect in many quarters, however, so it will
continue to be controversial. The idea of having publicly accessible
education standards makes sense when the work of school needs to be
explained to the public. Such standards would help answer the critics of
U.S. schools when the standards are adhered to. Having recognized
experts in education examine a school for compliance with the standards
helps the school improvement process, particularly when the public is
told which standards are met or exceeded. That is basically the concept
of instructional auditing. Certainly the idea of having experts share with
the administration and staff the best ideas from other schools is helpful.
Avoid calling the expert an inspector. Consider the concept but not the
name.

Nationalizing education is, at best, controversial. But the basic elements are largely in place: national frameworks, national assessment
(standardized achievement scores and NAESP), an attempt to develop
national teacher certification, and nationally published (but locally
marketed) textbooks, computer software, etc. Elementary school
leaders should keep abreast of these developments and align with the
standards when feasible.

9. *Teacher assignment in world-class schools facilitates the mobility*
of educators. Current efforts to develop a recognized national teacher
certification are commendable but incredibly cumbersome and expensive. World-class elementary school leaders recognize the national
mobility that characterizes our culture, and the leaders should support
reasonable efforts to have a standard teaching license among the states.
Perhaps the effort to develop such a license regionally is a better first
step in this direction.

10. *School charters are world-class. Elementary schools could*
validate the old adage that "the search is the treasure" by bonding with
their communities while collectively developing school charters. The
idea of telling the constituent groups what their rights and responsibilities
are makes sense. It fits with the visioning process of strategic planning.
It has intrinsic public relations value, appealing to parents, educators,

and the business community at the same time. Such contracts should not be drafted lightly, however, nor can they simply borrow from someone else. The values of the community should be reflected in these statements, that should be short, simple, and to the point. A world-class elementary school leader might consider a children's charter first, followed by a statement of parents' rights and responsibilities. A community group could draft the responsibilities section of an educator's charter, whereas the staff might draft the rights section. Possible starting points could be as follows: under rights, ''Teachers have the right to a safe and orderly climate in which to teach''; under the responsibility section, ''Educators are responsible for being prepared to teach all children every time they enter class.'' A school charter could be mutually developed by the school and its constituencies.

REFERENCES

Commission on Excellence in Education. 1992. *Schools for a New Century.* New Brunswick, Canada: Department of Education.

Commission on Excellence in Education. 1991. *Excellence in Education.* New Brunswick, Canada: Department of Education.

Department of Education for Nova Scotia. 1994. *Restructuring Nova Scotia's Education System. Preparing All Students for a Lifetime of Learning.* Nova Scotia: Author.

Department of Education for Nova Scotia. 1994. *What Work Requires of Schools: A SCANS Report for Canada 2000.* Nova Scotia: Author.

Education in Korea. 1993–1994. 1994. Seoul, Korea: National Institute of Educational Research and Training, Ministry of Education.

Eldar, Dorit. 1995. Interview (May 15).

Führ, Christoph. 1989. *Schools and Institutions of Higher Education in the Federal Republic of Germany.* Bonn: Inter Nations.

Glickman, Carl. 1994. *Restructuring America's Schools.* San Francisco: Jossey Bass Co., Inc.

Glickman, Carl. 1990. *Supervision of Instruction: A Developmental Approach.* Needham Heights, MA: Allyn and Bacon.

Government Information Office, Republic of China. 1995. *Republic of China Yearbook 1995.* Taipei: Author.

Hanley, Thomas. 1995. Interview (June 14).

Liao, C.-H. 1993. Interview (March 15).

Malcolm, Peter M. 1993. Interview.

McAdams, Richard P. 1993. *Lessons from Abroad: How Other Countries Educate Their Children.* Lancaster, PA: Technomic Publishing Company, Inc.

McGee, Clive. 1994. Interview.

Mortimer, Peter. 1992. In *Standards and Quality in Scottish Schools, 1991–1992.* Edinburgh, Scotland: The Scottish Office of Education.

Moyer, Francis. 1995. Interview (April 14).

Nielson, David. 1995. Interview (June 14).

Ott, Walter. 1995. Interview (June 14).

Rich, Thomas. 1995. Interview (June 12).

Standards and Quality in Scottish Schools, 1991–1992. 1992. Edinburgh, Scotland: The Scottish Office of Education.

White, Merry. 1987. *The Japanese Educational Challange: A Committment to Children.* New York: Free Press.

Young, J. Crumwell. 1985. "Canada" *Encyclopedia Americana, Vol. 5,* Danbury, CT: Grolier Publishing Company, p. 312.

Youngblood, Kennith. 1995. Unpublished monograph.

DEVELOPING WORLD-CLASS ELEMENTARY STUDENT ASSESSMENT

Some gates are so locked up they couldn't be doorways.

— Arnie

Chapter 6 builds on the definition of world-class elementary curriculum developed in the previous chapter, because the two components of a world-class system are interdependent. The chapter examines the world-class nature of elementary student assessment by giving the reader a glimpse of how each world-class country structures elementary student assessment. The chapter focuses attention on current attempts at international assessment, particularly the 1992 IAEP science and mathematics scores. A summary of assessment practices in the United States follows.

The agenda for action includes 10 suggestions that elementary leaders might use to install a world-class assessment system.

The United States has yet to come to grips with one of the most perplexing of educational issues, ''How do educators best measure what students learn?'' The issue remains perplexing because the political nature of assessment often takes precedence over sound educational issues. For example, legislators at the national, state, and local levels often propose tests that will tell Americans how well the country compares with other nations; how well students compare with other same-age students; and how one school compares with another. A sound educational purpose for testing is to design and use tests that can be used to assess student progress and establish goals for future learning. Educators cling to their assumed right to decide how students will be assessed and how the results will be used. These conflicting goals

149

produce division and seem often to remove all parties from the educational value of assessing learning and helping students grow.

THE WORLD-CLASS STATUS OF STUDENT ASSESSMENT

Student Assessment in the World-Class Countries

New Zealand is dedicated to national curriculum and national evaluation. Testing in New Zealand's primary schools is criterion referenced, and a student's achievement is compared with national standards. Teachers are expected to gather information about their students' progress in each learning area outlined in *The New Zealand Curriculum Framework* (1993). Happily, teachers use the testing information mostly to assist children in their learning and to report progress to interested parties. The department of education strongly recommends that educators move away from measuring one child's progress against another. Therefore, teachers describe what each child has achieved and comment on the success in relation to the national curriculum goals. Specifically, each primary school should provide a system that enables them to:

- identify needs
- show rates of progress
- provide a profile of each child
- demonstrate the degree of proficiency achieved
- supply evidence on which decisions have been made
- assist in the selection of appropriate teaching strategies
- report to children and parents
- complete the primary progress records (Faire and Yates, 1994)

Although the department of education expects teachers in New Zealand's primary schools to use a variety of student assessment methods, observation is perhaps the most commonly used method. Other methods include collecting work samples, interviewing students, taping learning events, keeping anecdotal records, providing self-assessment by students, and, of course, administering formal and informal tests. Teachers currently design their own tests, but they may soon have to deal with testing designed to monitor national standards. Plans call for teachers to take a light sample (probably 5 percent) of student achievement at ages 8 and 12. Teachers will collect the sample on a 3- or 4-year cycle to build up a national picture of student achievement. The purpose will be to improve the national standards (*The New Zealand Curriculum Framework,* 1993).

Teachers encourage students in New Zealand to regularly assess their own progress. Students often collect work samples, test results, and personal logs in a portfolio and use the portfolio to report to parents and perhaps the community (Faire and Yates, 1994). Again, American educators can learn from New Zealand the value of trusting teachers to conduct important educational experiences such as evaluation.

France disposed of national testing at the elementary level during the last decade. Twenty-eight regional academies (26 in France and 2 overseas) provide for the development and administration of primary tests. There are frequent tests over all subject areas causing many pupils to fail, with the result that they may have to repeat the grade (Cummings, 1994). Teachers design tests to measure the national curriculum. The national curriculum varies little from school to school but has some regional variation. Students spend their first 5 years in primary school (ecole primaire) where teachers spend approximately the same number of hours on each subject (*What College-Bound Students Abroad Are Expected to Know about Biology,* 1994). The French student cannot graduate from middle school without an in-depth knowledge of language usage. Before entering high school, teachers require the French student to recognize and develop allegories, metaphors, hyperbolas, oxymora, redundancies, euphemisms, antitheses, and paradoxes. French students will amass huge amounts of history, geography, science, math, and languages. The long-range assessment goal for students is to pass the baccalaureate after the high school years. The exams do not require the student to deliver memorized facts but to discuss, argue, and extract meanings (Marcus, 1994).

A World-Class Quote from France

''To the deepest circle of educational hell belongs the 'multiple choice' exam. French teachers abhor it and, as convenient as it is, they haven't succumbed to it yet'' (Marcus, 1994).

Because success in later schooling depends on the student's ability to analyze, create, manipulate, and evaluate, primary teachers use essay tests almost exclusively beginning in kindergarten. French teachers think that essay testing promotes thinking and writing (Gavin, 1995). Marcus (1994) explains, "To the deepest circle of educational hell belongs the 'multiple choice' exam. French teachers abhor it and, as convenient as it is, they haven't succumbed to it yet.''

In Germany, students move to a tracked program early in the educational experience. All students attend primary school, where teachers are responsible for test preparation and grading. After grade 4, educators at the Grundschule send students to the main school *Hauptschule* (terminal vocational school), the *Realschule* (intermediate school), or the Gymnasium (academic school). Once tracked, students have few examinations until the conclusion of the secondary experience when vocational tests are required for students in vocational schools, and the Abitur is required for those students in the Gymnasium. Each of the 16 Länder is responsible for curriculum development and test development, but the Länder work together, and the resulting tests are quite similar with the results mutually accepted. The Abitur is crucial for admittance to the university, and students take the test seriously and begin preparation early in their years in the Gymnasium.

Britain is the only world-class country to schedule national examinations twice during the primary years. The Educational Act of 1988 created national curriculum and attainment targets for each national subject. In England and Wales, for example, there are five major targets: (1) speaking and listening, (2) reading, (3) writing, (4) spelling, and (5) handwriting. For each of these targets, the Office for Education established 10 levels of attainment. Officials also established 4 key stages of educational experience:

- Key Stage 1: up to age 7 (infants)
- Key Stage 2: 7–11 (juniors)
- Key Stage 3: 11–14 (pre-GCSE)
- Key Stage 4: 14–16 (preparation for GCSE)

Teachers assess students at the end of each key stage by using a combination of teacher-made tests and standard national assessment tests. The combined assessment experience is called the Standardized Achievement Tasks (SATs) (*Education in Britain*, 1991).

Teachers integrate the tasks into everyday classroom practice and exploit a wide range of presentation modes such as oral, written, pictorial, computer, and demonstration. The intended use of the test results in England and Wales was diagnostic, but the government clearly intended to use the tests for comparing schools and evaluating the national education standards. Teachers consider the tests to be high stakes, turning up a notch the stress on teachers and students. In Scotland, the test procedures are similar, except the results are only intended to provide diagnostic and formative information to teachers. Therefore, the teachers view the Scottish tests as low stakes. Teachers in both countries found the 1991 tests difficult to administer and time consuming. In 1993 when the Key Stage 3 tests were scheduled, teachers in England, Wales, and Scotland refused to administer the examinations. The boycott received some support from parents in England and Wales and strong parental support in Scotland. Four reasons were given for the boycott:

- The tests in English literature are flawed and too narrow.
- The tests do not result in improved student learning.
- Local teachers administer and grade the tests, which requires excessive time.
- The purpose of the tests is to provide statistics for the construction of league tables used to compare schools.

The battle over testing at the primary level appears to be a much larger conflict—a conflict over local control of testing as opposed to national control of testing. The British media generally sided with the Department for Education, and a few local school boards (boards of governors) flirted with the idea of removing pay from teachers who refused to administer the tests (Chalker and Haynes, 1994). The testing scheme, however, remains intact in Britain as of this writing, but adjustments were made in 1994 after a blue-ribbon committee reviewed and reported.

In Japan, Korea, and Taiwan, instruction at the elementary level prepares students to take a high-stakes, national test at the conclusion of the elementary experience. In Taiwan, all students take a National Entrance Examination at the end of the junior high school experience. Virtually all students attend 6 years of elementary school and 3 years of junior high school. The National Entrance Examination is administered each year in July for a period of 2 days, and its composition is essay with some multiple choice. The exams are graded by teachers.

Huang (1995) claims that the exams are fair, for all students have the same opportunity to learn in Taiwanese elementary schools. Local teacher-designed tests in the elementary schools and junior high schools are patterned after the National Entrance Examination and measure success on the national curriculum. Many students also attend cram schools after regular school hours where the focus is preparation for the national exam. Class sizes in the cram school are in the range of 50−100 students, and the schools employ the best teachers available in the country. Superior students are sometimes granted free tuition, for there is competition for cram schools to produce students who score highest on the National Entrance Examination. Standards are high in both the regular school and the cram school, however, and those who fall behind might have to stay in elementary school an additional year. Students who work hard are the norm in Korea, however, for the culture rewards hard work rather than ability. Huang (1995) credits his success on the National Entrance Examination to hard work, cram school attendance, and tons of homework. He believes that when homework is absent, students cannot really understand.

A World-Class Quote from Taiwan

''Confucius should teach everyone the meaning of fair in the whole world. For example, it is not good to separate students into cow students and star students. Everyone should have equal opportunity. National exams, however, are fair; for standards are not lowered for slower students. Slower students just have to spend more time to catch up'' (Huang, 1995).

A similar educational climate exists in Korea. Chapter 2 develops the historical paradigm that made South Korea achievement oriented and a country where status equates to superior performance in school. That same paradigm explains the importance of testing to measure superior performance. Like Taiwan, students in Korea take a national test at the conclusion of the elementary years that determines placement at the secondary level into vocational school or the academic high school. Higher scores also mean acceptance into schools regarded as "star schools" because of their superior reputation. Students admitted to star schools will even move from home to live with a friend or relative to attend the more prestigious high school.

Like Taiwanese and Japanese students, students in Korea work hard to eventually achieve on the national examination. Cram schools are also prevalent in Korea and homework the norm. One survey showed that the average Korean student spent 57.58 hours a week or 8.23 hours a day on academic preparation outside of the 6.5-hour school day (Lee and Phelps, 1988). Students spend serious time studying to score high on the national examinations. Lee and Phelps also provided one answer to the American concern that Pacific Rim students become stressed by the pressures of preparing for tests that determine so much of their future. They administered the Test Anxiety Test (26 true and false questions designed to measure student stress about testing) to 118 male

This school trophy case is located in the main lobby of the school so everyone can see the success of Korean students in competition. Unlike many prominent U.S. trophy cases, these awards are for academic excellence (photo by Elliott).

and 119 female eighth grade students in Korean schools. The administrators gave the test at the time students were to take the national examination. Lee and Phelps report the following results:

(1) Test anxiety correlates negatively with intelligence, academic self-concept, and achievement.
(2) There is no anxiety variation among male and female students.
(3) The data did not support the perception that Korean students are more affected by test anxiety than American students.

Chalker and Haynes (1994) also compared the student suicide rates of the 10 countries noted for world-class education and found that in 1988, rates in the United States and Canada were higher in all categories than Japan, Korea, and Taiwan.

Soon after World War II, the Japanese followed the example of the French in developing a system of student assessment. Teachers test frequently during the elementary years and administer a final test at the end of the school year. Again, the goal of testing in Japan is to prepare students for the national examination at the end of the elementary years. The Japanese changed their assessment practice to adopt the principle of administering entrance exams that admit students to the next level rather than exams from the school level they were leaving. When students leave junior high school, they take an entrance exam administered by the receiving school, and the results of the exam along with their junior high marks determine acceptance to the school. The Japanese examinations are also extremely comprehensive, and students take an exam in every subject including physical education. As in Taiwan and Korea, attendance at a cram school (Juku) is common, and teachers require extensive homework. The same education ethic exists in the Japanese home that the previous paragraphs described in Korea and Taiwan. Parents consider hard work the behavior that leads to success. The exams are difficult, and numerous students do fail, however; teachers blame failure on insufficient effort and admonish the student to try harder and repeat the exam if necessary (Cummings, 1994).

The Israel Ministry of Education also tests all students in the eighth grade, with the results used to help determine placement at the secondary level. Israeli students (Sarfaty, 1995; Borochov, 1995) report that the test is very important and taken seriously by students. The students report their elementary testing experience as follows:

Every other day we had a test. Every semester had one or two weeks of hard tests. During the eighth grade, every student takes the Hadsa, a test that determines a student's secondary experience. The test includes sections on English, mathematics, Hebrew, and shapes. It is timed and speed is important. The test is called an American test for it is multiple choice.

There is considerable diversity in Canadian assessment. All but two jurisdictions (Prince Edward Island and the Northwest Territories) had some type of provincial assessment during the 1993 – 1994 school year. Testing focuses on the basics, but some provinces include other subjects. Jurisdictions usually test students at two levels during the elementary years; for example, grades 3 and 9, or grades 4 and 8 (*Pan-Canadian Education Indicators,* 1995). The Toronto Board of Education initiated a Common Curriculum in 1994 – 1995 that includes benchmarks. The Ontario Ministry has also written a Common Curriculum.

International Assessment

Two measurements of international achievement have had significant impact on the development of world-class schooling, but neither is well understood in the United States. American educators often hear that U.S. youths do poorly when compared with youth from other countries, but typically educators remain far removed from the tests, their content, and their interpretation. How can the United States rise to the top of the success list on international tests when educators do not know the content tested? Following is information considered minimal for elementary school leaders.

The International Association for the Evaluation of Educational Achievement (IAEEA) conducts the oldest assessment of international education. The IAEEA is a private organization with headquarters in the Hague that has been conducting international testing since the 1960s. The third international assessment of mathematics and science is just beginning in more than 50 countries and will involve more than one million students. Twenty thousand plus of these students will be U.S. students. Educators will administer the tests to 9-year-old students, 13-year-old students, and students in the final year of precollegiate schooling.

The basic test consists of 70 multiple choice questions and 30 longer open-ended questions. Test administrators will give smaller subgroups experiential assignments. Developers will translate the test into more than 40 languages. Those administering the tests will look at other aspects of each country's educational system. They will look at the student's home background as well as his or her classroom experience. Researchers will ask questions pertaining to curriculum and the opportunity to learn. The results of the study will be available in 1996 (Viadero, 1994).

Student success on past IAEEA assessments varied. Math results were below average in the 1981−1982 testing, but the United States ranked near the top in reading assessment in 1993. Because bad news sells newspapers, poor performance seems to gather more headlines than good performance. School leaders must analyze the results of the 1996 data and deduct from them statistics that will help education in the United States.

The second International Assessment of Educational Progress (IAEP) was administered in September 1990 and March 1991. The primary purpose of the study was to assess the mathematics and science skills of 9-year-old and 13-year-old students in 20 nations that volunteered for the project. Each country also gathered data about resources within the school and at home that may have influenced learning. Other questions

Computer education may not be stressed as much in Asian schools as it is in the United States. Computers are used primarily for teaching mathematics, as shown in this Republic of Korea school (photo by Elliott).

probed the students' attitudes about science and mathematics. The data produced valuable information about cultural values, investment in education, and the organization of schools. Additional data produced information about conditions beyond school such as student attitudes, out-of-class activities, and parental support for education. For example, background questions examined students' television habits and how these habits might affect the students' scores on the IAEP. Each participating country was responsible for sampling, survey administration, quality control, and data processing (Chu et al., 1992).

Reflections on Research

A 1992 study of students in 31 nations found American 9-year-olds second in the world in reading. American 14-year-olds finished ninth, in the top third, but with scores only three points farther out of first place than the 9-year-olds. The scores of 14-year-olds were tightly bunched together meaning that a difference of a few points made a big difference in ranking (Chu et al., 1992).

Every elementary school educator should study the results of the background questions, for they reveal comparative data about students more revealing than the test results themselves. The age groups tested, ages 9 and 13, correspond to the midpoint and the conclusion of the elementary experience, therefore, yielding evidence about the elementary years. The results are reported in *Learning Science* (Lapointe et al., 1992b) and *Learning Mathematics* (Lapointe et al., 1992a). Chalker and Haynes (1994) also report many of the results of the IAEP study and relate them to the development of world-class schools.

The development of the assessment instruments should be particularly useful to elementary principals. International developers used a consensus-building model to develop common IAEP frameworks. Many of the nations submitted questions from their own assessment instruments including the United States, which submitted questions from the National

Assessment of Educational Progress (NAEP). American students have taken NAEP tests since 1980. Table 6.1 shows the topics on the IAEP mathematics and science exams and the number of questions included to test each topic.

Representatives from each nation screened all questions and adapted them to the language and culture of the country. Officials formed the science questions into a multiple choice format. The mathematics questions contained about one-fourth constructed response questions requiring students to generate and write their own answers, whereas the remaining questions required students to choose from several choices (Askew and Mead, 1992).

Table 6.2 shows the results of the mathematics and science assessments for 9-year-old students. Twelve of the 20 countries participating in the IAEP assessment chose to test their 9-year-old students. The 12 countries administered the tests in 1991 in both mathematics and science.

Several countries selected by the authors as world-class countries did not participate in the assessment. Korea and Taiwan did participate, however, and both performed at or near the top of the list. Both are developing countries in which citizens regard the educational system essential to the future success of students and the country. Both countries emphasize mathematics and science curriculum in the elementary grades. Although the United States is near the bottom of the mathematics assessment, the high rank on the science assessment should be encouraging to educators who have emphasized the development of science curriculum in the lower elementary grades. The United States ranks third on the science assessment, higher than traditionally well-scoring countries such as Hungary, Israel, England, and Scotland.

The IAEP assessments for 13-year-old students provide an assessment of American students recently completing or in the final year of the elementary school experience. The assessment should be very meaningful to elementary educators, for it assesses students who are completers of elementary education. Table 6.3 lists the assessment results for 13-year-olds taking the mathematics and science exams in 17 participating countries.

The dominance of Korea and Taiwan is again evident within the 13-year-old group. The United States, however, falls below the median country on both the mathematics test and the science test.

Other world-class countries, France, England, Scotland, Israel, and Canada all scored higher than the United States on both the mathematics

TABLE 6.1 Distribution of questions for 9- and 13-year-olds by mathematics and science topics and processes on the 1991 IAEP assessments.

Mathematics Assessment			Science Assessment		
Topic or Process	Ages	Questions	Topic or Process		Questions
Numbers/operations	9	32	Life sciences	9	23
	13	28		13	25
Measurement	9	9	Physical sciences	9	19
	13	13		13	26
Geometry	9	6	Earth and space	9	10
	13	11	science	13	9
Data analysis, statistic,	9	8	Nature of science	9	8
and probability	13	9		13	12
Algebra and functions	9	7	Knows facts, concepts	9	26
	13	15	and principles	13	20
Conceptual	9	25	Uses knowledge to	9	23
understanding	13	25	solve problems	13	33
Procedural knowledge	9	22	Integrates knowledge	9	11
	13	27	to solve problems	13	19
Problem solving	9	15			
	13	24			

Source: Askew and Mead, 1992, pp. 127, 128.

TABLE 6.2 The mean percents correct of answers on the IAEP mathematics and science assessments taken by 9-year-old students in 12 countries.

Mathematics		Science	
Country	Mean Percent Correct	Country	Mean Percent Correct
Korea	74.8	Korea	67.9
Hungary	68.2	Taiwan	66.7
Taiwan	68.1	United States	64.7
Scotland	65.7	England	62.9
Israel	64.4	Canada	62.8
Spain	61.9	Hungary	62.5
Ireland	60.0	Scotland	62.2
Canada	59.9	Spain	61.7
England	59.4	Israel	61.2
United States	58.3	Slovenia	57.7
Slovenia	56.0	Ireland	56.5
Portugal	55.5	Portugal	54.8

Source: Dupuis et al., 1992, pp. 174, 184.

TABLE 6.3 *The mean percents correct of answers on the IAEP mathematics and science assessments taken by 13-year-old students in 17 countries.*

Mathematics		Science	
Country	Mean Percent Correct	Country	Mean Percent Correct
China	80.2	Korea	77.5
Korea	73.4	Taiwan	75.6
Taiwan	72.7	Hungary	73.4
Switzerland	70.8	Switzerland	73.7
Hungary	68.4	Slovenia	70.3
France	64.2	Israel	69.7
Israel	63.1	Canada	68.8
Canada	62.0	England	68.7
Scotland	60.6	France	68.6
England	60.6	Scotland	67.9
Ireland	60.5	Spain	67.5
Slovenia	57.1	China	67.2
Spain	55.4	United States	67.0
United States	55.3	Ireland	63.3
Portugal	48.3	Portual	62.6
Jordan	40.4	Jordan	56.6
Brazil	36.4	Brazil	51.9

Source: Dupuis et al., 1992, pp. 179, 189.

and science tests. In Canada, where the control of education is vested in each province, scores were considerably higher than in the United States. Canada desegregates the data by province, and each province showed a higher mean percent correct than the United States. The United States must look to Canada for experience in building state common curriculum. Science is again the brighter light for 13-year-old students in the United States, for the United States scored on a par with China and is much closer to the mean scores of the highest scoring countries. There is, therefore, less gap to close.

STUDENT ASSESSMENT IN THE U.S. ELEMENTARY SCHOOLS

In contrast to the other world-class countries previously presented, educators in the United States are often less certain about what teachers should teach and test at the various elementary grades. Most states have no prescribed curriculum and no meaningful test to assess progress in learning the curriculum. States usually develop tests to measure the achievement of minimum objectives, yet educators interpret the scores as if they measured optimum achievement. In the 1970s, 35 states established some kind of minimum competency test. An example of such testing is the Michigan Assessment of Educational Progress (MEAP) that is now in its second decade of use in Michigan. The MEAP measures minimal objectives in mathematics, science, reading, social studies, and writing. North Carolina has developed end-of-year tests for all students beginning in the third grade and end-of-course tests administered at the end of secondary courses. The tests measure the objectives of the state curriculum and include open-ended questions as well as multiple choice questions. The North Carolina State Department of Public Instruction continues to struggle with problems of grading and interpreting results, for the program simply tests students too often. The State Department of Public Instruction must realize that testing at the end of every year and every course is simply a case of overtesting. In fact, during the summer of 1995, the North Carolina General Assembly considered dropping the exams and finally did reduce their use. North Carolina is currently working to develop yet another measurement program. Administrators and teachers simply blink and wait for one initiative to pass and another to replace it.

Other countries produce world-class results without checking the progress of students so often. Germany and France, for example, delegate testing to the classroom until the national test appears at the end of the entire school experience. But the North Carolina effort does tie curriculum and testing together and is probably worth revising. Politics will prevail, however. Relative to the reporting issue, the North Carolina State Department of Public Instruction reports the results of each school system to the public on a report card that includes other measures of effectiveness such as student attendance and retention. Using the testing program to compare schools is a passion with North Carolina political leaders, but they are not alone.

Because agreement is lacking among the 50 states and thousands of local school districts, elementary teachers develop their own tests or use tests designed by textbook companies or testing companies. The authors believe it rare, however, when teachers develop questions aligned to national or international tests. School districts also select nationally normed achievement tests, ability tests, personality tests, career assessment tests, and others. In fact, the ninth Mental Measurements Yearbook lists 1409 published tests in use (Cummings, 1994). Bracey (1994) argues that with few exceptions, this system of assessment does not promote quality assessment. Multiple choice tests are common and are not good measures of quality assessment. Testing companies report scores in percentile ranks, grade equivalents, or curves referenced to a national norm. The child, teacher, or parent does not often know if the performance reported is good or bad. It is a well-known fact that nearly all schools using a nationally normed test can report scores above average. School boards listen to test presentations with an ear toward assessing the district's performance rather than trying to understand the quality of a child's performance. Commonly, tests do not measure the curriculum taught in the classroom, because test companies develop generic tests that will sell to thousands of local school districts. Teachers fight the suggestion that they should teach to the test, and often teachers hold standardized tests in such disdain that they simply go through the motion of administering the test and using the results. Educators often allow students to enter the testing room without proper preparation for a test. Often, teachers lead students to believe that the contents of a test are secret only to be discovered when the test package is opened. Bracey (1994) deals with the secrecy attached to test administration in the United States with this statement that all educators should internalize: "Why all the secrecy? The secrecy surrounding tests perverts the whole educational system. If tests are supposed to measure what we think is important, how can we possibly justify not telling people what is on them?" (p. 65). Elementary educators in the United States are examining and trying alternative assessment measures to supplement testing programs. Malehom (1994) identifies 10 alternative assessment measures currently in use in America's classrooms:

- contracted learning
- mastery learning
- credit/no credit learning
- multiple marks
- anecdotal records
- pupil profiles

- dossier
- checklists
- peer evaluation
- self evaluation

Malehom contends that grades interfere with pupil learning and can no longer be defended. The authors disagree. The authors contend that grades are a benchmark fairly well understood by teachers, students, and parents, and that all persons with a stake in education need benchmarks. Until other functional benchmarks can replace grades, the defense of grades is fairly obvious, and alternative measures of assessments will only complement, not replace, the testing system.

Assessing students in America's elementary schools has also been a function of the federal government since the U.S. Department of Education founded the National Assessment of Educational Progress (NAEP) in 1969. The NAEP measures what students might be expected to know in mathematics and science. The tests are administered to a sample of 9-, 13-, and 17-year-old students in all 50 states. Officials use results to compare student achievement in the current year with achievement in previous years. The press uses the results to show that schools in the United States do not function well, and, too often, educators either agree with the press or do nothing to counteract the criticism. A major problem is that officials do not report results to parents, teachers, or students.

Two education experts find the NAEP flawed and used improperly (Bracey, 1994; Jaeger, 1992). Common complaints are that it does not substitute for a national exam given to all students; it is not used to strengthen student learning; students and teachers do not take it seriously; and as previously mentioned, it is used to compare the wrong things. Bracey also alerts educators to the fact that the scores do not show the drop in achievement that other analysts claim.

Stedman (1995), however, takes issue with Bracey's views and proposes that educators face squarely the bad news about education. Stedman claims that achievement in the United States is dismal and in need of reform. He cites IAEP and SAT data to support his position on testing and the *Phi Delta Kappan* report card to show that the public has doubts about its local schools. See Figure 6.1 for a sample progress report.

166

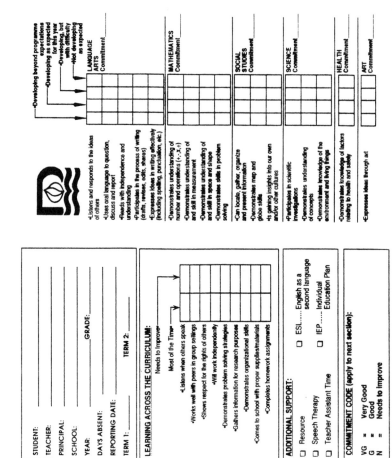

Figure 6.1 *Report cards around the world vary. Here is a copy of the Dartmouth (Nova Scotia) District School Board Progress Report for grades 3 – 6. Grades 1 and 2 reports are narratives on personal and social development, language arts/creative arts/social studies, and mathematics and science. A commitment code similar to the one shown previously is used on these report cards.*

STUDENT:

TEACHER:

PRINCIPAL:

SCHOOL:

YEAR: _____ GRADE:

DAYS ABSENT:

REPORTING DATE:

TERM 1: _____ TERM 2: _____

LEARNING ACROSS THE CURRICULUM:

Needs to Improve

Most of the Time

- Listens when others speak
- Works well with peers in group settings
- Shows respect for the rights of others
- Will work independently
- Demonstrates problem solving strategies
- Gathers information for research purposes
- Demonstrates organizational skills
- Comes to school with proper supplies/materials
- Completes homework assignments

ADDITIONAL SUPPORT:

☐ Resource

☐ Speech Therapy

☐ Teacher Assistant Time

☐ ESL...... English as a second language

☐ IEP...... Individual Education Plan

COMMITMENT CODE (apply to next section):

VG = Very Good

G = Good

N = Needs to Improve

- Developing beyond programme expectations
- Developing as expected for this year
- Developing, but with difficulty
- Not developing as expected

LANGUAGE ARTS
Commitment

- Listens and responds to the ideas of others
- Uses oral language to question, discuss and report
- Reads with independence and understanding
- Participates in the process of writing (drafts, revises, edits, shares)
- Expresses ideas in writing effectively (including spelling, punctuation, etc.)

MATHEMATICS
Commitment

- Demonstrates understanding of number and operations (+,–,x,÷)
- Demonstrates understanding of and skill in measurement
- Demonstrates understanding of and skill in space and shape
- Demonstrates skills in problem solving

SOCIAL STUDIES
Commitment

- Can locate, gather, organize and present information
- Demonstrates map and globe skills
- Is gaining insights into our own and/or other cultures

SCIENCE
Commitment

- Participates in scientific investigations
- Demonstrates understanding of concepts
- Demonstrates knowledge of the environment and living things

HEALTH
Commitment

- Demonstrates knowledge of factors relating to health and safety

ART
Commitment

- Expresses ideas through art

AN AGENDA FOR ACTION:
ELEMENTARY STUDENT ASSESSMENT

1. *Elementary principals must ensure that teachers conduct all testing in the school through the use of assessment devices aligned with the curricula.* Elementary leaders must see that teachers administer only tests that align with the curriculum. It makes no difference whether the test is internally or externally developed; competent educators should not subject children to a test that is not familiar to them. Curriculum and test alignment should be easy for the teacher, for the teacher knows what he or she has taught. The teacher can simply construct questions that reflect the content. Alignment becomes much harder when teachers administer state or national tests, for teachers usually do not know the content of the tests. Testing agencies often issue practice test questions, however, or release copies of past tests, and every school administrator should require teachers to use them. More important, students should know the structure of the test and as much about the content as possible. Unfortunately, many school administrators do not possess expertise in curriculum and testing alignment, but professional agencies such as AESP and AASA have consultants who can help teachers ensure alignment. Curriculum and test alignment should be common in staff development plans.

As stated earlier, American teachers love to keep test information a secret, and this borders on unethical behavior in such a high-stakes activity. Teachers should understand that students need to know what will be on a test.

Best Practice

Regardless of the tests used in the elementary school, all tests must be aligned with the curriculum. Students should know what portions of the curriculum will be tested. Teachers should receive staff development that ensures curriculum alignment and assessment.

---

2. *Because testing is high stakes for children and parents, school leaders must develop a policy that clearly defines ethical testing practices.* Every school district should have a "testing ethics policy" that guides the activities mentioned in number one. Many teachers and administrators yearly lose their jobs or face embarrassing discipline procedures, because they use questionable procedures to prepare students for tests. Furthermore, educators are not always clear about which practices are unethical and which are not. For example, teachers who do not take time to prepare students for tests display questionable behavior. Teachers who tell students that tests are not important and that they need not do their best, display unethical behavior. It is incumbent for every school principal to clearly articulate ethical and unethical practices to staff.

An ethics-in-testing policy should originate with the board of education. The authors developed such a policy based on the practices of teachers. The authors can lead practitioners to further information.

3. *Elementary school leaders should loudly lobby for national assessment that meets the definition of world-class.* Chapter 5 suggests that educators should endorse national curriculum guidelines so that the United States can identify curricula that every child should know and end the proliferation of thousands of local curricula that often are not very functional. Needless to say, the authors endorse the development of national assessment to measure achievement of national goals. Elementary school leaders should endorse the idea of national assessment and propose the development of national assessment inside the parameters of sound test development and usage. Members of professional societies should lobby their membership for support of national assessment and insist that the organization have a voice in the development of the process.

The development of national assessment is currently stalled in the Washington political arena. The Republican agenda calls for the return of educational decisions to the states. However, one must ask if the states have (1) developed a meaningful testing program during the 50 years since World War II, (2) provided guidance for local administrators and teachers needed to develop meaningful local assessment, and (3) cooperated with other states to develop similar assessment packages. The answer is probably no! Students move across state lines in huge numbers, yet state officials act as if education still operates in the 19th century. Before the United States embraces national curriculum and assessment, the country will need to endorse international curriculum and assessment. Educators must take the initiative in demanding national standards.

4. *Elementary school leaders must research world-class test construction and insist that teachers construct tests most beneficial for measuring learning.* Educators learned earlier in the chapter that most countries use objective testing sparingly. Essay tests, demonstrations, and experiential assessment are most common in the world-class arena. France begins essay testing in the early elementary years and continues its use throughout the school experience. Yet educators, textbook companies, state testing departments, and national assessment developers continue to develop multiple choice tests. Multiple choice tests do not permit educators to adequately judge student development.

Authentic assessment is the latest jargon developed by educators to present better ways of assessing students. Although educational jargon is symptomatic of a confused educational system—look how many innovative movements with catchy titles come and go in education—the ideas of authentic assessment seem useful. Authentic assessment measures knowledge and the students' ability to apply the knowledge. Teachers can encourage application in a variety of formats that use all senses, that include demonstration as well as written responses, and that allow students to demonstrate competence over a longer period of time. Because this book is not a "how-to-do-it" book, the authors suggest that every elementary school leader become familiar with more authentic ways of measuring student progress and how to apply them in the school.

5. *Student assessment at the elementary level should measure progress toward the achievement of benchmarks established at the conclusion of the early elementary grades—kindergarten through grade 3—and again at the conclusion of the upper elementary grades—4 through 6. In a middle school district or junior high school district, educators should develop benchmarks measurable at the end of the experience.* England established attainment goals at approximately the intervals suggested above. The English national tests measure student achievement of attainment goals, and the results are published for educators, students, and parents. The road to national assessment has not been easy in Britain, but educators in the British countries are working to perfect the system. The Toronto schools are also using benchmarks for the first time in 1994–1995. American educational leaders can benefit from both experiences.

Benchmarks reflect standards, and this chapter earlier established the need for standards. Benchmarks or standards give all students something to work toward. Although continuous progress is important, benchmarks help ensure that continuous progress results in learning appropriate for a given level of instruction and slows the problem of students continuing through the elementary years without progress toward literacy. Benchmarks should reflect literacy requirements, for literacy is the responsibility of primary schools in the world-class countries. If the state department of public instruction has not identified benchmarks for elementary students, then local educators must. The school should mobilize the best minds available on the subject of elementary learning to accomplish this task. School leaders should write grants, form consortia, hire consultants – do whatever is necessary – to establish benchmarks and to formulate a method of assessing them. School leaders must develop policies that specify the action the school will take when students achieve or do not achieve the benchmarks. Benchmarks are useless unless they help determine the educational experiences best suited for students at the next level.

6. *Elementary school leaders should regard the new wave of alternative assessment not as replacements for tests and grades but as a supplement for tests and grades.* Testing as a means of assessment is not going to disappear, and the use of letter grades, at least at the upper elementary level, is not going to vanish. Testing and grading form a paradigm that developed over many years in America's schools (see Chapter 2), and paradigms become part of the cultural expectations of the educational system. Besides, testing and grading prevail in all countries where achievement is world-class; and, in fact, tests increase in importance as international comparisons become more acceptable.

Portfolios are simply containers that hold student work, including the results of tests. Portfolios are not substitutes for tests. Experts who champion the use of portfolios in place of testing are leading educators down the wrong path. Also, peer evaluation at the elementary level will not replace the judgment of the trained professional. Experts who claim that alternative assessment can replace tests and grades are unrealistic in a society that values quantitative assessment and comparative data. New Zealand seems to have a good model for combining alternative methods of assessment with test assessment. In New Zealand one method of assessment complements other assessment methods, and national and local testing seem secure within a total package of assessment.

Elementary educators should develop such a package and cease trying to find a replacements for tests. Teachers should spend time making tests meaningful and legitimate. Although substituting progress reports for grades at the early elementary level might make sense, the practice loses practicality after the third grade.

7. *The results of tests administered to elementary students should be used to diagnose student problems and prescribe learning and to find weaknesses in the curriculum or methodology of teaching in the school. The practice of many countries to use tests to compare children, compare schools, or compare teachers should stop.* The term *student assessment* is key here. Purposely, the term school assessment, teacher assessment, or district assessment is not used, because tests are not intended as measurements of these elements. Because the central office, the state department, or some federal agency usually demands that test results be used for comparison of schools and teachers, local elementary educators have little influence over such a political decision. Educators should never embrace the idea, however, and lobby against such a practice whenever possible.

North Carolina, for instance, developed a report card recently that indicates the rank of a school compared with all other state schools. Schools are par, below par, or above par. The inference is that everybody knows what par means. The reality is that the report card is interpreted locally in a way that causes the least turmoil. Currently, the North Carolina General Assembly is considering the reduction of state testing and the report card. Testing would be returned to the local district.

8. *All teachers should be trained to properly construct tests, interpret them properly, and use the results to benefit children.* A course in tests and measurements is not common in the curriculum of teacher-training institutions. Pedagogy is unpopular with many university professors, and not enough hours exist to deal with the testing issue. This is unfortunate, and practitioners should insist that the local university prepare teachers better in the art of test construction and interpretation. With site-based management becoming popular, teachers will be given more responsibility for test development, a task for which they are ill-prepared. Staff development must pick up the slack and fill the void.

9. *Elementary administrators and teachers must take testing more seriously and pass that attitude to students.* Students in every world-class country pass through the elementary grades with a great reverence for tests. Teachers, beginning with very young children, teach the importance of tests. Teachers prepare students for tests diligently and give priority to test preparation in the daily school work. The authors inter-

viewed dozens of students from the world-class countries, and without exception, students showed great respect for testing in their home schools. Without exception, they also talked about the importance teachers attached to tests—a fact that affected the students' attitudes about the subject.

Feeling an overload of testing, American teachers develop an aversion to testing and then pass these negative feelings to students. Elementary students are quite impressionable and easily pick up the negative attitudes displayed by teachers. Testing becomes a chore to complete as soon as possible for teachers and students.

Elementary teachers and administrators must include improved assessment in their improvement plans. Educators must test just enough to convey to students the seriousness of the exercise. Testing should be relevant, serious, and useful for students, teachers, and parents.

10. *Every school in the United States should operate under the guidelines of an accountability plan.* Educators cannot escape accountability in today's world, so educators must face the music. Accountability helps ensure that school performance improves to meet the needs of each individual and satisfies the public's curiosity about school performance. In the current educational climate, state legislatures or school boards impose accountability. Chubb and Moe (1992) examined the British Reform Movement, compared it with education in the United States, and concluded that the best form of accountability is bottom-up, a concept foreign to bureaucrats and politicians in either country. The authors agree, but educators must strongly advocate for local accountability and start imposing a local model if educators are to keep the bureaucratic wolf away from the door. The authors favor a plan in which the people served would evaluate the schools using a variety of devices rather than just test results. As advocated earlier, test results are best applied to student performance and curriculum development.

REFERENCES

Askew, J. M. and N. A. Mead. 1992. "Part II: Assessment, Design and Implementation," *IEAP Technical Report*. Princeton, New Jersey: The International Assessment of Educational Progress, Educational Testing Service.

Borochov, E. 1995. Interview (April 28).

Bracey, G. W. 1994. *Transforming America's Schools: An RX for Getting Past Blame.* Arlington, Virginia: Excerpted with permission from the American Association of School Administrators, N. Moore Street, Arlington, VA.

Chalker, D. M. and R. M. Haynes. 1994. *World Class Schools: New Standards for Education.* Lancaster, Pennsylvania: Technomic Publishing Company, Inc.

Chu, A., D. Morganstein, and L. Wallace. 1992 "Part I: Sampling," *IAEP Technical Report.* Princeton, New Jersey: The International Assessment of Educational Progress, Educational Testing Service.

Chubb, J. E. and Moe, T. M. 1992. *A Lesson in School Reform from Great Britain.* Washington, D.C.: The Brookings Institute.

Cummings, W. K. 1994 "Evaluation and Examinations: Why and How Are Educational Outcomes Assessed," in *International Comparative Education: Practices, Issues, & Prospects.* R. Thomas Murray, ed. Tarrytown, New York: Pergamon Press Ltd.

Dupuis, R. F., E. G. Johnson, J. G. Blais, and R. Jones. 1992. "Part III: Data Analysis," *IAEP Technical Report.* Princeton, New Jersey: The International Assessment of Educational Progress, Educational Testing Service.

Education in Britain. 1991. Great Britain: Produced for the Foreign and Commonwealth Office by the Central Office of Information.

Faire, M. and R. Yates. 1994. "Assessing and Evaluating Student Learning," *The Professional Practice of Teaching.* Clive McGee and Deborah Fraser, eds. Palmerston North, New Zealand: The Dunmore Press Limited. The authors and publisher thank Dunmore Press for permission to use copyright material.

Gavin, S. 1995. Interview (April 10).

Huang, Alex. 1995. Interview (February 14).

Jaeger, R. M. 1992. "World Class Standards, Choice, and Privatization: Weak Measurement Serving Presumptive Policy," *Phi Delta Kappan,* pp. 119−128.

Lapointe, A. E., N. A. Mead, and J. M. Askew. 1992a. *Learning Mathematics.* Princeton, New Jersey: The International Assessment of Educational Progress, Educational Testing Service.

Lapointe, A. E., J. M. Askew, and N. A. Mead. 1992b. *Learning Science.* Princeton, New Jersey: The International Assessment of Educational Progress, Educational Testing Service.

Lee, Youngman, and L. Phelps. 1988. "Variables Related to Test Anxiety in Korea," *International Education,* 18(1):50−57.

Malehom, H. 1994. "Ten Measures Better Than Grading," *The Clearinghouse,* 67(6):323−324.

Marcus, E. 1994. "Doing It the French Way," *Educational Vision,* 2(2):18.

The New Zealand Curriculum Framework. 1993. Wellington, New Zealand: Learning Media, Ministry of Education.

Pan-Canadian Education Indicators: Academic Achievement. 1995. Toronto, Canada: Alberta Working Group, Canadian Education Statistics Council.

Sarfaty, I. 1995. Interview (April 28).

Stedman, L. C. 1995. "On Achievement Data: What the Evidence Shows," *Education Week,* 16(22).

Viadero, D. 1994. "Getting a Global View," *Education Week,* October 26, pp. 33−34.

What College-Bound Students Abroad Are Expected to Know about Biology: Defining World Class Standards. 1994. Washington, D.C.: American Federation of Teachers, Educational Issues Department.

WORLD-CLASS
ELEMENTARY STUDENTS

Our youths love luxury. They have bad manners, contempt for authority; they show disrespect for their elders, and love to chatter in place of exercise. Children are now tyrants, not the servants of the household. They no longer rise when their elders enter the room. They contradict their parents, chatter before company, gobble up their food, and tyrannize their teachers.

— Socrates, 265 A.D.

Chapter 7 explores the contribution of students to world-class elementary schools. The chapter recognizes the importance of parents and educators as caretakers and supporters of a student's life but also explores the student as an individual able to shape his or her own future. The chapter features research on student behavior and the student's use of time in school and out of school. Most important, however, the chapter presents the thoughts of several students who represent hundreds interviewed by the authors. The chapter concludes with an agenda for American elementary principals and teachers who wish to help their students become world-class.

Do not think for a moment that children fail or succeed only because they reflect the influence of parents and/or educators. Children can learn to control their own behavior and determine their own future even when parental influence is dismal and/or the school dysfunctional. Even children in elementary school have the capacity to learn right from wrong, to make hurtful or helpful decisions, to grow or remain as dependent as the day they were born. Children have the capacity to learn in school or waste the opportunity. Children have the capacity to control

175

their own destiny. The school must include students in any plan to improve and, in fact, make students key contributors to the success of the improvement plan.

Certainly the influence of the parent(s) is of prime importance, and the elementary teacher contributes mightily to the development of children. But youngsters must share a responsibility for growth along with parents and teachers. Chapter 7 develops the student's responsibility for growth in school. Before proceeding, however, the reader should return for a moment to Chapter 6 and review the contribution of teachers. Chapter 8 adds the contribution of parents, but a brief glimpse of that contribution follows shortly because of its importance.

First, let us preview the importance of home and community to world-class schooling. If America's schools are to survive, parents must send their children to school disciplined and ready to learn. They must support the school and the child through the educational experience. But, too many times they do not. In fact, they often influence their children to be negative about school. In Transylvania County, North Carolina, the school board passed a student accountability policy in 1994 that requires students to meet minimum scores on state standardized tests to pass the grade or course. Students may retake the tests or attend summer school, but they start all over if they fail. But several parents complained that students are stressed over the situation and they are circulating petitions to have the policy repealed (*Asheville Citizens Times,* 1995b). Although the authors do not encourage yearly high-stakes tests, the authors do encourage the establishment of standards and consequences for failure to meet the standards. So, although the testing program thrust on Transylvania County is flawed, so is the attitude of citizens worried about the stress on their son or daughter. Both should adjust, but certainly the school board should hang in there and not give up the idea of making tests truly important. Test scores improved in Transylvania County after the board of education passed the testing requirement; and given time, most students will feel good about doing good instead of feeling good about doing poorly. Students do better when parents raise them with the values of achievement and hard work. World-class parents produce world-class students.

Of course, educators also influence the development of world-class students. The reader just completed a chapter detailing a world-class agenda for teachers. Teachers have tremendous influence over the development of children. Many world-class teachers exist, but teachers who hurt student progress and produce negative results rather than world-class results do exist. For example, why do elementary teachers ignore the fact that nearly all countries depicted in the world-class research teach kids in a heterogeneous setting, yet these countries accomplish almost 100 percent literacy. There is no tracking or grouping in Japan, Germany, France, Korea, Taiwan, or New Zealand. Many American teachers, however, hang on to tracking practices religiously. Also, the world-class countries identify far fewer handicapped students than the United States, yet many Americans nominate students for special education the minute they falter, and the same teachers fume over attempts to integrate special education students back into the classroom. Even in the regular classroom, negative teacher attitudes often surface.

The school bureaucracy also contributes to student problems. Jennings (1995) reports that teachers in the United States appear to be teaching in the dark and students learning in the dark, although neither may understand why. For example, teachers using textbooks developed by commercial firms disconnect learning from tests developed by state departments of education. Well-meaning teachers and students end up guessing at expected learning. Politicians respond to the dilemma with more tests without a clue about how to fix the disconnected classroom, and educators respond with grade inflation to make the situation appear more positive. Political decisions sometimes appear more frequently used than educational decisions, so parents and educators are of prime importance to the success of students.

This chapter treats students as humans capable of becoming world-class students, and society must also view students as capable persons who can make a difference.

THE WORLD-CLASS STATUS OF STUDENTS

To determine the world-class status of students, the authors interviewed dozens of students from the research countries to complement the information gleaned from the printed word and opinions of significant adults. The interviews were most revealing, and summaries of many interviews are presented in this section. The chapter is organized a bit differently than other chapters, for the status of the United States on a presented issue follows closely the research on the other nine countries.

In every country where students come to school disciplined and ready to learn, students become successful learners (Chalker and Haynes, 1994). It is not difficult to describe a world-class student, and later in the chapter, educators will be encouraged to place the definition before students often throughout the school experience. The characteristics of world-class students analogous to all countries studied include the following. A world-class student:

(1) Respects and cares for people of every age, nationality, race, and gender
(2) Respects his or her own body and mind
(3) Treats other's property with respect
(4) Obeys the teacher, principal, and other adults in the school and treats school as a holy place
(5) Sets goals for himself or herself and works to achieve each goal
(6) Works hard
(7) Establishes high achievement expectations for himself or herself
(8) Turns on to homework and turns off the television
(9) Honors father and mother and all family
(10) Respects life as a gift not to be wasted

Hansen (1994) contributes to this process with the following message, "Values, beliefs, and attitudes are modeled every minute and second of the day. Teaching is continuous, and therefore, all methods of instruction are value laden." Students can be taught how to be world-class.

Students make choices that help them achieve success and world-class status. These choices deal with their use of time inside of school and outside of school. Several of these choices and their world-class status follow.

Student Behavior

World-class students see school as a rewarding experience. They view the teacher as a special, respected person who makes the rewards possible. They adjust their behavior to conform to school rules and teacher expectations. Pupils are not passive receivers of education. They have to participate in their own learning. They have a complete part to play in maintaining the behavior necessary to achieve high standards of learning (*Discipline in the Schools: Report of the Committee of Enquiry*

Chaired by Lord Elton, 1989). Educational leaders in Britain realize the importance of making students responsible for their behavior. Students in elementary school receive religious instruction that includes moral development and the responsibility of students to fellow human beings and to a greater power. In English elementary schools, teachers seem to have a high regard for a child's self-esteem and feelings. Teachers help students develop self control by (1) giving them more responsibility, (2) setting clear rules and consequences, and (3) simply by getting to know them and their background. Teachers have increased the use of rewards and communication and have decreased the use of capital punishment and use of penalties (Jambor, 1988).

New Zealand teachers also prefer preventive discipline rather than disciplining students in the heat of the moment. Vaughn and Weeds (1994) suggest that New Zealand teachers ignore disruptive behavior when possible but to have effective measures for dealing with behavioral problems that cannot be ignored. Although the experts list specific misbehaviors, methods of dealing with the misbehavior are not listed. The experts leave the method to the teacher. However, Vaughn and Weeds stress that intervention should not damage the teacher-child relationship and should not cast the teacher and student as "winners and losers."

In Japan, the approach to discipline contrasts with Britain and New Zealand. Japanese education is characterized by rote learning and regimentation prescribed by the central authority. Henshall (1992) attributes this in part to the teachings of Confucianism that stresses order and hierarchical relations. Whatever the cause, authorities characterize learning in Japan as a process controlled by teachers and supported by parents.

A World-Class Idea: A Profile of Students from Japan

Asuko Miyake remembers attending elementary school with an average of 50 students. This allowed for little discussion, and students took notes in textbooks published by the ministry and bought by each student. Asuko called her teachers by their first name, a surprise considering the formal nature of instruction. Teachers enforced the rules, however, including short hair for boys and uniforms for all students. She claimed that students respected some teachers but not all.

The teacher expected discipline, for the teacher had little time to tolerate poor behavior in such a large class with so much to accomplish. Asuko remembers student fights in elementary school and thought fighting fairly normal among young students. The teachers stopped the fights and called the parents if necessary. She recalled no suspensions for fighting.

Hitomi Kawaguchi confirmed the importance of homework, for she had regular homework in language, mathematics, and Japanese. Teachers assigned lots of homework over breaks. Hitomi did not participate in any extracurricular activity, so she had time to work at home. She did not feel that her parents influenced her to succeed and that her work ethic was self-imposed.

Asuko attended a commercial high school where few students matriculated to college. Hitomi attended a regular high school. Both students currently study at the University of North Carolina-Asheville (Miyake, 1995; Kawaguchi, 1995).

Schoollad (1986) believed that this strict regimentation in Japanese schools led to bullying. Children in the elementary school stand when the teacher enters the room. No one interrupts the teacher without being admonished. Teachers do not expect students to be different and have different needs. Teachers handle roughly children who rebel or attempt to do things differently. However, teachers often initiate bullying. Specific incidents exist of students being kicked, punched, and beaten by teachers. Teachers tell parents who complain about the beatings that it is the parents' fault for not raising the child properly. Schoollad believes that students, therefore, bully other students who are different because they see teachers doing the same. In fact, the use of corporal punishment is still acceptable in Japanese schools even though other tactics are gaining preference. Between April and October of 1985, authorities reported 155,066 cases of bullying in Japanese schools. Three percent involved physical harm. Hill (1992) wrote about bullying in Japan 4 years after Schoollad. He still saw the problem and added that Japanese educators must deal with the contradiction between institutionalized cooperation and the bullying of teachers and pupils.

Recently, Japanese educators have looked to other educational systems, including the United States, for ideas about including

Chinese schools have larger classes than the U.S. affords. These students are grouped for whole-class instruction and cooperative learning. Students use the textbooks for learning, and they are expected to be cooperative within their groups (photo courtesy of the Ministry of Education, Republic of China).

tolerance for individual differences in the curricula. But, although educators seek help, the fact remains that the number of bullying cases was still well below the number of similar discipline cases reported in the United States for the same year; and the Japanese schools report almost zero vandalism – 0.2 incidents per school per year (Henshall, 1992). Also, because citizens may not own guns, Japanese children do not grow up in a society in which adults covet gun ownership.

In Korea, the teacher also traditionally used corporal punishment, but the practice is decreasing because of parental protests. One authority believed that parents now give birth to one child and tend to overprotect them. Teachers, therefore, now sometimes hit students on the palm of the hand or make them stand if they misbehave. Again, teachers and parents teach students from preschool years throughout the elementary experience that school is the key to future success, and such cultural and religious values tend to diminish behavioral problems.

France is another nation with a prescribed learning process and high expectations that all children of primary age can achieve the same goals. Teachers can recommend retention for a student who fails a subject. The teacher and the parent meet to make this determination. It is possible for a student to fail more than once and to find himself or herself in a room with much younger students. Education is compulsory until age 16, however, and after a student misses the third day, a policeman arrives at home. If the student does not appear at school, the government cuts off the parent's allotment (Brahm, 1995). (In France, the government gives parents a monetary allotment for each child born.)

German teachers keep a class book that apparently influences student behavior. Teachers note in the book behavioral problems with students, and many students fear that the teacher will remember the misbehavior. One student reported that tests are essay, and the teacher can grade the student down if they remember behavior problems (Bruckhaus, 1995).

Israel presents an interesting contrast to the previous countries mentioned. Schools in Israel are relaxed. Students do not wear uniforms, and teachers encourage students to call the teacher by his or her first name. Instruction is often individualized and small group work is encouraged. Teachers teach students how to acquire knowledge and experience learning. Teachers encourage self expression and thought and teach intrapersonal relationships. Students receive biblical instruction yearly starting in the second grade. Every elementary school has a counselor (Eldar, 1995).

If an elementary student does misbehave, the teacher starts with a talk. If the misbehavior prevails, the teacher calls the parents and/or removes the student from the room. However, violence does not appear to be a major school problem in a country in which citizens carry guns as a necessary protection against violence. Sarfaty (1995), an Israeli student in the later elementary grades, states that teachers talk to students often about safety and search for student feelings about safety. Educators talk to students about Jewish tradition beginning in kindergarten with biblical stories and continue with lessons on Jewish tradition throughout the elementary grades. Sarfaty remembers the principal saying that, "School is like a greenhouse that keeps us warm." Students appear to feel safe in their environment and comfortable that their plans must include compulsory military service.

World-Class Quote

"School is like a greenhouse that keeps us warm" (Sarfaty quoting her elementary school principal, 1995).

In Alberta, Canada, an executive study comparing Alberta schools with schools in other nations warned that classroom discipline and violence was a growing and serious problem and other reforms could fail because of the problem (*International Comparisons in Education,* circa 1993). Rehner (1995), an assistant principal at the Dougall Public School in Windsor, Ontario, claims that the biggest change in discipline

Students in Brookhaven School in Dartmouth, Nova Scotia learn in settings much like U.S. classrooms. Principal Jean Llewellyn takes pride in her excellent faculty. The child at the rear of this photograph played the upright piano for one of the authors (photo by Haynes).

is the occasional student who explodes. Teachers are simply not trained to deal with such behavior, and it is not fair to expect them to disarm students or risk bodily harm breaking up student fights.

It might sound as if high school students are being addressed as dangerous characters. Not so, for during the past decade educators have seen violent behavior creep into the elementary schools. For several years the Lord Lansdowne Elementary School in Toronto, Canada, has addressed the issue of violence. The staff trains older students as mediators, teachers use learning circles in many classrooms to enhance self-image, and the school's code of behavior guides student behavior. The most interesting innovation, however, is the resource room where teachers send students for short-term remediation, counseling, or quiet time. The counselor, Special Education Learning Center teacher, and the English as a Second Language teacher, staff the room. The staff meets regularly with the vice principal, teachers, consultants, and the social worker. Administrators have been almost completely removed as the school disciplinarians (Friberg, 1995). The authors feature the Lord Lansdowne School in Chapter 13.

Reflection on Research

Violence in American classrooms is unlike that of other developed countries. The homicide rate for young men is four times higher than the next most violent industrialized country in the world, Scotland, and a rate 70 times higher than the rate in Austria. Each month about 420 children die from gunshot injuries, and the costs associated with violence are about $64 billion a year (Prothrow-Stith, 1994, p. 8). Reprinted with permission from the School Administrator (April 1, 1994).

In virtually every country, student behavior has become more disruptive or at least citizens perceive behavior as more disruptive. However, cultural and religious values keep the disruption minor in many countries. The amount of school violence is hard to discern in other countries, because the subject is embarrassing. The subject of discipline and school violence in the United States, however, seems to be on most people's mind. During the past decade, virtually every teacher and administrator has talked about declining discipline and the proliferation of violent behavior in America's schools. Prothrow-Stith (1994) claims that violence in American classrooms is unlike that of other developed countries. The homicide rate for young men is four times higher than the next most violent industrialized country in the world, Scotland, and a rate 70 times higher than the rate in Austria. Each month about 420 children die from gunshot injuries, and the costs associated with violence are about $64 billion a year (p. 8). Dunlap (1993) echoes the concern of educators about youth violence. He adds that violence is increasing at an alarming rate and that no one is exempt. There are too many guns, too many drugs, and too many temptations for youth. Unfortunately, elementary students exhibit these characteristics that formerly were problems for high school administrators and teachers.

The elementary educator in the United States deals with disruptive behavior much like educators in Britain and New Zealand. Teachers practice a proactive approach, and when that approach is unsuccessful, the teacher removes the students from the room, refers them to the principal, or the teacher calls the parent. A violent home environment, the availability of drugs and alcohol, and the violent nature of the community, however, work against changing the worst student behavior. The news is replete with examples of violent behavior. Many U.S. citizens have a love affair with guns, and the behavior of groups like the NRA is absolutely dangerous to the values adopted by elementary students. The emergence of militia groups is a new model for youth that is equally dangerous.

Truly, society should not require the teacher and principal to deal with violence. They are educators with little experience at handling extreme discipline cases. Society must find another way. Until that happens, however, the hard reality is that schools must deal with the problem. The blueprint later in the chapter offers some suggestions.

Homework, Television, and the Internet

Television

Television arrived on the international scene during the 1950s and since that time, has competed with the parent and school for the student's attention. Cable television has reached almost every developed country and has increased the entertainment available to school-age students. Figure 7.1 presents the percentage of 9-year-old and 13-year-old students in seven of the research countries who watched television 5 hours or more every day in 1992. The International Assessment of Educational Progress (IAEP) gathered the data. Students taking the tests reported their own viewing habits.

More 9-year-old and 13-year-old students from the United States reported watching 5 hours or more than any other country. Israel, however, is very close, and Eldar (1995), an authority on Israeli education, confirmed that television is as tempting in Israel as in the United States. She felt that Israeli parents are TV news junkies and that parents pass the value of watching news programs in the interest of assessing the status of national security to students. Sarfaty (1995), an Israeli student in her

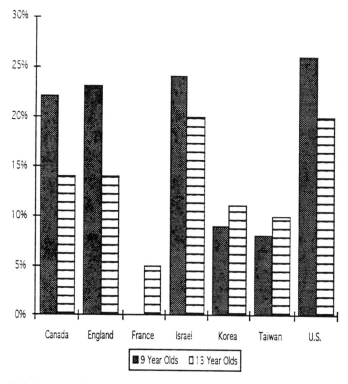

Figure 7.1 Percent of 9-year-old students and 13-year-old students in seven world-class countries who watch 5 or more hours of television daily, 1992 (data from Lapointe et al., 1992).

early teens, seemed to know that 77 television stations operated in Jerusalem and that two stations broadcast in Hebrew. Sarfaty stated that she returns from school about 2:00 P.M., eats lunch, does her homework, and then might watch television from about 8:00 P.M. until 10:00 P.M.

Nine-year-olds in France did not participate in the survey, but only 5 percent of French 13-year-olds answered the television question affirmatively. Why is television watching less popular in France? In the past, French educators expected their students to complete large quantities of homework. Students also apparently seek other use of their free time. Gavin (1995), a student who matriculated through the French public schools, felt that the statistics on French television watching were accurate and that French students do not watch television as much as students in neighboring countries. Gavin cited the need for French students to do homework and cited the social preference of young students to spend time together rather than in front of the television. Students gather in malls, theaters, and other locations that American students also find attractive.

A World-Class Idea: Profile of a World-Class Student from France

Sandra Gavin is a visiting undergraduate student at Western Carolina University. Sandra attended the Ecole Primaire Nieme primary school in Oyonnax, France. Kindergarten for Sandra was a 3-year experience with the last year devoted to learning basic skills of reading and writing. She remembers her kindergarten teachers telling stories and encouraging student drawings and paintings about the stories.

Elementary school meets for 6 hours a day and homework started in the first grade. Teachers fill almost the entire day with reading and writing. If you fail one subject, you must take the entire year over again. Teachers hold remedial sessions after school, but many students fail in spite of the attempts to remediate. This causes students of many ages to be in class together, and the older student often likes to show the younger students who is stronger. Most of the discipline problems stem from these students. If students fall at least 3 years behind, they seldom catch up and even have trouble learning in vocational school after the elementary experience.

Sandra felt that a student's social life in France centered around "interacting with friends." French students watch television much less than students in the United States, an opinion formed by Sandra's interaction with American students. Students also go to movies together. There is some focus on sports in French schools, but participation does not dominate the school day as they seem to in American schools.

Sandra felt strongly about her parent's influence in school life: "For my parents, teachers were always right, and if something was wrong, it was my fault. My parents didn't have to say anything to me because I respected them. Parents who take care of their children have no problems. Parents who don't come to school have problems."

Sandra left elementary school and entered a public boarding school specializing in arts. She will complete her higher education work after returning to France. Her respect for education continues to serve her well (Gavin, 1995).

In Canada, Parliament passed a law regulating violence on television, but to date, the extent of the regulation appears to be a warning stating that a program contains violence. Figure 7.1 shows that 14 percent of Canadian 13-year-old students watch television 5 or more hours per day. The figure is less than the 20 percent figure for the United States, even though cable has made television viewing in Canada and the United States quite similar. Friberg (1995), principal of Lord Lansdowne School in Toronto, had parents write a homework policy that included guidelines for television watching. The policy tells students that homework is important and expected of all students and that homework takes precedence over television.

Klevenz (1995), a German student, stated that television is not as important in German homes as it appears in American homes. Klevenz offered the opinion that German parents watch the news during the week but not too much other programming. He observed that American parents watch much more on a daily basis and even eat in front of the television. Bruckhaus (1995), also a German student, stated that he watches television mostly on weekends but prefers books. Both students sensed that television was much less important to German students than to students in the United States.

A World-Class Idea: A Profile of World-Class Students from Germany

Julian Klevenz and Christian Bruckhaus present an interesting contrast in educational background for researchers of comparative education. Both students studied together at Murphy High School in western North Carolina during 1994–1995 as exchange students. Before Murphy, however, Julian grew up in West Germany and Christian in East Germany. Julian, therefore, attended the Saxhsen Grundschule in Ansbach, Bavaria, and Christian attended Kemberg Grundschule in Kemberg, Saxton-Anhalt.

Julian attended Grundschule in classes from about 16 to 18 in size. He confirmed that the first day of school in the Grundschule is a day of celebration and that every student receives a cane of candy. He stressed that teachers treat students equally in the Grundschule. The day is short with no lunch hour, so students arrive home fairly early in the afternoon. Julian estimated that he did 1 hour of homework per day.

Christian also matriculated in small classes estimated at 20 students. Teachers do not group students; if a child could not learn, authorities sent him or her to a special school. Christian imparted this wisdom against the practice of grouping students, "If you put people in the lower group, they don't think they can do it." Christian remembers learning to read a watch and learning the alphabet in kindergarten. Because communism prevailed in East Germany, Christian learned Russian and clearly remembers an orientation toward Russian society and communist doctrine in all subjects. Teachers taught Marxist theory, which Christian found hard to read. The East German Grundschule did serve lunch and, in fact, provided day care for students during the afternoon hours so both parents could work. Christian remembers very little written work in the primary grades and, therefore, very little homework. What he could not finish in class, he could finish in day care. Leaders unified the schools in Germany when Christian entered the sixth grade in a prep school. Because the schools in East Germany adopted the organizational structure of the West German Schools, Christian found the first year confusing, but year 2 became more fun because teachers were not as strict.

Both students met with strict student behavioral expectations in primary school. Teachers keep a class book with details of student work, and students knew that breaches of discipline appeared in the book. Christian offered that a student would not burp in class, because the teacher would look at you; and students wanted to stay in good with each teacher. Every student knew that because the tests were essay, the teacher could grade the student down for misbehavior.

Even in the Grundschule, the Abitur looms in the distance, and students strive for a seat in the Gymnasium. Julian said that six or seven of his classmates in a fourth grade class of 18 went on to the Gymnasium. Christian echoed the amount for he estimated that 25 percent of his classmates went to the Gymnasium. Julian and Christian will return to their respective high schools and face the Abitur themselves. "I will take a written test and if I do well on that, teachers and administrators from the Educational Authority will give me an oral exercise," says Julian. Christian will open an envelope containing the test, will have a few minutes to organize his thoughts, and then must present on a subject. Christian relates, "You must study many subjects hard: that's why nobody skips school."

Neither student knows whether the year of school in the United States will count toward graduation. Both came to learn about the United States and accept whatever the future holds when they return (Bruckhaus, 1995; Klevenz, 1995).

American students watch too much questionable television. Students from the remaining world-class countries seemed to agree that being a serious student is not compatible with being a serious television watcher. Once students in the United States accept the above statement as the reality it seems to present, the student must then regulate his or her own television habits. The move to turn off the television must change some powerful paradigms. The typical elementary student in the United States clocks 35 hours of television watching per week. By age 18, a student has experienced about 12,000 hours of classroom instruction but has spent 25,000 hours in front of the television (McAdams, 1993). Preschoolers and elementary students are exceptionally vulnerable. On average, preschoolers watch 3 hours of television daily, and elementary students watch 5 hours a day. The research evidence is consistent on such heavy viewing. Children become more aggressive, get into more fights, and cause more physical destruction (*Asheville Citizens Times*, 1995a).

One factor that apparently affects viewing habits is the nature of the program selected for viewing. Recent data indicate that young children who watch public television educational programs perform better during the elementary years. Because television impacts student learning in a positive way when the programming is educational, television will certainly impact students in a negative way when the programming features violence and sexually oriented content.

World-Class Quote

By age 18, a student has experienced about 12,000 hours of classroom instruction but has spent 25,000 hours in front of the television (McAdams, 1993).

Internet

A new threat to the values developed by children emanates from the computer. Educators who worked hard to bring computers into the elementary school as a learning tool now find that students can use their computer skills to access violence and pornography. The Internet includes material that would cause the most hardened adult to blush. Both educators and parents must be alert to new media programs if computer usage is to remain a positive experience.

Homework

World-class elementary students do homework before considering television watching. Figure 7.2 includes the results of a second IAEP study in 1991 – 1992. The question asked of 9-year-old and 13-year-old students was, "Do you spend 2 hours or more on all homework every day?"

The figures for 9-year-old students show that at an early age, students spend serious time on homework. In Israel, over a third of the students

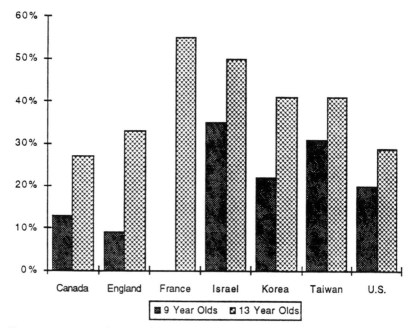

Figure 7.2 *Percent of 9-year-old students and 13-year-old students in seven world-class countries completing 2 or more hours of homework daily (data from Lapointe et al., 1992).*

surveyed said that they spent over 2 hours per day on homework with the percentage increasing to 50 percent for 13-year-old students. About one-fifth of 9-year-old students responded affirmatively in Korea and the United States. The United States shows the smallest percentage of increase from age 9 to 13, however.

Looking at the responses for 13-year-olds, again notice France where 55 percent of students reported doing 2 hours or more of homework daily. One would think that this fact undoubtedly compensates for the shorter school year in France. However, since 1994, the French Ministry of Education has forbidden homework in French elementary schools. Brahm (1995) reported, however, that teachers give it anyway because it is so ingrained into the learning process. Gavin (1995) confirmed that she had homework at the elementary level, but she did not feel that it was much. The homework was mainly mathematics and language that she took home. She considered visits to museums and other interesting places homework.

Nine percent of 9-year-old students and 34 percent of 13-year-old students in England reported spending 2 hours or more daily on homework. MacBeath and Turner (1990) studied the research on homework in Britain and the United States and concluded that (1) students who do homework perform better than students who do less homework, (2) greater effort on homework is related to higher expectations of parents and peers, and (3) homework may compensate for low achievement.

Reflection on Research

Research on homework in Britain and the United States concludes that (1) students who do homework perform better than students who do less homework, (2) greater effort on homework is related to higher expectations of parents and peers, and (3) homework may compensate for low achievement (MacBeath and Turner, 1990).

Students interviewed from other world-class countries confirmed that elementary and primary teachers expected homework. Miyake (1995), Japan; Huang (1995), Korea; Kleventz (1995), Germany; Osvath (1995), Canada; and Borochov (1995), Israel all received homework during the elementary or primary years—usually daily and in the range of 1−2 hours.

Friberg (1995), principal of the Lord Lansdowne Elementary School in Toronto, Canada, had parents develop a homework policy for the children. The policy identifies two kinds of homework, formal and informal, and includes guidelines for time spent on homework. Teachers and parents consider homework an important ingredient in the learning process. Notice, however, that Canada has the smallest numbers for students doing homework in both the 9-year-old category and the 13-year-old category.

The authors conclude that homework is a world-class learning tool. The agenda for action that concludes this chapter suggests that every school initiate a homework policy.

Extracurricular Activities

Few of the world-class countries provide an extracurricular program for elementary students. However, students in all countries report opportunities to participate in extracurricular activities outside school. If students choose to participate, they seem able to devote the time and still maintain their academic studies. Students in Japan, Korea, and Taiwan often attend Juku (cram school) to study the arts. Attendance might require extra time 2 or 3 days after school and on Saturday. Juku teachers assign homework just as the regular teacher does so that study time at home increases even more.

The authors interviewed about 20 upper elementary students from Israel touring the States with a dance troupe. The participants spend two afternoons a week practicing and were in the process of touring schools in the United States for a 2-week period. The school philosophy in Israel tolerates experiencial learning outside of the classroom.

A World-Class Idea: A Profile of World-Class Students from Israel

Inbal Sarfaty is a ninth grade student at the Hebrew Ginnasya in Jerusalem. She attended the Phola Ben Gurian Elementary School from kindergarten through grade 6. For Inbal, kindergarten began at age 3. "In kindergarten," says Inbal, "they talk to you about words, numbers, and stories. The kindergarten teacher tells stories about Jewish traditions." This teaching of values continues through the elementary experience.

Efrat Borochov, Inbal's friend and fellow dancer, currently attends the Dancing Academy, a private school where students study dance 2 hours a day after regular classes. Efrat attended her neighborhood elementary school as all Israeli students do. Only after the elementary years does choice become available to parents and students.

Both students remember clearly aspects of their elementary education. Class size was between 30 and 40 students who occupied a classroom similar in size to the average classroom in the United States. Neither had Arab students in their class, for they believed that living patterns and cultural differences caused Arab students to attend other schools. The teacher talked to the whole class sometimes but sometimes organized the students into groups and then moved through the groups. Both students bought their own textbooks prepared by the Ministry of Education. This made homework easier, and both agreed that Israeli students have more homework than the American students they had come across.

Because officials do not serve lunch in Israeli schools, Inbal arrives home by about 2:00 P.M. Her parents expect her to complete her homework before watching television. To Inbal, television rules were not necessary, because she respects her parents' wishes.

Both girls agreed on the formula for success in school—hard work plus listening to the teacher. Inbal summarized the formula in a novel way, "One must have a good butt and a good head." Although parental influence was an afterthought, Efrat said that she could go to her parents with a problem and that they would know what to do. Both girls clearly respected the importance of education for future success (Borochov, 1995; Sarfaty, 1995).

Miyake (1995) remembers training for a swim team 7 days a week after elementary school. She is now a successful university student in the United States. In Germany, an occasional school might maintain a soccer program, but usually students must take part in sports sponsored by city government (Klevenz, 1995; Wiegreffe, 1995). As in the United States, participation in recreation and sports at the elementary level is usually provided by the local government. Ontario, Canada, seems to be an exception. Most elementary schools in Ontario contain students in grades K–8. Interscholastic athletic participation is open to students in the upper elementary grades, but the presence of competitive sports carries pride to early elementary students also. Hewett (1995) and Ho (1995), fourth grade students at Annette Street Public School, Toronto, liked their school's athletic program. Kenny Ho is a swimmer, and Madeline Hewett prefers track, baseball, and swimming. A portrait of two older students at Annette Street Public School follows.

A World-Class Idea: Profile of World-Class Students from Ontario, Canada

Orion Osvath is a seventh grade student at the Annette Street Public School in Toronto, Canada. Jessica Denenberg is an eighth grader. Both attend the same gifted class, but not because the class is gifted. The staff at Annette purposely pairs classes throughout the elementary years. Placing two age groups together in every class-room allows for age appropriate grouping without the stigma of grouping same-age students. Both students live in the Annette Street attendance area located in metropolitan Toronto. They attend school with students from 40 different nationalities. Racial diversity is a given in each classroom.

Jessica thinks her school is a higher class school—a school with a reputation. Teachers make the program challenging, and teachers have a lot to do with her success. In fact, Jessica's parents moved, and she begged them to leave her at Annette. Her parents agreed. Jessica knows that her parents are proud of her and she feels fortunate. They trust her and support her. Because of a busy school schedule, Jessica doesn't watch much television—usually the morning news and some programs on weekends.

Orion also likes his school. He gives credit to a good principal who doesn't let students get out of hand. The previous year, he didn't really like the teacher too much, but his parents encouraged him to get good grades in spite of the situation. Orion does not watch much television either, for he prefers other activities. He estimated that he usually had about one and a half hours of homework per evening.

For both students, other activities center on the extracurricular. Orion stated that Annette had an excellent music program. But both students praised the athletic program that exists for students in grades 4−6 and in grades 7 and 8. The school won championships in volleyball and baseball. The teams have uniforms that are a source of pride. The school's reputation for excellence seemed enhanced by success on the athletic field as well as in the classroom (Osvath, 1995; Denenberg, 1995).

Participation in extracurricular activities seems to have appeal for students in all countries. Extracurricular activities can provide a student success and recognition that probably has carryover to the classroom. In the comparison countries, educators keep the programs outside the school day, and the perspective of extracurricular seems to prevail. For elementary age youngsters, the local government's recreation department usually provides sports. Where elementary schools include the seventh and eighth grade, interscholastic sports exist but normally outside the school day. The United States fits the same pattern. The United States has been fairly successful at keeping the overemphasis on athletics that exists in the senior high school out of the elementary school.

AN ELEMENTARY SCHOOL AGENDA FOR MAKING STUDENTS WORLD-CLASS

1. *Elementary school leaders should develop a profile of a successful, world-class student and continually teach children the contents.* Successful adults, especially those trained as teachers, know what behavior leads to success. Each elementary school faculty should develop a "successful student profile" and place it before students every day. The authors printed suggestions earlier in this chapter. Start in kindergarten with stories of successful students – remember the stories told in Israeli kindergarten. Have students write about success and discuss the profile with other students in groups.

Teachers must also model success and bring other adults to school that have success stories. In schools with multiage groupings, older students can help little ones understand the profile. Models are important to younger children so remember to provide models representative of all nationalities, races, and both sexes.

2. *Develop a student mediation program.* Older students in every elementary school can help fellow students solve disputes if educators train them to do so. Both the Lord Lansdowne Public School and the Annette Street Public School in Toronto, Canada, feature a Students as Mediators Program. Some schools in the United States adopted the idea several years ago (Ann Arbor Community Schools, Michigan, for example). Students who get into arguments and fights that could lead to disciplinary procedures can seek a trained student mediator who will attempt to solve the problem. This keeps many problems from reaching busy teachers and administrators and enhances the role of the student as a contributor to school success.

3. *Try a peer tutoring and counseling program in the elementary grades.* Although student mediation can be effective, it still kicks in after the fact. A peer tutoring and counseling effort can make a difference in a proactive way. Eastwood Elementary in Windsor, Canada, has a peer tutoring program in its open setting that serves as an example of students helping students with their schoolwork. Older elementary students spend part of the day with younger elementary students. The system can work as well in closed classrooms. C. Chalker (1996), Director of Alternative Schools, Metropolitan School District, Warren Township, Indianapolis, assigns at-risk high school students to work with kindergarten students in a nearby elementary school and finds that

the practice helps the small children as well as the at-risk students. The school is a model alternative school.

Ask the school counselor (if one exists) to develop and lead the peer tutoring and counseling program. There is much that elementary school counselors can do with groups that will prevent discipline problems.

4. *Incorporate character education into the school program in the regular classroom, in advisor-advisee programs, and through the use of "learning circles."* Other countries hold a distinct advantage over educators in the United States, because they teach values in the curriculum. Although citizens debate the practice in the United States, values are left to the home and church, and many students grow up without hearing that a civilized society is a society with a value system. American elementary schools cannot wait for special interest groups to agree on the importance of teaching values. Students in their early, formative years need to know right from wrong.

Advisor-advisee programs allow each student to meet in a small group with an educator each morning. Thousands of middle schools throughout the United States use advisor-advisee programs. They can be useful with younger students also. ''Learning Circles,'' where the teacher and students meet in an uninterrupted setting, can be better sources for developing self-esteem and communication skills. The teacher remains silent and permits each student to say whatever is on his or her mind. Trainers can train teachers to implement this process.

5. *Develop alternative programs for students who exhibit violent behavior and continually disrupt the class.* The disruptive child who continually keeps other children from learning can no longer remain in America's classrooms. Educators must develop alternative programs for such children. Principals should not allow disruptive students back to the regular classroom until they no longer disrupt the teacher and other students. School boards should expel students who bring weapons to school or pose a threat to the physical well-being of other persons. The parent should receive the same monetary allotment that the school receives for educating the child. The violence situation apparently is serious enough that elementary educators must adopt a ''tough love'' approach. If your state prohibits such action, then lobby the legislator with examples of students who are dangerous to themselves and others.

Best Practice

Educators must insist that disruptive students be removed from the classroom and placed in alternative settings. Students who break the law or bring weapons or drugs to school should be expelled. America needs a "tough love" policy in its schools.

---

6. Each elementary school should develop a homework policy that stresses the importance of homework for achieving maximum learning. An identical suggestion appears on the agenda for parents in Chapter 8. Students, however, can benefit from a homework policy written for them in their own language. In fact, students can help write the policy. First, the elementary principal must endorse the practice of homework and make it a nonnegotiable item for teachers. The value of homework is not debatable. It appears in every world-class country.

The homework policy should include (1) a schedule so that all teachers do not assign work on the same evening, (2) suggestions for students for successfully completing homework, (3) guidelines for the amount of time to be spent on homework, (4) lists of legitimate homework assignments that involve visits to interesting places and vacations, and (5) provisions for assigning homework during the summer months. The short school year in the United States makes homework a necessity. Teachers should guarantee students that their work will be checked. In other countries, teachers expect homework even when classes have 30–50 students. Seldom does an American classroom get that large.

Best Practice

Each elementary school should write a homework policy that

requires experiencial homework starting in grade 1 and progresses to 2 hours of homework by age 13. The homework requirement should not be negotiable with either teachers or parents. Homework helps achievement.

---

7. *Each elementary school should prepare a list of guidelines for student television watching that account for developmental learning.* Television so influences children's lives that the school must be clear about what television programs hurt children and what programs help. Teachers and administrators should prepare television guidelines along with the homework guidelines, for each competes for the student's free time. Again, students can help write the guidelines.

For early elementary children, educational programs seen mostly on public television can be helpful. Educational programs can be a source of homework if they become available after school hours. If not, suggest that parents tape educational programs for children. The school policy should take a stand against the violent and sexually oriented programming that children can watch after school and in the evening. In their own home, needless to say, children will watch whatever they wish, but perhaps the school can influence their thinking so that their choices improve.

8. *Elementary school leaders should encourage the development of extracurricular programs for students, but they should be available only after school and on weekends.* Although world-class educational programs seldom include extracurricular activities at the early elementary level, they do recognize the importance of play and cultural development outside the school and encourage student participation. By the time students reach the sixth grade, schools either sponsor a program of activities or cooperate with government authorities who sponsor programs. Teachers and parents should involve children in the arts at an early age. American schools usually have specialists in art and music who teach children during the day, but schools could offer enrichment after school. The Juku in Japan offers this service.

Athletics teach students lessons that are difficult to match in the classroom. School personnel must closely monitor the events, however, so that they are available for every child and do not become too competitive. On the athletic field, students learn fair play, organization, and the value of hard work. Students normally enjoy athletics, and programs offer relief from the less attractive work of the classroom.

Officials in too many American high schools overemphasized athletics, and elementary educators must be alert to attempts to overemphasize them at the elementary level. Principals should always schedule events outside the school day. Students should understand that participation depends on satisfactory completion of all academic work. Sponsors of activities, whether they be parents or teachers, should be responsible adults who know exactly what the school expects from the program.

9. *Elementary educators should discontinue any practice that labels students.* If America's students are to receive equal opportunity and contribute to the development of world-class schools, they must all feel equally welcome and special in the school. If teachers and parents expect students to take responsibility for their own learning, they must not handicap students with low expectations and labels that hinder the student's development.

A kindergarten teacher profoundly influenced one author and his wife by telling them that their 5-year-old son would never be a scholar. The son recently received a doctorate from the University of Georgia. Too many elementary teachers rush to decide which students are gifted, which are handicapped, and which are better than others in so many ways. World-class schools do not group youngsters but expect all to achieve according to their own unique abilities. World-class school leaders will ensure that their school is a school for all children whom a great leader assured everyone long ago are indeed created equal.

10. *Elementary school principals should restructure their administrative staff to change the role of the assistant principal from chief disciplinarian to child development specialist.* In most American elementary schools, the assistant principal assumes the role of disciplinarian and spends most of the day monitoring and correcting behavior. Chalker (1992) developed a new role for elementary school administrators for the 21st century. The time to plan for the change is now. Chalker proposes that the assistant principal become a child development expert and an advocate for children in the school. The principal would remain an instructional leader and advocate for teachers. Discipline would become a responsibility of the entire staff, thus releasing the assistant principal of full-time discipline responsibilities. Before you dismiss the idea as impractical, meet Peter Friberg, principal of the Lord Lansdowne Public School in Toronto, Canada. Friberg (1995) explains that the school's assistant principal is no longer the school disciplinarian. A resource room exists where teachers or administrators take children who misbehave. A counselor and two special teachers staff

the room and deal with learning problems and behavioral problems. There appear to be fewer to cope with than the average elementary school. Chapter 11 features the Lord Lansdowne School as an example of a world-class school.

EPILOGUE

The following letter is for persons who have doubts that early elementary students can contribute to the decisions made by school administrators. Thomas Rayner (1995), principal of the Annette Street Public School in Toronto, Canada, received the letter from Keisha, a midyear second grade student at the school. The child printed the letter very neatly, and the letter was practically mistake free except for a couple of letter reversals that the author could not duplicate in the copied version. The principal keeps the letter on the office wall as a reminder of Keisha but also as a reminder that students can do marvelous things if teachers and administrators remain open to students, and maintain high expectations. Every school has Keishas. Every school needs teachers who care and develop a mission to help kids be the best that they can be.

January 30, 1995

Dear Mr. Rayner

Here are some things to think About for next year!!
I have a Birthday on November 3rd AND Mrs. Sullivan Does too.
My 2nd NAme is Evelyn AND Mrs. Sullivan's 2nd name is Evalyn.
My J.K.-S.K. TeAcher was Mrs. Masellas AND her Birthday is November 3rd too!! So Please Hire a Gr. 3 Teacher that either Has a November 3rd Birthday or Evelyn As her 2nd name.

Your Friend,

Keisha

REFERENCES

Asheville Citizens Times. 1995a. Asheville, North Carolina (January 26):2C.

Asheville Citizens Times. 1995b. Asheville, North Carolina (May 31):3B.

Borov, E. 1995. Interview (April 10).

Brahm, B. 1995. Interview (May 22).

Brukhaus, C. 1995. Interview (April 3).

Chaer, C. S. 1996. *Effective Alternative Educational Programs. Best Practices from Planning through Evaluation.* Lancaster, Pennsylvania: Technomic Publishing Company, Inc.

Chaker, D. M. 1992. "Refocusing School Leadership for the 21st Century across the Board," *The Education Digest,* 58(3):4−8 (Condensed from *Thresholds in Education,* 1992, pp. 26−30).

Chaker, D. M. and R. M. Haynes. 1994. *World Class Schools: New Standards for Education.* Lancaster, Pennsylvania: Technomic Publishing Company, Inc.

Denenberg, J. 1995. Interview (June 13).

Discipline in the Schools: Report of the Committee of Enquiry Chaired by Lord Elton. 1989. London, England: Her Majesty's Stationery Office, Department of Education and Science and the Welsh Office.

Dunlap, E. 1993. "Violence, Values, and Human Decency," *Voice,* 6(1):7.

Eldar, D. 1995. Interview (May 23).

Friberg, P. 1995. Interview (June 12).

Gavin, S. 1995. Interviewed by Charlene Martin (April 10).

Hansen, D. D. 1994. "Public Education and Shared Values," *Divergent Views on the Control of Schools: An Iowa Dialogue,* Cedar Falls, IA: Institute for Educational Leadership, 5(2):64−66.

Henshall, K. G. 1992. "Education in Japanese Society: Lessons for New Zealand," *Delta,* 46:15−19.

Hewett, M. 1995. Interview (June 13).

Hill, P. B. 1992. "Looking at Japan: Historical Imperatives and Contemporary Realities," *International Education,* 22(1):49−55.

Ho, K. 1995. Interview (June 13).

Huang, A. 1995. Interviewed by Deborah Hall (February 15).

International Comparisons in Education−Curriculum, Values, and Lessons. Circa 1993. Alberta, Canada: Alberta Chamber of Resources.

Jambor, T. 1988. "Corporal Punishment and Other Classroom Discipline Alternatives: A Survey of Elementary School Teachers in Norway and England," *International Education,* 16(1):5−13.

Jennings, J. F. 1995. "School Reform Based on What Is Taught and Learned," *Phi Delta Kappan,* 76(10):765−769.

Kawaguchi, Hitomi. 1995. Interviewed by Kim Kisner (February 28).

Klevenz, J. 1995. Interview (April 10).

Lapointe, A. E., N. A. Mead and J. M. Askew. 1992. *Learning Mathematics.* Princeton, New Jersey: The International Assessment of Educational Progress, Educational Testing Service.

MacBeath, J. and M. Turner. 1990. *Learning Out of School.* A Research Study Commissioned by the Scottish Education Department. Glasgow, Scotland: Jordanhill College.

McAdams, R. P. 1993. *Lessons from Abroad: How Other Countries Educate Their Children.* Lancaster, Pennsylvania: Technomic Publishing Company, Inc.

Miyake, Atsuko. 1995. Interviewed by Kim Kisner (February 28).

Osvath, O. 1995. Interview (June 13).

Park, Hee Choung. 1995. Interviewed by Deborah Hall (March 7).

Prothrow-Stith, D. 1994. "Building Violence Prevention into the Curriculum," *School Administrator,* 4(51):8–12.

Rayner, T. 1995. Interview (June 13).

Rehner, M. 1995. Interview (June 14).

Sarfaty, I. 1995. Interview (April 10).

Schoollad, K. 1986. "ISIME: The Bullying of Japanese Youth," *International Education,* 15(2):5–28.

Vaughan, L. and A. Weeds. 1994. "Managing an Effective Classroom," *The Professional Practice of Teaching.* Palmerstown North, New Zealand.

Wiegreffe, C. 1995. Interviewed by Darrell McDowell (February 12).

Young, M. 1993. "The Dark Underside of Japanese Education," *Phi Delta Kappan,* October.

WORLD-CLASS PARENTS, HOMES, AND COMMUNITIES

Train up a child in the way he should go and when he is old he will not depart from it.

— Proverbs 22:6

Chapter 8 explores the concept of world-class parents, their homes, and their communities. The authors emphasize the roles of the parent as first teacher and later as supporter of the child and his or her school. The chapter first explores the status of parent and community activity in the countries of Canada, Britain, France, Germany, Japan, Korea, New Zealand, and Taiwan. Parenting and community support for education in the United States receive a similar examination. Finally, Chapter 8 presents an agenda for making the parents, the home, and the community in the United States world-class.

National efforts to form world-class schools will be successful only if the role of the home and community rises to the top of the education agenda. Chalker and Haynes (1994) hypothesize that a positive parental influence, a stable and caring home environment, and a supportive community determine success in school more than any other factor. The school restructuring suggestions contained in earlier chapters pale in significance when compared with the importance of the parent, home, and community in developing world-class schools.

THE WORLD-CLASS STATUS: PARENTS, HOME, AND COMMUNITY

"It takes the whole village to raise a child." The phrase might be

205

overused, but no other explains better the importance of parents, home, and community to the future success of children. Regardless of the country studied by the authors, children became successful in school when the parents in the home and citizens in the community valued education and passed that value on to children. Parents who take seriously the role of the child's "first teacher" prepare children well for school. They discipline the student, challenge the student intellectually, read regularly to the student, provide for the student's health and welfare, and instill in the child a love for learning and a respect for teachers. This rigorous preparation for life continues as the child progresses through school where parental support for the school actually strengthens the values. Nations with world-class schools have an abundance of these parents and students.

Parents and Communities in the World-Class Countries

The Asian Pacific Rim countries appear to have an abundance of such parents. In Japan, Korea, and Taiwan, parents assume responsibility for the child's education from birth through the school experience. The child learns early in the maturation process that the family values education and that school success honors the family. The mother assumes prime responsibility for school success and tenaciously leads the student through the educational process. Parents place adequate but well-defined pressure to succeed on the student, but the pressure seems to produce positive results with little negative influence on the child. Community values in the Asian Pacific Rim countries support the high esteem placed on education in the home.

Korea presents an interesting example of parental influence on the education of children. The structure of the Korean family makes parental pressure intense yet effective. Korean parents expect to be cared for by their children in old age, so they consider their relationship with the children an investment. Parents make a heavy economic investment in the child's education, often including support of the child in a "cram school" outside the regular school day. As mentioned previously, the mother usually remains home and assumes of the role of making sure that the children succeed educationally. In so doing, the mother can assume autonomous power known in Korea as "shirt wind." The Koreans often describe this power as "the force of a woman on the rampage." Children usually acknowledge the powerful influence of their

World-class learning requires time and support from the home. This Chinese mother spends time with the children at home, supporting homework and encouraging the children to be diligent learners. The portable textbooks come home every night so parents expect homework. One Taiwanese parent was asked what complaints Chinese parents have about the schools; his reply: "Not enough homework, not enough work, not enough tests!" (photo courtesy of the Ministry of Education, Republic of China).

parents and assume responsibility for working hard at school (Sorensen, 1994).

In Japan, parents play a major role in ensuring that their children meet the demands of the school in terms of attendance, timekeeping, and homework. Parents often pay for some of the resources children need to experience success in their studies (*Teaching and Learning in Japanese Elementary Schools,* 1992). Japanese parents also sacrifice to send their sons and daughters to cram schools (Juku). Japanese mothers appear to be particularly significant in establishing the "education ethic" in the minds of children. The "dragon mother" often observes the child in school and may even attend school for the child if illness prevents the child's attendance (Katsula Setsuo, 1992). Stevenson and Lee (1990) observed that parents in Japan and Taiwan consider academic pursuit of knowledge the most important goal in their child's life. When the child enters the elementary school, Japanese and Taiwanese parents mobilize themselves to assist the child and to provide an academic atmosphere in the home. Mothers in both countries hold higher standards for their children's achievement than American mothers, but at the same time, hold more realistic evaluations of their child's academic, cognitive, and personality characteristics. Japanese and Taiwanese mothers stress the importance of hard work as an ingredient of success in school rather than the ingredient of innate ability so often found in the beliefs of American mothers.

In New Zealand, it is becoming common for primary teachers to meet with parents and the child at the beginning of the year to set goals for the child's learning. The teacher benefits from the parent's knowledge of the child and is able to make the parent part of the yearly plan for learning. Teachers hold interviews and conversations with parents regularly to share information on the child's progress. Some schools schedule a meeting of the parents and student on or near the child's birthday. This is a longer meeting focusing on the child's progress, and the teacher often permits the child to present his or her own evidence of learning to the parent. In New Zealand, school leaders expect teachers to participate in the preparation of a report to the community. The report emphasizes student achievement (Faire and Yates, 1994).

In the European countries, parents of primary youngsters are more prone to leave the education of their youth to professionals in the schools. In Germany, the Grundgesetz (Constitution) of the Federal Republic of Germany gives parents the care and education of their children. Parents and the state community have a joint education commitment to cooperatively provide the child's education. The constitutions or legislative laws of the Bundeslander (states) explain the basic principles of this cooperative effort. All Bundeslander provide for representative parent bodies (Neuber, 1991). McAdams (1993), however, found that German parents generally prefer to leave education in the hands of educators. The strongest role that parents now play in German involves the selection of a school or program for the child leaving the Grundschlen. Parents are increasingly demanding placement in an academic setting that has caused great consternation among German educators. These demands have caused a drop in enrollment in the main school or Hauptschulen from 2.5 million in 1975 to 1 million in 1989. As in the Asian Pacific Rim countries, the primary contribution of parents is the development of an "education ethic" in the home. Parents instill a strong work ethic in students from their earliest school days. The German family views education as the most important responsibility of the adolescent and teaches the adolescent that school will have a dramatic effect on their future livelihood. The result is a preponderance of students who take school seriously. The German culture also seems to place a high value on education, a fact reflected by exceptionally good working conditions and pay for teachers (McAdams, 1993).

The French also demonstrate a high regard for education despite a school year no longer than the 180 days scheduled in the United States. Children start their education early. The French government provides a public, all-day kindergarten for children ages 2−6. Nearly all 3-year-old children are in kindergarten, and they remain in kindergarten through age 5 (Fowler, 1988). Students in kindergarten phase in academic study rather than wait for the students to enter elementary school. The French are proud of their early education experience and consider it largely responsible for the success of children in elementary and high school. Once in elementary school, students work a long day but a day broken into modules so that students will not become distracted. Tutoring is available after school for students who require extra work.

In France, the home environment also strongly orients students to the education ethic. In France, divorce is far less common than in the United States, and most children live with two parents. In fact, the extended family influences the child through close kinship networks, and a more traditional family life exists with families eating together and children vacationing with grandparents (Lees, 1994). Zeldin (1982) reported that half the families in France lived within 13 miles of parents. The IAEP survey shows that homework in the French home is world-class and that students watch television less than students in any other world-class country (Lapointe et al., 1992).

But, like German parents, French parents have historically little direct involvement in their schools. Parent-teacher organizations are relatively new in a system so tradition bound that parent input almost seems superfluous. Parents, however, now hold membership on the Conseil de Classe with administrators, teachers, and students. The Conseil de Classe decides on a child's promotion from certain levels of the student's schooling and eventually decides what type of secondary school the child will attend. In 1990, the French government established a goal to increase the number of students reaching the Baccalaureate level (Pierre and Auvillain, 1991).

The government's adoption of the parents' charter in Britain in 1991

TABLE 8.1 The Scottish parents' charter—your rights and responsibilities.

Your Rights	Your Responsibilities
A free school place for your child	To provide education for your child
A choice of school for your child within the limits of availability	To ensure that your child attends school regularly
To obtain information about your child's progress	To take an active interest in your child's education, for example, by encouraging learning at home and talking to the school about any problems or difficulties your child may have
To appeal if things go wrong	
To vote and stand in school board elections	
To receive information from the school board about its activities	
To receive help with assessment or special education needs that your child may have	To attend parents' meetings called by the school
To explore the possibility of self-governing status for your school	To participate in voluntary activities supporting the school
To receive, depending on income, an assisted place for your child at an independent school	To support the work of the school board and consider standing as board member

Source: The Parents' Charter in Scotland (1992, p. 3).

demonstrates a full commitment to parental involvement in the four nations forming Great Britain. Table 8.1 presents the Scottish parents' charter. Others exist in England, Wales, and Northern Ireland.

The parents' charter in all British countries gives to parents responsibilities far beyond those of the other world-class countries compared by Chalker and Haynes (1994). First, elementary parents sit on a governing board with considerable authority over decisions made about the schools. Parents can require the board to seek "grant status" for their school by a majority vote. Grant status gives the governing board authority to bypass the regional governing body and absorb all decision making at the local level. Second, the charter strengthens the concept of school choice for parents. Third, the charter guarantees parents reports of standardized examination results, budgets, and other reports issued by the governing board. And fourth, the charter makes available to parents information about independent schools, special education programs, and self-governing schools.

One correlate of the Scottish parents' charter is to encourage learning at home. In 1990, the Scottish Education Department conducted research on homework, a piece of the parent puzzle that should be of interest to all parents in the United States. MacBeath and Turner (1990) reported on the comparative status of homework in several European countries. In Belgium, officials do not permit homework below the age of 10, and in Spain, homework is forbidden for all ages. Luxembourg sets a maximum of 30 minutes for first year students. Most countries, however, provide no guidelines at all. As a result of the study, the authors found support among students, parents, and educators for homework if educators structured the homework properly. The research produced numerous suggestions for all concerned with homework and is worth further study by educators in the United States. The primary conclusion is as follows: "Rather than debating the pros and cons of homework, discussion should occur on questions of purpose and quality, acknowledging that independent learning out of school is a vital ingredient in education motivation and achievement" (p. 63).

Britain, however, reports problems with parental authority and control of school-age youth. A substantial number of youth who have developed an antischool attitude plague British schools today. The department for education reports a substantial number of early school leavers and a relatively small percentage of students matriculating to the university. Socioeconomic class still partially governs opportunity in spite of attempts to democratize the system. Parents often do not take advantage of the opportunities afforded by the parents' charter.

Closer to home, reports from Alberta, Canada, indicate that there appears to be a deterioration of the parenting role as it pertains to education. Too many parents apparently give less time and interest to the child's educational achievement, resulting in a child who enters school unmotivated and unprepared. In Alberta, concern for the deterioration of education resulted in a cooperative study conducted by the Chamber of Resources and Alberta Education. The study found family problems in Alberta almost identical to those reported in the United States: (1) a high divorce rate, (2) a majority of children living in a family where both parents work, and (3) 15 percent of children living in families below the poverty level. The study concludes that the importance of parenting to academic achievement deserves publicity and that the government encourage parenting programs (*International Comparisons in Education*, circa, 1992).

In Toronto, Ontario, however, one author discovered two elementary schools where the principal worked hard to develop a disciplined climate. Parents were involved in writing homework policies, parents helped determine the staffing of the schools, and parents volunteer regularly in the schools. Ontario schools will have mandated school councils composed of parents, community representatives, and a student by the 1995 – 1996 school year (Friberg, 1995; Rayner, 1995).

Lewin (1995) reports that all developed countries are experiencing drastic changes in the structure of family life. Lewin gathered data from the report, "Families in Focus," published by the Population Council, an international group in New York. The report found that (1) marriages are dissolving with increasing frequency, (2) parents are burdened with child care as well as aging parent care, (3) poor families with only a mother present are increasing, (4) unwed motherhood is increasing, and (5) more mothers are working. Foreign consuls interviewed by the authors confirmed the fact the family is changing often in the way described in "Families in Focus." For example, in Taiwan, 40 percent of the families with children in school have both parents working (Li, 1995). The likely conclusion is that all countries studied must adjust the educational system to compensate for changing conditions in the home.

Parent and Community Involvement in the United States

The elementary school in America is in a strategic position to mold the homes and communities served by the schools. Parents, for example, are more involved in their child's education during the elementary experience, and the smaller service area allows for the easier development of a sense of community. Elementary school leaders can no longer afford to remain in the confines of the school if they desire world-class education. Parent involvement in the PTA, parent-teacher conferences, and the annual open house, although important, are no longer sufficient to ensure a successful school liaison with the home and community. New knowledge shows that the interaction taking place between the parent and the child at home is crucial to the student's success. The quality of that interaction in the preschool years seems to be the most crucial of all. Likewise, the positive value placed on education in the community correlates to success in school. The phrase, "it takes a whole community to raise a child," therefore, gains new meaning in the quest for world-class school status.

Fairview School in Sylva, North Carolina invites parents to the school for food and a homework session where parents and students work together. Staff members and student teachers from Western Carolina University work with parents and students to develop good homework habits (photo by McNair).

World-Class Quote

"Never doubt that a small group of thoughtful, committed citizens can change the world; indeed they are the only ones that ever have" (Margaret Mead).

Preschool Parenting

First, consider the status of preschool parenting in the United States today. The first national education goal—by the year 2000, all children will start school ready to learn—has perhaps the most potential for ensuring world-class education in America's elementary schools. The three objectives of the goal call for (1) education and support for parents, (2) attention to health and prenatal care, and (3) universal access to appropriate educational environments. Kagan (1994a) suggests that the goal sparks a national commitment to all young children and highlights the critical role of parents in the educational process.

How does the United States compare with the other research countries in terms of enrollment in preprimary education? Figure 8.1 shows preschool enrollment percentages for the combined total of 3-, 4-, and 5-year-old students for 1990–1991. Similar data were only found for five countries.

France is proud of the fact that that 100 percent of 3- to 5-year-old children are in school. Brahm (1995) states that 60 percent of 2-year-old students are in school and in 1 or 2 years, all 2-year-old youngsters will attend school. Socialization and integration are goals during the pre-school years, and 5-year-old students can read in France. The government believes that the child has the best possibility of learning during the preschool years.

Germany is also moving toward preschool for all children. Parents used to pay for the kindergarten experience, but the government is now more and more providing preschool education. Educators in Japan still consider preschool education to be the responsibility of the parent, but

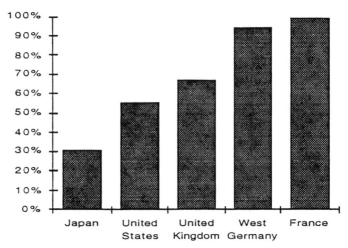

Figure 8.1 *Gross enrollment ratio (%) for children ages 3–5 in preprimary education, 1991–1992, for five world-class nations (data from Husen and Postlethwaite, 1994).*

parents place more and more children in preschool as the mother joins the workforce. The percentage will increase in Japan.

Meaningful statistics come from world-class nations not represented in Table 8.1. In Korea, a country with the shortest compulsory attendance laws, a majority of 4- and 5-year-olds now attends kindergarten. In Israel, 96 percent of Jewish youngsters, ages 0—6 are in the Early Childhood Network. Fifty percent of Arab youngsters are in the network. In New Zealand, 73 percent of Maori children under age 5 attend preschool. In Canada, 4- and 5-year-olds attend kindergarten in Manitoba, Quebec, and Ontario. Also significant is a law recently passed by The Department of Education in Ontario, Canada, requiring new school construction to include a preschool center (Innerd, 1995).

The preprimary experience of children in the United States, however, varies in quality and quantity. In the United States today a child's educational experiences from birth to age 5 primarily come from three sources: the home, day care, and the preschool. The quality and the range of each child's experience in these settings cause the child to enter formal schooling with different backgrounds and different expectations. It is the quality of these differences that send the child to school with sound adjustment mechanisms or the potential for problems. Too often, the school knows little about these early experiences and does little to adjust the program for children who experience difficulty in preschool.

The home is the child's first learning environment. Although some homes are excellent classrooms, the literature clearly describes the deterioration of many American families causing little positive learning at home. The divorce rate is the highest of the developing countries. The number of families surviving below the poverty level is on the increase. Child abuse has increased at an alarming rate, and many parents seem to have little time to develop the education ethic in their children. Many family practices have a positive influence on the child's readiness for school, but too many have a negative effect. Even some parents who seem to be comfortable in life financially often do little to establish readiness for school. The intensity of parenting for learning found in Japan, Korea, Germany, and other world-class countries is missing in many American homes. Parents, even those with the best of intentions, function in a society where education lacks priority on the community agenda and in the home. In fact, too many times parents negatively influence children about education. Parents tell children about their own negative experiences in school, the terrible teachers that they have had, and the fact that school is not fun.

Day care centers and preschools grew so fast during the1980s and 1990s that they still struggle to develop appropriate developmental activities. Kagan (1994b) characterizes the reality of the child care and preschool movement as follows: "Today's early care and education efforts represent a collection of comparatively isolated events, taking hold idiosyncratically throughout the nation in schools, child care centers, resource and referral agencies, and Head Start programs" (p. 227).

Kagan notes, however, that child care and preschool efforts are gaining media attention and are found increasingly on the agenda of educational conferences and in the educational journals. Corporate leaders have become involved, and the government agenda often now includes the early childhood years. Much needs to be accomplished, however, and Americans need to totally accept a social responsibility for all children.

Parents of Elementary Students

The influence of parents at home continues to be important after the child enters school. Parents must continue to support teachers and administrators and continue to insist that the child learn to the best of his or her ability. Parents must insist on homework and provide a quiet study area for the child. The United States leads the world-class countries in youthful television watching, and parents are the only ones who can reverse this harmful practice. Bennett (1994) states the case for a supportive home environment this way, "Family structure has an enormous amount to do with education, and the values taught at home have an enormous amount to do with education" (p. 23).

Wildavsky (1994) reports on an impressive study conducted by *Reader's Digest* that reveals what is behind student success in school. The study invited 2130 high school seniors to take a special academic test and then answer a list of personal questions. The data related to the home environment follow: "Strong families give kids an edge in school. For instance, students who lived with two parents scored high more often on our test than students who didn't. Students who regularly shared mealtimes with their families tested better than those who didn't. This 'family gap' showed up for students of all backgrounds" (p. 49).

Although parental influence at home is important, encouraging news about parent involvement in school affairs is also beginning to surface. Educators have always assumed that students do better in school when parents become involved in the school agenda, but research on the subject has been rare. As noted previously, other nations where students excel do not always encourage a great deal of parental involvement, leaving Americans to wonder if parental involvement in the school is really world-class. Americans are beginning to find that parental involvement pays. Concluding a study of American families in all 50 states, Zill and Nord (1994) reported that all parents expect their children to complete high school, and nearly three-fourths anticipate a college degree for each child. But do parents follow up on these high expectations by becoming actively involved in their child's school program? Figure 8.2 shows the level of involvement in school activities for U.S. students in grades 3−5. All 50 states participated in the research.

The researchers asked parents if they attended three different kinds of school activities, (1) parent meetings, (2) school events, or (3) volunteer activities. High involvement means parents participated in all three activities. The study defined moderate involvement as a parent who participated in two of the three categories, and low involvement as a parent who participated in one activity or none at all. Figure 8.2 shows that 42 percent of the parents with students in grades 3−5 claimed high involvement in school activities, and another 32 percent claimed moderate involvement. Furthermore, a high level of involvement existed for parents of children enrolled in private school and/or when both

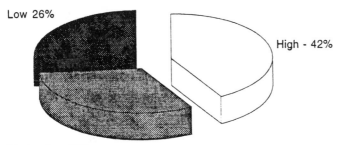

Low 26%

High - 42%

Moderate - 32%

Figure 8.2 Level of parent involvement in school activities for U.S. students in grades 3−5. (Note: U.S. Department of Education, National Center for Education Statistics, 1993. National Household Education Survey, School Safety and Discipline component, calculated by N. Zill from public use tapes.)

parents were college graduates and earned a comfortable income, and/or when both parents were present in the household.

But do students whose parents are highly involved in school activities achieve better in school? Zill and Nord reported conclusive results. Students from low-involvement families were twice as likely to be in the lower half of their class as students from high-involvement families. Students from low-involvement families also experienced more discipline problems. The survey supports perceptions that parents involved in the school can make a difference.

Reflection on Research

Seventy-four percent of parents with children in grades 3–5 are highly involved in school activities in the sense that they attend PTA meetings; go to school plays, sports events, or science fairs; and act as volunteers or serve on committees. Students whose parents showed low involvement are twice as likely to have been suspended or expelled from school (21 percent versus 7 percent) as students with highly involved parents (Zill and Nord 1994).

Schools, however, must create these opportunities if parents are to participate. Weiss (1994), director of the Harvard Research Project, found that many schools have a piecemeal approach to parent involvement, and that less than half of the states mention any form of parental training programs. Parents often feel unwelcome in their local school, and teachers sometimes feel that parents only come to school to complain. The finger pointing must stop, and the local school, with support from the central office, must lead the way to a cooperative arrangement. In most schools where successful alliances between educators and parents exist, the school describes the alliance in writing, both educators and parents value the role played by each party, and training is available for both educators and parents.

From 1986–1988, the Southwest Educational Development

Laboratory (SEDL) sought to identify the characteristics of "promising parent involvement programs" in the five states of Arkansas, Louisiana, New Mexico, Oklahoma, and Texas. SEDL staff visited selected programs across the region and interviewed local educators. They found seven essential elements common to all promising programs (Williams and Chavkin, 1989):

(1) Written policies legitimized the importance of parent involvement.
(2) Administrative support was evident in the areas of funding, material and product resources, and people to conduct the programs.
(3) Promising programs made training available for staff and parents.
(4) A partnership approach made both staff and parents feel a sense of ownership.
(5) Two-way communication between home and school occurred frequently and regularly.

The United States must also continue to attack the problem of illiteracy in the country. In 1991, the literacy rate in the United States was 96 percent (*World Education Report,* 1993). Illiterate parents will seldom be effective partners with the school. Schools simply need to continue family literacy programs until illiteracy becomes nonexistent and parents feel comfortable helping teach their children basic literacy. In the most recent study based on information from family literacy programs in Atlanta, Rochester, and Richmond, improvements were impressive. "Parent/child book reading time increased by 70 percent; parents took their children to the library twice as often; children's reading of books increased by 80 percent; and parents became increasingly aware that their children learn better through activities and play" (Darling, 1994, p. 31). Sometimes schools must help parents learn if schools are to be successful in ensuring that the child learns. Adult literacy is one key to a student's success.

Of all educational factors affected by community and home influences, the one factor with the most focus is the political, social, and economic factor of family status and family values. The United States struggles with one of the highest divorce rates in the world, and the nation has an abundance of one-parent families. Regardless of the effectiveness of the one parent, the child misses the double effect of two parents encouraging and guiding the child. The number of births to unwed mothers is staggering, and this conditions only adds to the number of one-parent families. Children often have inadequate supervision at home, and violence in the schools has become the number one concern of parents, students, and teachers. Henderson (1994, p. 8) gathered the following information that dramatically presents the impact of society on education:

(1) Adolescent suicide rates quadrupled from 1960 to 1988.

(2) Teenage homicides more than doubled from 1960 to 1988.

(3) The percentage of parents whose children divorced within a year's time more than doubled between 1960 and 1988.

(4) Births to unwed mothers increased fivefold, and the percentage of children in households with one adult tripled from 1960 to 1988.

(5) The percentage of children under 6 whose married mothers were in the workforce went from 18.6 to 57.1 during the years 1960 to 1988.

(6) In 1991, no books were purchased in 60 percent of American households.

(7) Today about 10 million children between the ages of 6 and 13 are without adequate supervision after school.

(8) Parents rather than supporting teachers and schools frequently undermine academic affairs by speaking or acting negatively about education.

(9) Every 8 seconds a child drops out of school.

(10) Every day thousands of children bring guns to school.

Recently, the U.S. Department of Education gathered research from 30 years of research on the effects of family involvement in children's learning (*Strong Families, Strong Schools: Building Community Partnerships for Learning,* 1994). Some caveats from the research follow:

- Three factors over which parents exercise authority—student absenteeism, variety of reading materials in the home, and excessive television watching—explain nearly 90 percent of the difference in eighth grade mathematics test scores across 37 states and the District of Columbia on the National Assessment of Education Progress (NAEP). Thus, controllable home factors account for almost all the differences in average student achievement across states (Barton and Coley, 1992).

- Studies of individual families show that what the family does is more important to student success than family income or education. This is true whether the family is rich or poor, whether the parents finished high school or not, or whether the child is in preschool or in the upper grades (Coleman et al, 1966; Epstein, 1991; Stevenson and Baker, 1987; de Kanter et al., 1987; Henderson and Berla, 1994; Keith and Keith, 1993; Liontos, 1992; Walberg, n.d.).
- The single most important activity for building the knowledge for eventual success in reading is reading aloud to children (Anderson et al., 1985).
- If every parent of a child aged 1−9 spent 1 hour reading or working on schoolwork with his or her child 5 days a week, American parents would annually devote at least 8.7 billion hours to support their children's reading (U.S. Department of Education, 1994).

Reflection on Research

Three factors over which parents exercise authority—student absenteeism, a variety of reading materials in the home, and excessive television watching—explain nearly 90 percent of the difference in eighth grade mathematics test scores across 37 states and the District of Columbia on the National Assessment of Educational Progress (NAEP). Thus, controllable home factors account for almost all the differences in average student achievement across states (Barton and Coley, 1992).

In all 50 states, educators accept parent involvement as one ingredient that should increase student success. Thousands of programs about parental involvement appear in the literature, and school and community classes exist in most preparation programs for teachers and administrators. The following agenda for parent and community involvement does not attempt to repeat information about these many admirable attempts to involve parents and community. They are readily available to educators. The agenda does reflect the world-class practices discovered by Chalker and Haynes (1994) and suggests new standards for making America's elementary schools world-class.

AN ELEMENTARY SCHOOL AGENDA FOR MAKING PARENTS AND COMMUNITY WORLD-CLASS

1. *Elementary educators should develop a plan for appointing preschool parents as adjunct faculty and supporting their work as the child's first teacher.* Elementary school leaders must help parents prepare their preschool youngsters for a successful transition to school. The elementary principal must mobilize staff to lead the home-to-school connection. Try this agenda. First, identify all parents of preschool children living in the school catchment area, including those who move to the district during the preschool years. Second, give them the title of adjunct faculty by sending an official letter of appointment and welcome. Third, invite the new adjunct faculty to a faculty meeting and present them a "parent as teacher" certificate enabling them to teach the child in the home. Appoint a mentor from the teaching staff to help them during their parenting and teaching years. Fourth, provide staff development opportunities that focus on teaching the child at home and in the community. Stress reading to the child, game playing, and activities to teach the child how to live in harmony with others. If the budget permits, place books in the school library that parents can check out, or better yet, encourage the parent and child to visit the school library. Finally, bring the new adjunct faculty to school periodically for roundtable discussions in which parents can share successes and generate new ideas. Have children attend enough of these meetings so that children can gain a feeling for the school environment and an appreciation for teachers and administrators.

Best Practice

Elementary administrators should appoint all parents of preschool youngsters as "adjunct faculty" and develop a program (materials and methods) for these parents that encourages them to work with their youngsters at home and in the community.

---

2. Elementary educators can take the lead in developing materials for preschool parents. Many parents need reference materials that might help them prepare their child for school. The elementary school should take the initiative to provide these materials. The ideal method of developing the materials, however, would be through a cooperative effort with the local school, the nearest university that trains teachers, and local business. Many of these collaborative arrangements exist, and where they are not in place, they should be.

The Alliance of Business Leaders and Educators (ABLE) at Western Carolina University is such a collaborative. The leadership of the Alliance developed a booklet, *Getting Your Child Ready for School* (1993) that contains chapters on preparing the child to read, developing a positive self-image, teaching the child to live in harmony with others, building a support group for the family, and enhancing the child's health. A video is a companion to the booklet and provides a visual resource for parents reluctant or unable to read the booklet. The booklet and video are both professionally produced and contain material developed by local experts. Local business organizations made the ABLE resources available to schools, hospitals, preschools, and others invested in the growth of children.

ABLE also maintains a library of materials developed to promote effective parenting. Every elementary school in the United States should have access to such a library collection. The ideas that such materials spawn can be sent to parents in a variety of creative ways. The following research moment is an example of an idea that if adopted by parents, can make a difference.

The development of materials for parents of preschool children compliments the first suggestion on the agenda—the suggestion to make all preschool parents adjunct faculty and to provide them with the expertise necessary to prepare their children for the transition from home to school. Blending the two agenda items can help create the education ethic that world-class countries have so firmly entrenched in their social mores. Without the education ethic, America's schools will not likely reach world-class status.

Reflection on Research

Four things parents can do to raise achievement 38 percent:

1. Have a daily conversation with your child about events at school. (Recall emotional events, not judgments.)
2. Have your child teach you the most valuable thing he has learned today.
3. Treat your child "as if," not "as is." The ratio of compliments to criticism should = 2 for 1.
4. Model learning by learning one thing each week important enough to be useful for a lifetime as a parent (Phillips, circa 1994).

3. Each elementary school should develop a "parents' charter." Earlier in Chapter 8 the authors presented the Scottish parents' charter. The charter includes the obligations of the school to the parent as well as the responsibilities of the parent to the school. Although these obligations and responsibilities are often present in America's elementary school, they are often not in writing and often not presented in charter form. Both of these factors seem to be important if educators are to convince parents that they are valuable members of the school team.

Elementary principals should develop a parents' charter that goes beyond the information provided in the Scottish charter. Parents, teachers, and students should be involved in the development of the document so that all concerned have ownership over the product. The charter should contain the school's commitment to parents, including the commitment to provide parents information necessary to guide parental decisions about learning in the home. The charter should encourage involvement in school activities by identifying these activities and also should contain the parents' responsibility to become involved in these activities. The charter should be attractively printed and presented to parents of kindergarten children and parents of children new to the school.

4. *Elementary school leaders can develop creative parent-teacher conferences and activities for parents and teachers to share.* New Zealand educators have developed some innovative approaches to the typical school conferences that offer an excellent model. For example, on each child's birthday, the teacher can invite the parents to school for a celebration of the child's accomplishments and the opportunity to establish goals and objectives to ensure continued success. Students with summer birthdays can be assigned a special birthday during the school year. Older elementary students can chair the meeting and take responsibility for presenting their portfolio of significant work. The teacher, parent, and child should set goals as a team. As in France, the parent should be involved when significant decisions about the child's future are made. The parent should always be present when the possibility of retention is discussed, and the parent should be available when the elementary experience is complete and plans are made for entrance into secondary education.

The elementary teachers and principal should work together to develop creative parent-teacher conferences. Primarily, it is the school's responsibility to keep conferences from becoming repetitive and meaningless. When parents cannot come to school, the teacher should be released to visit the home.

Also, each elementary school should create activities that parents and children can share together. Schools do well scheduling activities such as science fairs, musical productions, and award ceremonies. Often, however, parents of children at-risk do not attend. Fairview elementary school in Jackson County, North Carolina, created an experience for students and parents (Parents Involved in Education) that holds promise for all elementary schools in the United States. Teachers first identified students and their parents who could benefit from additional learning experiences. School officials sought input and support from local business, local citizens, and the local university. The Jackson County Board of Education pledged support and finances beyond the donations of the community. The board of education supported a weekly program in which the identified students come to school once a week with their parents. The parents, children, and educators eat dinner together and then work together on homework and learning activities designed for family involvement. Children then meet together and learn study skills, while parents discuss parenting skills together. Students who complete all requirements of the program receive an attractive desk that they take home and use for study. The program is an excellent example of educators helping to establish the education ethic in homes where parents and children need extra help.

5. *The school community should encourage the business community to provide released time for parental involvement in the child's school.* Business and industry should provide released time for employees to spend time in school. Research shows that involved parents usually have children who perform better, and when students perform better in school, the employee usually performs better at work. The school principal should lead a delegation that approaches the chamber of commerce and the management of local businesses about the establishment of released time.

If some businesses do not provide released time, the school should keep visitation hours flexible so that parents can participate in school activities without missing work. When parents cannot or will not come to school, the faculty should consider a visit to the workplace or the home.

Business and school partnerships have become common in the elementary school. Although some are superficial, others can have great value. The principal should foster partnerships that promise academic help for students. Adults from the business community can serve as tutors, teachers of business-related subject matter, and partners in the school planning and evaluation processes. In Germany, business and labor become partners in the school learning process during the elementary years. German educators and representatives of the business community jointly structure a vocational program that is highly regarded as a world-class effort.

6. *School board meetings should rotate among the elementary schools in the district.* This has already become common practice, so schools that have not yet implemented the idea should do so. Parents living in the school site selected for the board meeting should receive a special invitation to attend and should be recognized by the board. The board of education is the community's link to the educators in the school, and the board should constantly preach the value of respect for education in the home and community. Unfortunately, board of education members often encourage criticism of the schools or of specific administrators and/or teachers. Although it is difficult for the school administrator to control the behavior of board members, the administrator does have influence over the elementary school community. The administrator, therefore, must accent the positive and devalue the negative even if it comes from board members.

7. *The elementary school should be in touch with community services for children and help parents understand the nature of the services and where and how they can be accessed.* Communities have several agencies other than the school that operate programs and services for children. The school staff should be aware of these agencies and work with them whenever possible. Among those agencies whose agenda include children are the recreation department, the department of social services, the juvenile court, the community churches, day care centers, and area colleges and universities. Personnel in these agencies can help school leaders develop programs and materials for parents, can provide facilities for gatherings involving youth, and can provide direct services beyond the scope of the school such as health services and counseling services.

Schools need all the help they can get, and the community should feel an obligation to assist with the education process. School administrators too often hide within the confines of their school. This must change.

8. *Each elementary school in the United States should establish a goal of 96 percent adult literacy. In districts where the literacy rate is already 96 percent or above, the school system should aim higher until the United States is 100 percent literate.* In virtually all of the world-class countries researched by the authors, the country assigned the job of developing literate adults to the elementary or primary school. The goal of 100 percent literacy is obtainable. Britain reports 100 percent literacy, and France, Germany, New Zealand, and Japan report 99 percent literacy. The literacy rate in the United States is 96 percent (*World Education Report,* 1993). In the United States, literacy is a worthy goal for elementary educators, for the definition of literacy generally includes those skills taught at the elementary level. The elementary administration should accept this obligation and establish a literacy goal within the guidelines suggested above.

Elementary schools in the United States must deal with the issue of retention, for the research is not conclusive that retention severely harms or benefits the child. If elementary schools wish to practice social promotion, then they should put in place mechanisms for ensuring that all students reach literacy before leaving elementary school programs. To clarify the recommendation, elementary schools must establish alternative programs or schools, tutoring programs for students, or post-elementary programs for students who enter the secondary school without reaching an acceptable level of literacy. However, the answer to the literacy problem is not to increase the number of students placed in special education because the number is presently excessive. The intent is to have each elementary school in America take responsibility for the literacy of its membership.

With 4 percent of the American population illiterate, the country can expect illiteracy to breed continued illiteracy. Children with illiterate parents will likely miss the interaction with words and numbers and the learning environment established by the literate parent. Part of the puzzle needed to make America's schools world-class, therefore, is the eradication of illiteracy among the population. Elementary educators must meet the challenge.

9. *Elementary educators must give parents guidance on the subject of television watching and homework.* Homework is world-class, and elementary educators must establish a homework policy that holds students and their parents accountable for homework. The authors visited the subject of homework in Chapter 7 from a student's point of view, but homework is important to world-class status and is, therefore, repeated again with emphasis on the role of parents. Homework should start in kindergarten where teachers can give children simple exercises to perform at home with their parents. As teachers introduce reading, writing, and arithmetic into the curriculum, they should develop homework related to these subjects. By the end of the elementary experience, children should be doing homework each evening up to a maximum of 2 hours.

Homework should allow children to research subjects or to practice subject matter introduced in school. Teachers should check homework as much as possible within the time constraints of the job. Teachers should give students and parents feedback.

The short school year in the United States makes homework absolutely necessary. The other world-class country with a short school year, France, makes homework an extension of the school day. All of the other world-class countries with the exception of Canada also make homework routine, thus allowing students the opportunity to extend their learning time beyond the school day. This additional learning time takes on increased meaning in countries like Germany with 220 days of school and Japan with 228 days of school. Homework extends over the additional days of school, compounding the additional practice offered students.

The role of the parents is key for this current discussion of homework. Once the child starts school, the parents should provide the child an adequate place to study that includes a desk and hopefully resource materials. A computer is now a valuable resource. Parents must make homework a part of the child's daily routine and insist that it be completed before other activities take place. Parents must check homework to ensure that it is complete. Certainly parents should permit television only after the child completes homework.

More needs to be said about television watching. Compared with the other nine world-class countries, the United States had more television sets in 1990, 812 per 1000 inhabitants, than the other nine countries (*World Education Report,* 1993). This figure is approaching one television per person. When 13-year-old students responded to a survey administered during the assessment of the International Assessment of Educational Progress (IAEP) about television watching, 20 percent of students from the United States said that they watch television 5 hours or more per day. No other country had as high a percentage; among the French students, whom you will remember excelled at homework, only 5 percent of the students watched 5 hours or more of television each day (Lapointe et al., 1992). Except for a handful of programs on public television and cable and rare documentaries on the major channels, television has become a vast wasteland for elementary youth in the United States. Students watch too long, and most of the time, they watch programs depicting gross violence and dehumanizing experiences. But, for elementary age children, much of the responsibility for controlling television rests with the parent. Much of the time, the child is unsupervised at home, but just as often, children watch along with parents. Students watch television rather than do homework, multiplying the problem, and educators will confirm that the parent often condones television watching and condemns homework as unnecessary.

Elementary principals need to develop television guidelines for parents incapable of developing guidelines for their own children. The guidelines should include (1) suggestions for limiting time children spend in front of the television, (2) the programming that children at various ages should watch, (3) rules placing homework and home chores before television watching, and (4) alternate activities for children that can replace television. Perhaps if educators go to war against the television industry, the industry and the consumers will think twice about the quality of television in the United States for young school-age children.

10. *Elementary educators should develop procedures for helping*

dysfunctional families, including provisions for removing dysfunctional children from the regular classroom until such time that they become functional. Earlier in the chapter attention was given to the impact societal problems have on kids. The elementary school experiences daily disruption due to the behavior of children that are the victims of these societal problems. Needless to say, the elementary teachers and administrators want to help these students because of their desire to teach and nurture young people. But the baggage children bring to school in our modern world is debilitating and often causes problems beyond the capabilities of the teacher or administrator to solve. The result is that dysfunctional children are stealing valuable time from others in the classroom.

The authors believe that educators must remove seriously disruptive children from the classroom. The board of education must be brave enough to legislate this action. Because these children are young and must usually remain in school, educators should craft alternative programs for the disruptive youth. Programs for parents should accompany these programs, and, if possible, parents should volunteer in the alternative program. The process, however, requires a cautious approach to identification of students. Elementary principals must be vigilant about controlling teachers who might refer students to the alternative program for violations that the teacher should control in the classroom. This has often been the situation with referrals for special education, and the percentage of American students in special education classes far exceeds the special education population in the other world-class countries. Administrators must develop strict guidelines that ensure the students' and the parents' rights and that adhere to minority equal opportunity rights. All things considered, however, disruptive students must be removed from the regular classroom when the rights of the majority are impaired.

The authors propose funding alternative elementary programs by varying class size. For example, principals can increase elementary class size by one or two students without a decrease in student productivity. Administrators, however, must apply the savings to alternative programming. The class size of alternative classes should be small. Elementary school leaders must also pressure universities to develop training programs for teachers of alternative school programs. Alternative school programs should be as important to the board of education as programs for the gifted student. The stakes are greater, and the rewards can be significant.

World-Class Quote

"You can take all your opportunity to learn standards, you can take all your technology, you can take all your class size. You give me children from a two-parent Asian American family, and they will outscore almost everybody in the environment, because they are taught at home that school is a special and holy thing, [and] teachers must be respected" (William Bennett, 1994).

REFERENCES

Anderson, R. C., E. H. Heibert, J. A. Scott, and I. Wilkinson. 1985. *Becoming a Nation of Readers: The Report of the Commission on Reading.* Washington, D.C.: National Academy of Education in *Strong Families, Strong Schools.* 1994. Washington, D.C.: U.S. Department of Education.

Barton, P. E. and R. J. Coley. 1992. *America's Smallest School: The Family.* Princeton, New Jersey: Educational Testing Service in *Strong Families, Strong Schools.* 1994. Washington, D.C.: U.S. Department of Education.

Bennett, W. 1994. In *The Third Annual Conversation with the Secretaries of Education.* Produced by SCIS, The Southern Center for International Studies, in cooperation with the College Board, Atlanta: The Southern Center for International Studies.

Brahm, B. 1995. Interview (May 22).

Chalker, D. M. and R. M. Haynes. 1994. *World-Class Schools: New Standards for Education.* Lancaster, Pennsylvania: Technomic Publishing Company, Inc.

Coleman, J. S., E. Q. Campbell, C. J. Hobson, J. McPartland, A. M. Mood, F. D. Weinfeld, and R. L. York. 1966. *Equality of Educational Opportunity.* Washington, D.C.: U.S. Government Printing Office in *Strong Families, Strong Schools.* 1994. Washington, D.C.: U.S. Department of Education.

Darling, S. 1994. "Literacy Is the Key, a Family Plan Involving Parents in Education: 10 Ideas That Work," *Education Week,* October, pp. 29–33.

de Kanter, A., A. L. Ginsberg, and A. M. Milne. 1987. *Parent Involvement Strategies: A New Emphasis on Traditional Parent Roles.* Washington, D.C.: U.S. Department of Education in *Strong Families, Strong Schools.* 1994. Washington, D.C.: U.S. Department of Education.

Epstein, J. L. 1991. "Effects on Student Achievement of Teacher Practices of Parent Involvement," in *Advances in Reading/Language Research. Vol. 5. Literacy Through Family, Community and School Interaction.* Greenwich, Connecticut: JAI Press in *Strong Families, Strong Schools.* 1994. Washington, D.C.: U.S. Department of Education.

Faire, M. and R. Yates. 1994. "Assessing and Evaluating Student Learning," in *The Professional Practice of Teaching*. Clive McGee and Deborah Fraser, eds. Palmerston North, New Zealand: The Dunsmore Press.

Fowler, F. 1988. "In Search of Equality and Competitiveness: French Education after 58 Reforms," *International Education*, 18/1:5–14.

Friberg, P. 1995. Interview (June 13).

Getting Your Child Ready for School. 1993. A Publication of the Alliance of Business Leaders and Educators, College of Education and Psychology, Cullowhee, North Carolina: Western Carolina University.

Henderson, A. T. and N. Berla. 1994. *A New Generation of Evidence: The Family Is Critical to Student Achievement*. Washington, D.C.: National Committee for Citizens in Education in *Strong Families, Strong Schools*. 1994. Washington, D.C.: U.S. Department of Education.

Henderson, B. 1994. "Do We Care about Kids," *Western*. Spring.

Husen, T. and T. N. Postlethwaite (eds). 1992. *The International Encyclopedia of Education*, 2nd Edition. Tarrytown, New York: Pergamon.

Innerd, W. 1995. Interview (June 14).

International Comparisons in Education – Curriculum, Values and Lessons. Circa 1992. Alberta, Canada: Alberta Chamber of Resources in Partnership with Alberta Education.

Kagan, S. L. 1994a. "Early Care and Education: Beyond the Fishbowl," *Phi Delta Kappan*, 76(3):184–187.

Kagan, S. L. 1994b. "Readying Schools for Young Children: Polemics and Priorities," *Phi Delta Kappan*, 76/3:226–233.

Katsula Setsuo. 1992. Interview (October 9).

Keith, T. Z. and P. B. Keith. 1993. "Does Parent Involvement Affect Eighth-Grade Student Achievement? Structural Analysis of National Data," *School Psychology Review*, 22(3):474–496. In *Strong Families, Strong Schools*. 1994. Washington, D.C.: U.S. Department of Education.

Lapointe, A. E., N. A. Mead, and J. M. Askew. 1992. *Learning Mathematics*. Princeton, New Jersey: Educational Testing Service.

Lees, L. H. 1994. "Educational Inequality and Academic Achievement in England and France," *Comparative Education Review*, 38(1):65–87.

Lewin, T. 1995. "Worldwide Study Finds Traditional Family Structure Dissolving," *Raleigh: The News and Observer* (May 30):2A.

Li, Chen-ching. 1995. Interview (May 22).

Liontos, L. B. 1992. *At Risk Families and Schools Becoming Partners*. Eugene: University of Oregon, ERIC Clearinghouse on Educational Management in *Strong Families, Strong Schools*. 1994. Washington, D.C.: U.S. Department of Education.

Macbeath, J. and M. Turner. 1990. *Learning Out of School: Homework, Policy, and Practice*. A Research Study Commissioned by the Scottish Education Department, Glasgow, Scotland: Jordanhill College.

McAdams, R. P. 1993. *Lessons from Abroad: How Other Countries Educate Their Children*. Lancaster, Pennsylvania: Technomic Publishing Company, Inc.

Neuber, M. (ed). 1991. "The School System in the Federal Republic of Germany," *Education and Science*, Nr. 3/4 (e), Inter Nationes Bonn Press.

The Parents' Charter in Scotland. 1992. Edinburgh, Scotland: The Scottish Office of Education.

Phillips, G. L. Circa 1994. *What's a Parent to Do: The Home-School Conspiracy.* Produced by Gary L. Phillips.

Pierre, B. and S. Auvillain (eds). 1991. *Organisation of the French Educational System Leading to the French Baccalaureat.* Washington, D.C.: Embassy of France, Office of Education.

Rayner, T. 1995. Interview (June 13).

Sorensen, C. W. 1994. "Success and Education in South Korea," *Comparative Education Review,* 38(1):10−36.

Stevenson, D. L. and D. P. Baker. 1987. "The Family-School Relation and the Child's School Performance," *Child Development,* 58:1348−1357, in *Strong Families, Strong Schools.* 1994. Washington, D.C.: U.S. Department of Education.

Stevenson, H. and S. Lee. 1990. *Contests of Achievement: A Study of American, Chinese, and Japanese Children.* Monographs of the Society for Research in Child Development, Vol. 55, Nos. 1−2, Chicago: University of Chicago Press.

Strong Families, Strong Schools: Building Community Partnerships for Learning. 1994. Washington, D.C.: U.S. Department of Education.

Teaching and Learning in Japanese Elementary Schools. 1992. Edinburgh, Scotland: Her Majesty's Inspectorate, Department for Education, The Scottish Office Education Department.

U.S. Department of Education. 1994. Calculations based on information from the *1994 Condition of Education,* the *1993 Digest of Education Statistics,* and the *1993 Statistical Abstract of the United States,* in *Strong Families, Strong Schools.* 1994. Washington, D.C.: U.S. Department of Education.

Walberg, H. J. (n.d.). "Family Programs for Academic Learning," prepared for the Office of the Under Secretary, U.S. Department of Education, in *Strong Families, Strong Schools.* 1994. Washington, D.C.: U.S. Department of Education.

Weiss, H. B. 1994. "We Must Move Beyond Finger-Pointing, a Family Plan Involving Parents in Education: 10 Ideas That Work," *Education Week,* October, pp. 5, 31.

Wildavsky, R. 1994. "What's Behind Success in School?" *Reader's Digest,* pp. 49−55.

Williams, D. L. and N. F. Chavkin. 1989. "Essential Elements of Strong Parent Involvement Programs," *Educational Leadership,* 47(2):18−20.

World Education Report. 1993. Paris, France: United Nations Educational, Scientific, and Cultural Organization.

Zeldin, T. 1982. *The French.* New York: Pantheon Publishing.

Zill, N. and C. W. Nord. 1994. *Running in Place: How American Families Are Faring in a Changing Economy and an Individualistic Society.* Washington, D.C.: Child Trends, Inc.

Chapter 9

NEW ZEALAND ELEMENTARY SCHOOLS[1]

The study of educational systems in other countries has reshaped our views about what is needed to help American schools continue to be world-class.

— Haynes and Chalker, 1994

By world standards, New Zealand's elementary schools are world-class schools. The purpose of this chapter is to describe some of the characteristics of New Zealand schools that might give some insights into why they are successful in producing world-class achievement in their students. These observations come from long experience of schools in New Zealand and elsewhere. In a brief chapter it is necessary to generalize, which is always risky and open to challenge, for generalizations can hide complexities that exist within any education system. However, I hope the reader can sense something of the particular character of the schools and classrooms.

BACKGROUND

New Zealand is a democratic country in the South Pacific. Its population of nearly four million people has one of the highest literacy rates in the world. About 85 percent of the population is made up of people of European descent. Indigenous Maori people comprise 12 percent of the population. English is the main language, and Maori is a joint national

---

[1] Authored by Clive McGee, Centre for Primary Education, School of Education, The University of Waikato, Hamilton, New Zealand.

language. Although Maori is spoken by a small percentage of the population, recent school policies have been enacted to encourage its expansion, especially among Maori themselves, for only a minority of Maoris speak the language.

New Zealand was one of the first countries in the world to put in place a system of compulsory elementary education funded by the government. Most children attend schools in a three-tier system. Elementary schools usually cater for grades 1 – 6, intermediate (middle) schools for grades 7 and 8, and secondary (high) schools for grades 9 – 13.

One of the features of elementary schools is that they have always been required to base their learning program on a national curriculum. To American readers, it may seem strange to have a single curriculum for an entire country. However, it needs to be noted that the population is small, and a national curriculum has certain advantages. All children are given a general education, so there is equality of opportunity to access a good quality curriculum. No matter where they live or what their personal circumstances, government-funded schools are available to all children. Over the years the government has carefully monitored standards of teaching and learning through a system of inspectors of schools. Curriculum changes were easily disseminated to all schools, and the change process has always included teachers. Furthermore, any major curriculum changes have traditionally been followed by the production of government-funded resources and in-service teacher education.

To readers who are unfamiliar with the New Zealand system, a national curriculum may seem like a recipe for control and the stifling of school and teacher initiative in planning innovative programs. To the contrary, elementary schools have enjoyed a considerable amount of freedom within broad national guidelines. It has to be acknowledged that there have indeed been tensions between the central authorities and local schools and teachers over what should be done and how it should be done. Nevertheless, elementary teachers have a long history of innovation and flexible approaches in the way they teach.

It is difficult to say for certain how this came about, but here are some speculations. Partly it is because New Zealand teachers have looked to other parts of the world for inspiration and ideas and incorporated them into their own beliefs and practices. Perhaps this relates to the geographical isolation of the country, which produces a yearning to know what is going on elsewhere. Partly it is due to the nature of the curriculum documents. For many decades, syllabuses of instruction have been

New Zealand's parents and extended families are actively involved in their schools. The national curriculum reflects public input, and parents expect to be a major force in their children's education (photo provided by McGee).

written in a concise, general manner, very much as sets of suggestions rather than detailed prescriptions. Therefore, the door is open for in- novation. Another reason for the innovation and flexibility is the strong development of a liberal tradition. The influence of great educators like John Dewey has been remarkable. Taking these factors together, elemen- tary teachers have forged an ethos in their teaching that is child-centered, and their curriculum is based on a model of adaptation and modification as against slavish following of textbooks or detailed curriculum guides. Indeed, teachers view with some suspicion curriculum packages that provide every step for the teacher to follow.

RECENT CHANGES

In 1989, major changes were made to the way New Zealand elemen- tary schools are governed and managed (the proposals are summarized in Lange, 1988). Previously, each elementary school had a small school committee elected from local householders. Its functions were limited to decisions about school facilities. The real power lay with regional education boards elected by school committees and the government's central education department.

All this changed in 1989. After pressure over a number of years, schools were finally given greater legislative power over their own affairs. Each elementary school now has an elected board of trustees. The boards are required to write a school charter that states the school's goals, taking into account the needs of the particular community. In effect, the charter is a contract between a school and the community and the government. Money to run a school is now bulk funded to its board. Under the terms of the Education Act 1989 and Education Amendment Act 1990, boards now make the major governance decisions, and the school principal is the site manager. Teachers' salaries continue to be paid out of a central fund in accordance with a national salary scale.

Although school boards have considerable powers, the government also continues to exert its authority. School boards must operate under many legal requirements as to how a school is operated. The national curriculum must be the basis of any school's curriculum, although local variations are encouraged. In this situation, it is not surprising that there is some tension between the Ministry of Education and schools. Schools sometimes feel that the government has passed responsibility to them and is only too ready to blame schools when something goes wrong, and only too ready to impose further requirements. To add to this, the reforms included the establishment of an independent Education Review Office with responsibility for carrying out regular — every few years — assurance reviews and effectiveness reviews. Assurance reviews check to see if school boards have met their statutory requirements. Effectiveness reviews determine how well schools have met their charter objectives, for example, the achievement of the students in meeting curriculum objectives. Research (Mitchell et al., 1993) has shown that the administrative reforms have resulted in greater work pressures on schools, particularly principals. Teachers have felt the pressure over the last 2 years as the whole national curriculum is being rewritten and they must adapt their programs.

The tension between the center and the schools has always been a factor affecting the quality of schools. Yet, curiously, it has probably contributed to the maintenance of a world-class system. How is this possible? On the one hand, the government has taken steps to check on schools to try to ensure the delivery of quality education. Before the Education Review Office, it did this through a system of school inspectors who regularly visited schools and gave advice to teachers and principals about how to deliver effective curriculum. In the main, this was a benevolent approach. Although some individual inspectors may have tried to mold teachers in their own image, they generally encouraged teachers to reflect the qualities already referred to: innovation, flexibility, and initiative in designing curriculum suited to children's particular needs. This is hardly surprising because inspectors themselves were recruited from the teaching profession.

On the other hand, elementary teachers have always been conscious that they work within national guidelines provided by a national curriculum, yet enjoy the professional right to practice as extended professionals. They have generally not felt overly constrained by limits from outside, even though they know that they are accountable to teach a coherent, balanced curriculum. Under these conditions, children in elementary schools have had the best of both worlds: a national curriculum that ensures some similarity no matter what school is attended and teachers who feel the freedom to use their talents to modify the curriculum to suit themselves and their students.

SITE-BASED MANAGEMENT

The move to site-based management has had the positive effect of causing elementary school authorities to develop a sharper focus on their goals and strategies for achieving them. Now it is common to find written strategic plans that state what a school claims to do best. Here is an example of a few priorities from one school which are communicated to parents in an information booklet. The school:

- offers a balanced curriculum to educate the whole child: intellectually, physically, socially, culturally, and emotionally
- has children of different abilities and working habits in the same class, resulting in a range of working levels
- has a strong emphasis on individual achievement, initiative, and success
- has a highly dedicated and well-qualified staff
- provides access to new technology to all students

In the same booklet, some of the goals the school board and staff have collaboratively developed are:

- The school will develop an atmosphere of warmth, security, and acceptance.

- The school should be sensitive to the individual learning capabilities of thinking, growing children, each developing toward their full potential.
- The school should try to be a positive model of society and help children to develop personal skills in interacting with other people, which may be used increasingly as they grow into the wider community.
- Each child should be aware of his or her own self-worth as a human being. The school should encourage each child to have a high level of self-esteem about their achievements and confidence within their peer group.
- The school should value the diverse ethnic and cultural heritage of families in the school community and encourage the sharing of different cultural backgrounds.
- The school environment should be educationally functional, aesthetically pleasing, and a source of pride within this community.

TEACHER APPRAISAL

Most elementary schools have a system of staff appraisal. It involves careful writing of job descriptions and recording of annual targets for staff development. Boards of trustees are required to financially support teachers' access to staff development (Education Review Office, 1995). The process of appraisal usually involves a school principal observing classroom teaching, follow-up discussion, goal setting, and peer appraisal with another colleague. This sometimes includes teachers observing each other.

Schools are required by law to engage in self-review under the direction of the board of trustees. Essentially, it involves an analysis of a school's charter goals to assess how effectively they have been met (Education Review Office, 1994). Although some refer to schools as self-managing, there are many legislative restrictions on schools. Every school must have a strategic plan and an advantage is that it causes a school board to engage with teachers to set school goals, including targets for students' learning. Thus, there is a connection between setting goals and self-review, which increases the potential for more effective student learning.

SUCCESSFUL SCHOOLS AND TEACHERS

In spite of a large body of research, it is not easy to list the characteristics of successful or good schools, because schools vary in their aims and ideals. Nevertheless, successful New Zealand elementary schools reflect a balance in their program by focusing on personal, academic, and social goals. In these schools, students are prepared for citizenship as well as for jobs and further education. To capture something of the nature of good elementary schools and teachers, I will look at some features that characterize them.

Getting to Know the Children

Effective New Zealand teachers pride themselves on teaching to the whole child. This means learning about each child: their home and family situation, interests and preferences, and abilities and needs. Planning an individual program for each child is the ideal of every teacher. Although in practice, it is impossible to do so, even young elementary students can be organized to individualize a certain amount of their program.

One of the keys to successful teaching is the kind of classroom environment that is established. Every child needs to feel safe and valued. The classroom needs to have clearly defined rules and routines that are understood by the children. Within these guidelines, there should be a high degree of warmth, spontaneity, and humor. Children should be taught self-discipline so that they can assume as much responsibility for their own learning as possible. When they have self-discipline, the teacher can become less dominant and the children more able to make decisions about their learning in many specific ways.

Learning Styles

New Zealand elementary schools have been influenced by a range of learning theories. In recent decades two particular theoretical orientations have shaped schools and teachers. First, humanistic psychology has led to an emphasis on child-centered classrooms in that children are able to develop their uniqueness and individuality. Second, constructivist learning theory has caused teachers to lessen their emphasis on rote learning of prescribed information and increase their emphasis on children's present ideas or constructions. Teaching becomes a quest to discover what a child knows and to utilize these constructions to help the child build further constructions. Science and mathematics are two subjects that have been affected by this approach.

Teachers' Planning

Elementary teachers work in a tradition of planning their classroom program from national curriculum guidelines in each subject. The guidelines have, until recently, been general so that teachers have had to construct detailed plans for particular classes. In the 1990s, each subject syllabus is being rewritten into a more specific format that suggests objectives and learning activities. Even so, the objectives remain reasonably broad, so that teachers have retained a good deal of planning freedom.

In many elementary schools teachers plan in teams or syndicates. They collectively decide on topics and select suitable resources. This reflects another characteristic of New Zealand schools; textbooks are used sparingly, even in mathematics. Most resources are chosen by teachers with principal approval, and parents have generally accepted this situation. Four levels of planning in schools is common. First, a school has an overall plan of what will be taught in each subject in a school year. Second, each teacher will develop an annual classroom plan from the school plan, sometimes as part of a team. Third, teaching units are planned in particular topics, covering a certain number of lessons, for example, six lessons on mammals in science. Fourth, a weekly plan is drawn up by each teacher, which specifies what will be covered by the class, groups, and individuals.

A feature of elementary school programs is that teachers frequently integrate curriculum. Even though there are curriculum statements in each subject, teachers often combine elements and knowledge into themes or centers of interest. Again, teachers have a tradition of using their own initiative to combine with flexibility to incorporate aspects of different subjects into coordinated units. One of the tensions in the 1990s is whether teachers will be constrained by the new curriculum statements that appear to have reasserted the dominance of separate subjects, on paper at least. It is difficult to imagine that New Zealand teachers will relinquish their accustomed freedom to plan in their own individual or team manner.

Good teachers involve children in planning. From grade 1, children can make decisions about what they learn and how they learn it. It is common for teachers to brainstorm with their students before beginning a teaching unit. The teacher outlines the topic, in general, to build up student interest. For example, planning a unit on road safety can result in numerous student questions about what they would like to know more about: laws, regulations, bike riding safety, how to ride defensively, and so on. Together, teachers and students can suggest where resources might come from. Following this kind of planning, the teacher writes the plan for the unit, which commences some days later. In this way, students feel greater ownership of their study and learning. It is not always imposed by the teacher and the textbook. The approach requires teacher faith in the ability of students to engage in such active planning and learning. Most children are capable of it. At first, teachers sometimes need to work hard to get children to participate, especially if they are unused to being involved in that way.

Classroom Interaction

The above comments about planning give a clue to the kind of classroom interaction sought by effective teachers. Although there is always a tension between cooperation, competition, and individualization, there are strategies that can allow each to exist in the same classroom.

In their own classroom, teachers make decisions about the best ways to group their students. Elementary teachers typically teach some lessons as whole class lessons. However, because it is recognized that there are wide differences among students, more frequently the class will be divided into smaller groups, or even individuals working on their own program. Groups are often ''fluid'' with flexible movement between groups according to the topic or subject. Few teachers would create groups that did not have the mechanism to change the membership according to factors like interests, achievement, maturity, motivation, and learning needs. In this way, students get to work closely with a variety of other students.

Some schools and teachers use vertical grouping where multiaged students are in the same class. The method results in a family-like atmosphere but is more challenging for teachers because the range of differences is greater than in a one-level class. With New Zealand's tradition of using relatively few compulsory textbooks, the vertical groups are less complex than might be imagined.

Physical Layout

The layout of the traditional elementary classroom included desks in rows and lines facing the front of the room. As can be imagined from what has been said already, classrooms have moved a long way from this layout. It is likely that desks or tables are formed into small groups. Various centers will occupy particular spaces, such as a science center, mathematics center, and reading center. During a typical day, desks and tables may be moved several times so that different forms of lessons can occur. Doing an achievement test in rows might give way to a social studies lesson requiring clusters of five or six desks. In turn, this might change to an art lesson requiring three groups of desks in long rows to set out art resources. Following art, a music lesson may require that the desks be moved to the perimeter of the room to enable folk dancing to occur. This flexibility is typical of most New Zealand elementary classrooms.

Movement and Noise

Flexible classrooms require well-established routines and procedures so that children know the limits within which they work. They must be trained in these routines, and they can be!

Two aspects require both teacher and student decisions. First, a flexible classroom involves a lot of student movement. If children are to accept responsibility for their own learning, they need to be free to move when necessary without always seeking teacher approval. For example, it is necessary to fetch books and equipment. When students are well trained, they will move only when they need to move. Second, students need training about what level of noise is acceptable for different kinds of activity. Clearly, some kinds of tests require silence. Discussion requires the noise of voices, and so on.

The test of whether movement and noise are appropriate is whether each child is sufficiently on task without adversely affecting the work of others and whether the noise level allows students to successfully achieve the purposes of a particular activity.

Aside from whole language and reading recovery teaching, New Zealanders use field trips and outings for learning out of school (photo provided by McGee).

Integrating Children's Learning

Skillful teachers are able to pull together the various elements described so far. In a grade 1 class I know, Judy, the teacher, will often spend the entire morning session on needs-based teaching and learning. It works something like this: because Judy has kept detailed records of each child's achievement in all the areas of language and literacy, she is able to plan a morning based on a complex mix of grouping and learning activities. Often, she will begin with a whole class session to introduce a topic of interest for the day, for example, springtime. A model of how to write a story will be demonstrated. Charts are used to record concepts and key words or phrases. From there, the class disperses to engage in independent learning areas such as an art and craft center, a math center with building blocks, manipulative materials, etc., a writing table, a home corner, a natural science center, and so on. The children are taught to be self-reliant. They are often supported by parent helpers, so in small groups they can cook, construct, paint, draw, watch a story on TV, listen to tapes of songs, poems and stories, and so on. While all this is going on, Judy withdraws particular groups of children for particular skill-based teaching on the basis of their needs, for example, a group needing help with concepts of print.

At some stage, the whole class will experience shared book reading (where phonics are introduced in context). The class will do worksheets for guided reading. Every child will read from an individual box of readers at the correct level. And by the end of the morning, their individual stories will be finished, and a sharing session allows Judy to reflect with them on what has been achieved. This kind of program, is I believe, whole language at its best. All through the morning Judy will have recorded data on children's achievement, which will be the basis of her next day's teaching.

Whole Language

The prevailing view of elementary teachers is that schools should get children to increase their functional literacy; more than that, however, is the belief that they should also demonstrate active, critical, and productive literacy (Cambourne, 1988). Cambourne has carefully identified the principles of whole language, and he has argued that the emphasis is on "demonstrating wholes of language" (p. 205) as opposed to more traditional approaches of fragmenting wholes into small parts to teach grammar, phonics, or spelling.

The philosophy of whole language fits well with what has been said in this chapter about good teaching practice in New Zealand schools. Although there is continuing debate over a phonics approach and the whole language approach, there is evidence that the whole language approach is successful for most children. In a recent international study of achievement in reading literacy, New Zealand 9- and 14-year-old students had scores that were among the highest internationally (Wagemaker, 1993). However, Maori and Pacific Islands students were behind the other New Zealand students, as were students from non-English-speaking backgrounds. The study linked several characteristics of New Zealand classrooms with literacy success: frequent silent reading, regular book borrowing, frequent story reading by the teacher and more scheduled hours on language teaching.

Another probable factor in reading success is the Reading Recovery program. A nationwide program offered to over 20 percent of 6-year-olds (nearly all children begin school as 5-year-olds) is based on intervention when a child is not responding adequately to the regular class program. It is daily individual tuition, highly structured, differentiated to suit each child after diagnosis, and aimed at reading independence. Every child is thoroughly assessed on or near their sixth birthday, using techniques developed by Marie Clay (1993). Those who enter the program are taught by specially trained teachers who work closely with the classroom teacher. Evidence of the success of the program has come from independent observations by two inspectors of schools from England (HMSO, 1993).

It can only be assumed that the drive toward independence in reading and the encouragement to choose books from an early age carries over into adulthood where the country is noted for the high reading involvement.

ASSESSING AND EVALUATING STUDENT LEARNING

Elementary teachers in New Zealand have enjoyed a tradition of assessment and evaluation that has enabled them to avoid the excesses of testing seen in some countries. Formal standardized tests have been used—by a school's choice—for many years. These norm-referenced tests are diagnostic in intent, for example, Progressive Achievement Tests to assess percentile ranks for aspects of language, reading, and study skills.

In recent years, a new national system of criterion-referenced assessment has been put in place to emphasize achievement in relation to a student's work rather than to compare children (Ministry of Education, 1994). Teachers record assessment data on each child in each subject and in personal and social development.

Teachers have systems that enable them to identify students' needs, provide a profile of each student, show achievement with clarity, make curriculum decisions on the evidence they gather, assist in school reviews, report to students and their parents, and complete official school records. Good teachers use the following strategies:

(1) *Observation:* Alert teachers continually observe their students. Informal observation may result in a recorded comment like, ''Lisa enjoys reading and likes getting information from books to use in her projects. She prefers to read than play sports.'' More formal observation may be, ''Lisa is able to decode text to work out new

words. She has developed skills of trying a section of text in any new book to assess whether she can read it reasonably fluently.'' When observations are recorded, they form an invaluable emerging record of learning in each subject that can be used when reporting to parents, students, and principals.

(2) *Conversations, conferences, and interviews:* Elementary teachers spend a lot of time talking with individuals and groups. Teachers can assess a rich source of information about thoughts, understandings, attitudes, and feelings. Students receive valuable feedback from their teacher and can be encouraged to focus on particular aspects of learning. Normally, conversations arise more or less spontaneously, whereas interviews tend to be planned in advance. As with observations, these strategies result in teachers recording data for subsequent analysis.

(3) *Collecting and analyzing work samples:* Elementary students typically do written work in exercise books or on loose-leaf paper. Teachers make regular collections of a student's work, date it, and sometimes make anecdotal comments on it. Running records of reading achievement is a feature of classrooms, so that the information can be used for future curriculum decisions.

(4) *Portfolios:* A portfolio is an innovative way of collecting and showing off a student's work. It can be a collection of various kinds of work, including audio and video productions and art and craft work. Children can take part in assembling a portfolio so it is a collaborative effort. This aids self-assessment by students, which is a growing trend. If children are conscious of their own learning, they are more likely to take responsibility for their learning and from the earliest grades, good New Zealand teachers train children to these ends.

(5) *Testing:* Apart from the use of standardized diagnostic tests, teachers use informal tests or specific tests such as a pretest and posttest in units in some subjects. I believe the low-key emphasis on formal, standardized achievement tests is one of the reasons why New Zealand schools are successful. This may sound paradoxical to educators in countries where tests are more prevalent. The problem with using regular standardized tests is that the tests themselves come to dominate the school and class programs. Teachers teach for tests! Parents, students, teachers, and education authorities get pulled into a system in which the test becomes both the means and

ends of schooling. I imagine that most children soon learn where they stand in the ranking system of test results. Those who fail in first grade, will usually fail in second grade. Fortunately, New Zealand teachers are largely free from this constraint, although they do test. Currently, the Ministry of Education is funding the development of two new kinds of tests that will soon be available to schools. Resource banks of assessment tasks will cover two important transition stages, grade 7 and grade 9. They will be directly related to the national curriculum statements. For younger children, a grade 2 standardized observation survey will be extended to include item banks of assessment tasks that are typical of the learning activities to be found in elementary classrooms. In summary, teachers take assessment very seriously, but because formal testing does not dominate, teachers are free to focus on learning experiences considered most suitable for their students. As has been shown, international evidence suggests that this approach is successful. National standards will be monitored by a light sample of probably 3−5 percent of grade 4 and 8 students on a 3- or 4-year cycle. Test items will be of several kinds, including pencil and paper tests, group tasks, interviews, and learning tasks, and the items will relate to curriculum goals and content. Test items will be available for teachers to use as a natural part of their classroom program.

REPORTING TO PARENTS

The procedures of gathering information relate to a professional task that elementary teachers have always engaged in, that is, reporting students' progress to their parents and families. The most common strategy is for a school to provide two written reports each year, using written comments and checklists and focusing on personality factors as well as academic factors. To be useful, the reports have to be accurate, honest, relevant, and appropriate (Department of Education, 1989).

Another strategy is to hold an interview with parents. One approach is to hold an interview that coincides with the written report, usually at midyear and the end of the year. Another approach, which is now quite common, occurs early in the school year. It involves a meeting of the student, the parents, and the teacher to discuss prospects for the year, identify learning needs, and set targets.

Yet another strategy is to combine oral and written reporting. Some schools spread the workload on teachers by holding an interview on or near a child's birthday. In this way, more time can be taken, and the portfolios mentioned previously can form an interesting source of discussion, and students can explain the portfolio to their parents. This collaborative approach usually means that all parties feel a closer connection with a student's schooling. It also demonstrates to parents that the school and the teacher are committed to the learning of the student.

One area of controversy in assessment is the use of levels of achievement in the recent curriculum framework. New curriculum statements divide content into eight achievement levels. A danger is that teachers will see the levels in absolute terms and link the age of a child to particular levels. It is hoped that teachers' traditional practice of matching the child and the learning activity will continue, not matching the child and some artificial, nebulous level.

RESOURCES

A feature of most New Zealand classrooms is the plentiful supply of resources for teaching and learning. For many years, teachers have benefited from a continual supply of resources that have been paid for by the government. Resources are therefore relevant to the national curriculum. Two examples demonstrate the relationship. The *Ready to Read* series of early grades readers were published to take account of research into reading and learning, and their content was distinctly New Zealand. Science units were published to give teachers suggestions that were deliberately connected to the topics in the national syllabus. A feature of resources produced in this way is that they are subjected to pilot studies before final publication. It is teachers who do the trials, and teachers are usually included in writing teams. This government publishing role has overcome a problem of how to get quality resources in a small market. Having the resources available does not mean schools are obliged to use them. It is their right to pick and choose. However, because the quality of government-funded resources is high, most schools readily adopt them.

Teachers are great collectors of resources, sometimes jokingly referred to as the ''blotting paper'' attitude because they ''soak up'' whatever they can find. Teachers have an ethos of using a combination of resources funded by the government and resources purchased by schools. They also have an ethos of sharing ideas and resources, which is evidenced in school-based curriculum development plans.

OUTDOOR EDUCATION

Elementary schools have a long tradition of education outside the classroom (EOTC). In many schools most of the students experience EOTC each year. Junior elementary students frequently embark on day journeys or sometimes overnight camping. Middle students may go on camps for a day or several days and senior elementary grades often have 1-week camps. Most teachers are therefore experienced in leading camps. There are many benefits for children, including experiencing enjoyable activities not otherwise available, developing an appreciation of nature and heritage, responding to challenges, and solving problems in groups. Typical activities are forest walks, kayaking, horse riding, repelling, camping, and curriculum studies in science and environment.

A particular advantage of EOTC is that many worthwhile classroom studies can be linked to the outdoor experience. Most teachers construct units that are cross-curricula, incorporating knowledge from different subjects in themes. For example, a conservation theme can involve children in planting trees, studying the effects of trees on the environment, water studies and testing, learning about plants and animals and their place in the environment. The landscape can inspire creativity, too, and much writing, music, dance, and art can result from the stimulus of the outdoors: the forests, farms, lakes, rivers, and mountains.

There are, of course, strict procedures and rules that need to be applied in EOTC. Safety and common sense are paramount, but teachers are well trained in these matters and mishaps are rare. A special feature of EOTC is that parents of children are part of the adventure, acting as helpers, guides, and supporters as they, too, take part.

MAORI EDUCATION

In recent years, there has been a policy commitment by the government to increase the success rates of Maori students. Initiatives to do this include the creation of more opportunities for Maori students to learn their own indigenous language as well as English. Under threat, Maori language is now in a resurgence with a number of schools in which Maori is the language of instruction. In regular schools with Maori students, bilingual language units have been established. However, these developments are slow because there are still too few teachers who speak both Maori and English. Gradually, teaching resources are being translated into Maori from English.

School boards are required to show in their charters how policies are to be developed to take account of Maori culture and language and to show progress toward offering lessons in Maori for those parents who want them for their children. Providing an impetus for elementary schools is the development over the last decade of many Maori pre-schools in which Maori children learn Maori language. There is evidence that these "language nests" have raised children's self-esteem and confidence. They have become bilingual children.

COMMUNITY INVOLVEMENT IN SCHOOLS

For many years a feature of elementary schools has been the high level of involvement by the parents of students and a school's community. At the national level, several major inquiries into education in the last 20 years sought public reactions to questions about the purposes of schools, what they should teach, and how they should teach it. This was done through booklets that identified educational issues and raised specific questions for the public to answer in groups or as individuals. Typically, response levels are high, so there is a tradition of public interest.

At the school level, elementary schools usually encourage parental involvement and include parents in various ways. There is a legal requirement for a school board to consult its community when contemplating any charter revisions. More specifically, many schools have an "open door" policy under which parents are free to come and go in classrooms as long as there is no hindrance to the teacher's work. Although this may seem threatening to some teachers who are not used to such a strategy, most teachers find that involving parents in this way helps to develop a mutual interest schooling enterprise. When parents understand what a teacher is trying to do, they usually become advocates and supporters and help to improve the quality of the class program. Sometimes parents help out, for example, with grade 1 attempts at cooking or woodwork. Grandparents, too, are sometimes invited.

EFFECTIVE CLASSROOMS AND
EFFECTIVE SCHOOLS: SUGGESTIONS

There is a relationship between effective classrooms and effective schools. There are some critical factors that seem to distinguish effective schools, and New Zealand research bears this out (Ramsay, 1993). These factors are listed below and some suggestions made for educators to consider in relation to their own school or schools.

(1) An effective school needs a clearly articulated philosophy. It should be a written document, which, in New Zealand, is called a school charter. It should outline the school's intentions and hopes and policies. It should be a document to which teachers and school personnel have ready access. It should be read!

(2) To be effective, a school needs a collaborative culture. To achieve this, teachers need to be involved in collaborative goal setting and be committed to the school's goals. Principals need to learn to share power and decision making, and teachers need to experience the benefits of working in teams to develop school policies and class-room programs.

(3) Good communication systems are needed. Regular newsletters to parents are necessary. Regular staff meetings help communication, for they are a time for sharing information and promoting the feeling of belonging to a team. But they need a clear focus and purpose. Staff support systems help, too, sometimes being based on ''buddy support.'' When all teachers feel they are kept fully informed, they are more likely to feel the school is theirs and increase their sense of commitment.

(4) Teachers need to accept responsibility for their students' learning and not make excuses and blame other factors.

(5) Teachers should have high expectations of all students. Given a need for realism, teachers should expect every child to achieve what they are capable of achieving.

(6) Effective schools should have in place a good system of appraisal. Teachers should take time to reflect on their practice and have others comment on their practice in a supportive, nonthreatening setting. The appraisal system should be connected to opportunities for staff development.

(7) The major task of an effective school is children's achievement. Classrooms should be challenging and exciting places where children are taught self-discipline and routines so that they can make decisions about their own learning. Teachers are facilitators—artists who guide learning and do not dominate it.

(8) In an effective school teachers should create orderly and safe classrooms that children enjoy, for it is the whole child that a school should develop.

(9) An effective school is an attractive place. A school's physical environment has a powerful effect on those who work in it. Classrooms should be colorful places with plenty of children's work in sight.

(10) Effective teachers need to have a commitment to the job and be prepared to work hard. They need to develop an interest in new ideas about teaching and learning. They need to take some risks in trying out ideas, for only in this way will alternative successful teaching strategies be found.

(11) Finally, as is well established internationally, the school principal is a key factor in creating an effective school. Every principal needs to work with teachers to develop a shared vision of a school and to work collaboratively to achieve it.

New Zealand now has site-based management schools. A good board of trustees will make sure that it develops efficient systems that enable teachers to focus on their teaching. It is difficult to say how much boards have contributed to the development of effective schools, for long before boards were established in 1989, elementary schools in New Zealand were regarded as world-class schools. The hope is that good boards will create the conditions for good teaching to continue to flourish. Already there is evidence that this is, indeed, the case. Good boards are helping to foster the characteristics described in this chapter that mark a good school.

REFERENCES

Cambourne, B. 1988. *The Whole Story.* Auckland, New Zealand: Ashton Scholastic.
Clay, M. 1993. *Reading Recovery: A Guide Book for Teachers in Training.* Auckland, New Zealand: Heinemann.

Department of Education. 1989. *Keeping School Records: Principles and Practice of Assessment and Education.* Wellington, New Zealand.

Education Policy Studies Group, University of Auckland. 1990. *What Makes a Good School.* Auckland: GP Books.

Education Review Office. 1994. *Self-Review in Schools.* Wellington, New Zealand.

Education Review Office. 1995. *Managing Staff Performance in Schools.* Wellington, New Zealand.

HMSO. 1993. *Reading Recovery in New Zealand: A Report from the Office of Her Majesty's Chief Inspector of Schools.* London: HMSO.

Lange, D. 1988. *Tomorrow's Schools: The Reform of Education Administration in New Zealand.* Wellington, New Zealand: New Zealand Government Printer.

Ministry of Education. 1994. *Assessment Policy and Practice.* Wellington, New Zealand: Learning Media.

Mitchell, D., C. McGee, R. Moltzen, and D. Oliver. 1993. *Hear Our Voices: Final Report of Monitoring Today's Schools.* Hamilton, New Zealand: University of Waikato.

Ramsay, P. D. K. 1993. *Teacher Quality: A Case Study Prepared for the Ministry of Education as Part of the OECD on Teacher Quality.* Hamilton, New Zealand: University of Waikato.

Wagemaker, H. 1993. *Achievement in Reading Literacy: New Zealand's Performance in a National and International Context.* Wellington, New Zealand: Ministry of Education.

SUGGESTED READING

Assessment: Policy to Practice. 1994. Wellington, New Zealand: Ministry of Education.

Dancing with the Pen: The Learner as Writer. 1992. Wellington, New Zealand: Ministry of Education.

McGee, C. and D. Fraser (eds.). 1994. *The Professional Practice of Teaching: An Introduction to Teaching, Learning and Curriculum.* Palmerston North, New Zealand: The Dunmore Press Limited (this book is available only from Dunmore Press, P.O. Box 5115, Palmerston North, New Zealand).

Mooney, M. E. 1988. *Developing Life-Long Readers.* Katonah, NY: Richard C. Owen Publishers, Inc.

Mooney, M. E. 1988. *Reading to, with, and by Children.* Katonah, NY: Richard C. Owen Publishers, Inc.

The New Zealand Curriculum Framework. 1993. Wellington, New Zealand: Ministry of Education.

Reading in Junior Classes. 1985. Wellington, New Zealand: Ministry of Education.

Smith, J. W. A. and W. B. Elley. 1994. *Learning to Read in New Zealand.* Katonah, NY: Richard C. Owen Publishers, Inc.

Chapter 10

ONE AMERICAN FAMILY'S EXPERIENCE IN A JAPANESE ELEMENTARY SCHOOL[2]

Our new van is a Chrysler with a Mitsubishi engine. It is just like me: American on the outside and Japanese at heart.

> — Marie Moyer, age 12, upon returning
> to the United States after 7 years
> of elementary school in Japan

This chapter was written by an American family who lived in Japan for 14 years. Although an American school was available across the street where they lived in Tokyo, Tony and Frances Moyer decided to send their child "down the street, around the corner" to a Japanese elementary school. Tony Moyer is the assistant director of the North Carolina Japan Center in Raleigh, North Carolina. This is the story of their experiences with two daughters who attended a private, nondenominational Christian elementary school. Marie, the oldest, attended 3 years of preschool and kindergarten and 4 years of elementary school. Anna experienced 3 years of preschool and elementary education in Japan. On their return to the United States, both girls experienced American education for the first time. Marie continues her Japanese education as the only American in the "Saturday School" Japanese nationals established in Research Triangle Park, North Carolina.

In their own words, the Moyer family tells the reader why they chose a Japanese education and what the cultural impact of that decision was on the family. The family then discusses experiences with school climate, time on task, students and teachers, learning ethos, parents and community, curricula, and student assessment. Finally, the family offers suggestions for American elementary school leaders who wish to improve their schools.

[2]Authored by Francis A. (Tony), Frances E., Marie, and Anna Moyer.

INTRODUCTION

Zadankai

Tony: We are going to conduct a zadankai, a group discussion of our family's experiences between 1982 and 1989 when we lived in Tokyo and our two older girls attended Japanese kindergartens and elementary school.We speak about experiences that our girls had in private schools in Japan. The vast majority of kindergartens in Japan are private, so the private school experience is normal at that stage. Also, the fact that there is a national curriculum in Japan and that none of the experiences that our girls had seem to be at odds with our other observations of Japanese schools, lead us to believe that we can generalize broadly. We believe our experiences provide a good indication of the nature of Japanese education.

The School Choice: American or Japanese

Tony: When we arrived in Tokyo in 1982 we expected to be in Japan for an extended stay (we left in 1989). I studied the language extensively in graduate school, and Frances studied it when we were in Japan during earlier visits. We decided to place our children in Japanese schools in order to enrich their lives and help them to meet Japanese friends. We did this rather than send them to one of the fine English language international schools available in the Tokyo area.

Frances: We were concerned also that our children have an opportunity to become fluent in Japanese. Many Western foreigners residing in Japan feel that Japanese is an impossible language; we now know that for a child it is not. Still, this was not an easy decision. We questioned it every year and by the time Marie was in fourth grade, teachers from the international schools and various friends were telling us that we should "get her out of there!"

We always spoke English at home, and it was the first spoken language for both girls. We taught them to speak English at home. They picked up their Japanese at school and while it was their second spoken language, it was their first language for reading and writing. The first books both read were in Japanese, not English. Marie read *The Three Little Pigs* and Anna read *Snow White,* both in Japanese translation.

The children from one elementary grade pose with their teachers for a class picture. Marie Moyer, the sole Anglo in her class, is on the top student row, farthest left (photo provided by T. Moyer).

ACCEPTANCE

The Insular Nature of Japanese Society

Tony: Japanese society tends to be relatively homogeneous in its makeup. Japanese people are not homogeneous in the sense that they are all cut by a single cookie cutter. There are 129 million of them with a lot of personal variety. However, they have a very strong sense of Japanese identity, and this sense of Japaneseness often makes them feel very different from others, both in negative and positive ways. Also, as a society they have not had a great deal of experience with non-Japanese living in their midst and participating in their native institutions, such as schools. The idea of a non-Japanese attending their schools is something of a novelty that can involve putting the non-Japanese child on a pedestal or not accepting him as fully a member of the class.

Frances: It is not uncommon to have Japanese children turn and point to you and shout *"Gainin! Gainin"* (Foreigner! Foreigner)! Of course their parents do not control them; perhaps the children are acting out some parental sense of shock. On one occasion I remember Marie throwing her hands over her ears and bursting into tears because she ''wasn't a foreigner!'' and how dare they make her feel like an outsider! But those were not her classmates, who really did accept her.

Tony: Our experience of acceptance of the children in Japanese schools was good. But I'll never forget the first day that Marie attended, and we went to observe the children. Japanese children and Japanese society are very curious about Caucasians, and they tend to stress differences that distinguish themselves from other peoples. Marie was playing at a sandbox, and the other children were checking out this new addition to their class. The girls would hang around and look at Marie, but the boys were more intrusive. They would come up to her and poke and look and interfere. Finally, this got to be too much for this little 4-year-old, and she turned around with a great big 3-foot plastic shovel and threatened them. So I figured, ''Hey, this kid is going to be able to take care of herself.''

Marie came to see herself in some ways as Japanese. While she was in kindergarten and her hair was still very blond and curly, she drew pictures of herself with straight, black hair. We had a very interesting lesson in the development of identity.

Marie: When I first entered elementary school most of the students didn't have any problem with me being an American. The only trouble was with some of the third and fourth grade boys who would come by and tease me because I was a Ganin. However, no one in my class seemed to mind. There was one girl in my class from the first grade whose grandfather had lived in Hiroshima when the bomb had been dropped, and she really seemed to hate Americans in general. She probably had never had any contact with Americans before that and was probably real bitter because of what she felt we had done to her grandfather.

She didn't want to have anything to do with me for a long time, but we ended up being friends. I just wouldn't let her alone. I decided that I was going to be friends with her and that was it. When I left Japan her mother made me a *yukata* (summer kimono) and gave me a letter with it in which she thanked me for being one of Aya's first friends. Aya had a hard time making friends in first grade. Her mother was very glad that I had stuck to this girl and made her be my friend.

Culture and Acceptance

Tony: Confucianism, which came from China to Japan, says that all relationships are hierarchical. Somebody is above and somebody is below, and the person below owes loyalty and obedience and support to the person above. The person above can expect this kind of behavior, but also in turn, must foster the well-being and the interest of the person beneath. This is, of course, the ideal.

Marie: Even in a friendly situation you are always conscious of who is above and who is below. There is nothing wrong with that. You can get along perfectly well.

Tony: Do you think this helps kids learn authority and obedience?

Marie: Probably. I think it helps them to learn to take orders. Many American students don't want to be told what to do. I see a lot of them being really rebellious for no reason except that they feel they want to be the one to decide.

Culture and School

Frances: What makes children see the school as a place of study with respect for teachers? What did the students do when the teacher first comes in the room?

Marie: We stood up and said, "Good morning," and bowed; then the teacher would bow back and say, "Good morning," and then everyone would sit down.

Frances: One of the theories about wearing uniforms is that it sets school aside as a distinct and special place. You wear very nice, dignified, navy blue uniforms with blazers and hats with the school insignia, a sunflower, on them.

Marie: We'd come to school in our nice dressy uniforms, and then we'd change into our gym clothes that we'd wear all day. In high schools and junior highs you wear your uniform all day except for PE.

Tony: Americans worry about such things as the amount of time spent in school. These discussions forget the importance of the social context in which Japanese schools operate. Like any institution, a school is a reflection of the values that exist in that society that creates and maintains it.

Marie: School is a priority in Japan. Children do not have to do chores when they come home, even in high school, unless both parents work. Besides your own room, your mother takes care of everything. When you come home from school your mother brings you a snack.

Frances: But you are expected to help clean the school.

Tony: What's the price the students pay for this?

Marie: They have to study. School is important, and you want to get into a good school because both you and your parents want you to. Sometimes the pressure gets to be too much, and students feel they are doing it because their parents don't want to lose face in the community. The parents are competing and want to outdo each other.

Tony: The whole society's basic message is that education is very important.

Marie: That doesn't mean that Japanese students never play.

Frances: Oh, no. I think one thing that we pointed out is that the elementary level is not the kind of grind people imagine. It is enjoyable. The children like their teachers.

Tony: Japanese schools are very consciously committed to teaching their students the behavior patterns expected of good Japanese. This starts very early in kindergarten. One aspect that we have mentioned before with regard to the boxes for shoes and cubbyholes for personal equipment, is the emphasis on compulsive behavior. Japanese society stresses learning to do things correctly or having a place for everything and putting everything in its place. This is attributed by some to the crowded conditions under which Japanese live, but it is certainly a trait that the society finds desirable and encourages.

Marie: That sounds like me. I have to have everything straight.

Tony: You can find other symbols of this type of order throughout Japanese education. Everyone wears the same size backpack and all textbooks are designed to fit the backpack. There is a pattern here of getting everything organized.

Frances: And everything has to go into a drawstring bag of specific proportions; your lunch, your cup, your gym clothes. When Marie went to the summer camp, we were sent a 30-page book listing everything that had to be packed for her: seven shirts, seven pants, on each shirt a sewn on white cloth name tag of specific size indicating name, school, class, and student number. There must be a drawstring bag 20 × 30 cm. Immense detail.

Marie: That is the way it should be. It just makes sense. You are describing this as though this is so unusual, but everything should be organized this way. I find it helpful now when I pack for a trip.

Tony: One of the other characteristics that defines Japanese society is its strong emphasis on membership in groups. Here American society with its stress on the individual is at the other end of the continuum from group-oriented Japan.

In schools this starts with uniforms. Most elementary students do not wear a full uniform as ours did, but they do have a uniform hat that identifies what school they belong. There is also an emphasis on eliminating behavior that disrupts the group or even sets some members of the group apart.

We had a beautiful illustration of that when Marie started to attend kindergarten. When she joined the class, there was another American family of friends who sent their two girls to the same class. Frances and the other mother gave our three girls toothbrushes so they could brush their teeth after lunch. At the end of the first week, both of our families received a note advising us that no other children brought toothbrushes to kindergarten and that this was disruptive, exceptional behavior. We should refrain from sending toothbrushes to school with the girls. Frances and the other mother complied and the children brushed their teeth when they got home in the afternoon.

A couple of months later, on Dental Health Day, a dentist visited the kindergarten and gave each child a quick check and sent home a report to the parents. All three of the American girls had a good report with no cavities. Soon we all received a note from the teacher to the effect that only three children received a "no cavities" report (no names, but guess who?) and starting next week all students were to bring in a toothbrush so they could brush their teeth after lunch.

The critical lesson is not about the objection to toothbrushes but the unacceptability of a few children doing something different. If we all brush together it is fine.

Frances: What fosters togetherness? How about school assemblies?

Marie: Yes, we had an assembly of the entire student body every Saturday, at which we all sang the school song that everyone knew by heart. Keeping the class together each year also helped to develop group ties. This shows in the fact that we are all still so close, even though it is 5 years since the class graduated from sixth grade and the Japanese students are all scattered among many different high schools. We write to each other regularly, and everyone always includes news of other students and reports who they met last weekend. I still write to them; they still write to me; and when I went back to Japan for visits a bunch of them would get together. They still have reunions periodically.

THE SCHOOL SETTING

Transportation

Tony: Let us talk about getting to school. Japanese deliver themselves to the school. While kindergartens often operate buses to collect students, we knew of no cases where Japanese elementary, middle, or high schools had school bus systems. Children walked, rode bicycles, rode public buses or trains. Some schools have rules forbidding parents to bring their children to school in order to foster independence. You often see mothers walking their youngsters to the end of the block and watching there while the child hikes the last few yards alone and makes an independent entrance. Remember that most residential streets lack sidewalks. Later, children in upper grades can apply for permits to ride a bicycle to school.

Buildings and Grounds

Marie: Most Japanese schools have their own pool and many have a gym. We did not have either. We had a hall with a stage, a piano, and wrestling mats. We did PE in there if it was raining. The kindergarten had its own part of the grounds with equipment: a slide, swings, monkey bars, and a tree house. The school had a big open area with trees along the side and gymnastics bars. We also had vertical bamboo poles to climb and two sets of swings. Later basketball goals were added. There was an equipment shed that contained wooden vaulting horses and balls. And there was a baseball backstop and soccer goals.

Frances: When the students entered the school building, there was a vestibule where they took off their outside shoes. On either side the wall was lined with little boxes containing their room shoes — identical cheap, white, canvas sneakers.

Anna: But they had different color toes!

Marie: At our school there were no color codes, but at middle and

Eastern Pacific Rim school children normally leave street shoes off while in class. The penchant for order is seen in this cubby, with shoes paired neatly, resting on a tray in each cubbyhole. Concerns about shoe security are nonexistent (photo by Elliott).

high school, each grade had a different color toe. You know when you see someone coming down the hall what grade the student is in.

Everyone has his or her assigned little cubbyhole for their shoes – the younger students lower down, the older ones higher up, and you know where your shoes are going to be. Whenever you go outside for recess, you have to change into your outdoor shoes. Whenever you come inside you put on your indoor shoes. The shoes are just there. Most people don't make the mistake of taking someone else's shoes. It is organized and it is hard to mix up shoes, anyway. The outside shoes were all different. The inside shoes were all the same, but they had our names written on the heels.

Frances: The school halls are pretty bare with an occasional poster, announcement, or bulletin board. The interior has a look of institutional, gray utilitarianism. There were a few calendar pictures and a couple pictures of Jesus in this Christian school. But when you walk into an elementary school in America, it is almost solid construction paper. One might find autumn leaves, snowmen, or Abraham Lincoln all in bright and solid colors. But in Japanese schools there is very little of this.

Marie: Sometimes, if we did a class project in art, they would hang our pictures along the art room walls or in our classroom.

Tony: The rooms and halls were not bare but the decorations were simple, sparse, and homemade.

Frances: This school did not have central heating, did it?

Marie: No, when it got cold the fifth and sixth graders would get the stoves out of the storage area and attach the tin pipe chimneys to an outlet in the ceiling of each classroom. Then they would set up a big kerosene stove in the corner of each classroom with a high fence around it.

CLASSROOM CLIMATE

Class Setting

Frances: When you entered the classrooms, the younger grades sat at tables arranged together where students worked in groups. The upper grades had individual desks. It was interesting to us that the children put all of their supplies, pencils, paper, and books in individual cubbyholes around the room.

Marie: When we got our desks in the upper grades, we put our books in the desk but kept our backpacks in cubbyholes. Each child had several cubbyholes in a vertical row. In one we put the bag containing our gym clothes, in another we put our uniform hat, in another our book bag, and in yet another we put any books that we would leave overnight.

Tony: The conviction that teachers should decorate the place, make it cheerful, appealing, and educational was not evident in any Japanese school that I've ever been in. What about the supplemental classroom supplies and resources of many American schools?

Marie: In our classes we had shelves full of books. There were no learning centers. No computers anywhere. There was a television in the science room for various educational programs we watched sometimes during class, and there was a television and VCR in the library. Of course, no one uses calculators in Japan at the elementary level. Everybody had a jump rope that we kept on hooks outside the classroom along with our towel and a reversible cloth gym cap. One side was white and one side was red so you could define teams. Each class had its own set of balls.

Work during the School Day

Anna: In Japanese schools, the children eat in their classrooms. They do not go to the cafeteria. The students serve the meals.

Marie: The elementary schools have a kitchen and serve a hot lunch. The students do not have a choice of food. Students assigned for that week go to the kitchen, bring the food to the classroom, and dish it out to their classmates who line up. We all drank tea.

Tony: Many writers note that Japanese children clean their own schools, but student involvement in the actual management of the school itself is much more extensive than that. Do you remember any other assigned responsibilities?

Anna: We cleaned the school every day including Saturdays. In the first grade, we wiped the bookshelves, and a couple of students would wipe the hall in front of the classroom with damp rags. Then we would move all the desks and clean the floor with dry rags and do the blackboards.

Marie: The fifth graders did the area around the outside of the school. They also had to do the art room. The fourth graders did the assembly hall. Before athletic events, everyone would line up at one end of the school grounds and walk across it picking up rocks. We would weed the planted areas and plant different things and care for them.

Tony: I am aware of cases where Japanese middle schools engaged in periodic neighborhood cleanups. Their responsibility to society extended not to particular disadvantaged groups, such as the homeless, but to being good citizens in the immediate community. This approach is more insulated from the greater world and the larger social issues on which we tend to focus attention here in the United States, but it does teach a kind of practical group citizenship in the immediate community to which people belong.

TIME ON TASK

The School Year

Frances: The academic year starts in April and ends the second week in March. It is divided into three quarters. Summer vacation comes after the spring (April—July) quarter and before the autumn (September—December) quarter.

Marie: During summer vacation, depending on the school, the students have 2 or 3 days when they must come in to check up on each other and have the teacher see how their homework is going. Our school never had this. However, at my kindergarten, we came in 2 days in the middle of vacation to play in huge pools they brought in.

Our elementary school had a week-long camp at the beach during vacation. Everyone went and everything was organized by classrooms: tables, activities, sleeping. The third graders learned how to swim. We did our own laundry. We had fireworks. It was great.

Frances: The teachers took part in this, too, during their vacation. They really participated in the experience of being with the children the entire week.

After the autumn quarter there is a 2-week vacation at New Year's. After the completion of the winter (January—March) quarter, there is a vacation for the last 2 weeks of March that comes between the end of one school year and the beginning of the next. The major vacation was 6 weeks in the summer. The same teacher who says good-bye to the children in mid-July greets them when they return at the beginning of September.

Marie: You always have homework over summer vacation.

Frances: One year you had to write four essays. That was a bit much. Another year you had a little workbook containing math problems and Chinese characters to practice.

The School Day

Marie: The Japanese day was not like an American school where after a 45-minute period the teacher says, ''That is the end of math; now we will study spelling.'' In the Japanese school we had breaks in between classes. Before we played we were expected to go to our cubbies and get our books for the next class.

Tony: My impression was that one of the things that they tried to teach the kids was to regularize their study patterns. That it wasn't a question of just finishing the assignment but of spending a certain amount of time working on their studies. You do your assignment and then review. You set aside a period of time for study.

However, there was a seriousness of purpose about study. When children started school, there was a whole ritual surrounding the transition from child to member of the larger community: buying bookbags, buying uniforms, and organizing family space around a desk. This last point is a major imposition on a Japanese family living in a small space. It certainly sends a concrete message as to just how important education is considered to be.

Marie: That's what I was going to say. Everything the American schools do bites into class time. Seriously, in the case of the trips we went on in Japan, we would have a day and then everything was over. You quickly went back to academic work.

In the United States, programs often take a lot of time. The only exception in Japan was the annual Sports Day in October. That was on a Sunday, but preparations took time. Here in America, even in high school, I find many things that take away from class.

I should explain about the breaks. At the end of each 40-minute study session there was a 10-minute break. We could go to the bathroom or to get a drink and then go out and play on the swings or in the sandbox. In American elementary school, the students work straight through until lunch and then go back to their desks for another several hours. I think that affects how the students act in class. If you have that time to blow off steam, then you are refreshed and ready to go back and study. You know that when you finish your study time you can go out and play again. We had a full hour for recess and lunch. We could eat at our own pace, but we had to spend the last 10 minutes doing exercises with the whole school.

Tony: Americans who are concerned about academic performance frequently look at how few days each year our students go to school. My impression is that it is not only a question of time in school, but the use of the time itself. In the United States, we are engaged in broadening horizons, and in the process of doing so, we fail to preserve enough time for basic skills.

The Japanese have agreed to make basic skills their top priority, especially in the first years of elementary school. Socialization takes place, too, and children learn to be good Japanese. But the actual content of the work is focused on academic subjects, and that is reflected by good performance in those areas.

STUDENTS

Student Attitudes

Marie: Children know that when they are in school they are there to study. More people in American classes are more laid back and relaxed. "Who cares about classes?" I am not saying that the Japanese are thrilled to be in school, but they take it seriously. Many American students talk like they do not care. They are a lot less respectful to the teachers. Not that they trash the teachers, but they are not as worried about the teachers. They will take notes, but certain students will lay back and sit there and do nothing. They will be talking to their friends. Of course, I am comparing high school in America to elementary school in Japan.

Tony: This goes back to the ways students encourage each other in the two cultures, "Take it easy" in the United States or *Gambate,* (persevere) in Japan. The cultural context requires these expressions of attitude from you.

TEACHERS

Teacher Esteem

Tony: The Japanese made a decision in the postwar period to put money into human resources. I have heard that the ministry pays teachers in the public school system 10 percent higher than civil servants in their community with comparable qualifications and longevity. This automatically places the Japanese teacher in the position of an esteemed community resource; qualified teachers are guaranteed premium pay by virtue of the fact that their job is to mold the future of society by training its children. This is not only a gesture of respect, but it subsidizes teaching as a sustainable career path.

Marie: I really liked my teachers. I liked my third year kindergarten teacher very much. After I left for elementary school I visited her at home, and she sent me a New Year's greeting card. And every time I have visited Japan since we moved back to America in 1989, I have gone back to the elementary school to visit with my teachers. I have written them often and received letters and cards over the years from several of them.

Anna: Since leaving Japan, I got letters from my teacher and a Christmas card from my kindergarten teacher. During vacation your teachers sent you postcards.

Marie: The teachers would play with us during recess and breaks between classes. They would be out there playing dodge ball or tag with us, or play card games.

Tony: Japanese society is more formal than American. Were the teachers formal in their relationship with you?

Marie: I feel that the students had more respect for their teachers, but it was not the sort of distant respect where you could not be friendly.

Anna: It was not a distant relationship at all.

Frances: How can you keep discipline and control in the classroom when the teacher is that friendly and involved?

Marie: Like you said before, society shows respect for teachers, and the students are part of that. They know who the teacher is. In general, the students obey the teacher during class. Then during breaks they go out and blow off steam. They know the difference between class time and play time.

Frances: One interesting thing about the class breaks was the level of chaos that was allowed during those 10 minutes. It would drive Americans crazy. I think we have an underlying fear that discipline is going to get out of control! I think an American teacher or parent would fear that control once lost would be very difficult to regain. The Japanese teachers I saw, both in kindergarten and elementary school, seemed to have a capacity for allowing the students to generate tremendous noise and chaos.

Frances: Can you comment on the fact that your teacher would come out and play with you? A lot of Americans would say that a teacher who plays with the students is going to lose their authority and the child's respect.

Marie: No, you like the teacher a lot more for that.

Frances: Yet, you still respect the teacher and see the school as a place of learning?

Marie: Definitely! In Japanese society people respect the older person. Especially in middle or high school, 1 year makes a difference in who is in charge and has authority. Respecting your elders and respecting authority is definitely there from the beginning.

Tony: I think Japanese adults are very effective at organizing group projects in which they divide responsibilities, assign tasks to members, and contribute effectively to the completion of the whole project. What I see in adults relates very directly to what I think I saw being taught to children at a very early age. What about planning parties?

Marie: Once or twice a year we would have class parties in which we would form groups and decide what act to perform. A group of us would put on a play or tell jokes. We would also form little committees. The decoration committee would make decorations and decorate the classroom. Some would set up the desks. Others would be the MCs of the party. Others would be in charge of bringing the food. We did this in second or third grade. Teachers brought candy but really didn't do that much.

Teacher Assignment, Specialty Teachers, and Teacher Assistants

Tony: One impression I have is that, outside of the kindergarten, there are no assistants in the classroom. One teacher ran a class. Specialists in reading, science, art, and music would work with the students. Anna's first grade class had 36 students. The public school in the neighborhood averaged 40 to a class, which is standard in Japan.

Frances: Marie's kindergarten class did have an assistant for 42 children.

Marie: In our Japanese elementary school, it was the practice for a class to be assigned a teacher upon entering the school. That class would keep that teacher for first, second, and third grades. Then upon starting fourth grade, they would be assigned a new teacher who would stay with the class through sixth grade. The teacher who had been with them the first 3 years would rotate to a new incoming first grade class. The preferred pattern was to have a teacher stay with the class for 3 years at a time.

Frances: The school gave the children a female teacher for their first 3 years, because they are supposed to be more nurturing and supportive of the younger children. The teachers for fourth through sixth grade were usually males who were thought stricter and more demanding of the children.

Teaching Methods

Tony: I think the Japanese let children learn through hands-on experiences with these responsibilities more than we do. Americans want them to have experiences, but we tend to structure and feed these experiences to students. The Japanese see the planning and doing as valuable and emphasize groups dividing tasks and coordinating the processes.

Marie: Let us return to the reading teacher. He would come to the first grade class and during reading period, he would come to each student and listen to us read. He would highlight words we did not know, drill us when we had run into problems, and generally help us one at a time. The regular class teacher would be going around at the same time doing this with other students.

Students read at their own pace. When you finished your textbook, you could choose whichever book you wanted out of a series of story books. Your goal was to read all the books in the series. Then we did the same thing with another, more advanced series. From then on we read aloud together.

Tony: Was there streaming in language classes?

Marie: No, in the first two grades we all worked at our own pace. Some people finished the material faster than others. Nao was really fast, and when she finished a book, she would go on to the next one. From the third grade we all worked together and read aloud as a class. There were no groups. When we worked together on math assignments or for chores, we formed groups, but there was no streaming. The groups were assigned by seating or by the Japanese equivalent of alphabetical order.

Frances: Did the teachers help students with difficulties outside of class hours?

Marie: Yes. The teachers were always around school, and you could stay after hours and they would help you with problems.

Tony: Do you think Japanese students have a higher tolerance for drill and repetition?

Marie: Yes, definitely. The people in my class in America get bored easily.

Frances: When our younger children went through first, second, and third grade here, the classes' progress seemed slow, and they were bored especially with math.

Anna: Every year, after we drew the ambulance and fire truck, the art teacher would pick out the best pictures for each grade and send them into the city. They had competition, and the winners were put on display in the city hall. In first grade, I won first place.

Frances: One thing that really struck me about the Japanese is that some of the things that were done lacked imagination and were very repetitive. It went beyond constructive drill. Every year the fire engine came. Perhaps that gave everybody a sense of tradition or continuity. Every year the same thing was done. On the other hand, that lowers the need to expend energy in planning. Every year at our American school there are many, many different things going on. There is something every month for the whole school. It is creative and demanding. The teachers are always frantically trying to catch up.

The Japanese school always had the same activity. Our school always went to a certain park and a certain picnic spot; always went to the cemetery and prayed at the founder's grave on his death anniversary; always went to the same mountains for an outing; always had the fire engine come. There was a lack of imagination in planning these activities.

GRADES AND LEARNING ETHOS

Grades

Tony: Did grades create tensions within the class? Japanese schools are very achievement oriented and yet seek to foster a strong sense of membership with the class. Do these two forces work at cross-purposes?

Marie: Certainly by the time you get to middle school, there is a lot of emphasis on grades and performance. Middle schools regularly post lists of grades so everyone can see how they are doing compared to each other. Nobody gives the good academic performer a hard time like you see here in the United States. The general feeling is that if your performance disappoints you, it is up to you to try harder and get better grades.

Tony: I think that there is a cultural difference in response to under-performance. In the United States, we tend to worry more about hurt feelings and a bruised self-image. We comfort each other, excuse the problem, and explain away the disappointment. My impression is that the Japanese recognize disappointing performance for what it is and encourage one another to greater efforts.

Tony: What about grade failures or grade repetitions?

Marie: There were never any in our school, but failure to advance with your class does exist in Japan. You hear about students who skip school all the time and do not have enough days to complete the grade, or someone who has been very sick and in the hospital a long time. Students who return from living overseas may have to drop back a grade.

Frances: What about students who just don't do well in school?

Marie: I don't know, but I don't think it is very common in elementary school. Everyone seems to move along together. The classes stick together, and by the time you are in the fifth and sixth grade, everyone is working on qualifying to go to a particular middle school. Your teacher and your *Juku* (supplemental school) teacher advise you on which schools you have a realistic chance of entering.

Frances: Do they tell you which schools to try for?

Marie: Somebody has to do it. The teacher and your Juku teacher know you and your work, and they act as counselors to point you toward places where you can succeed.

Tony: You did not get report cards until the fourth grade. Was there any sense of how you were performing relative to others?

Marie: Of course. Students always know that. We knew that Nao was one of the smartest in the class, but no one ever made fun of her for doing well. One of the boys did not read as well as the rest of us, but we were all friends. Maybe someone would tease him a little when he had to read aloud, but not much. The teacher told us to stop.

When we got report cards (see Figure 10.1), we would immediately compare and see how we all did. Most Japanese schools use a 5-point grading system. Ours was different in that we used a 10-point scale. Obviously, you want 9s and 10s. Those were especially good. Eights are acceptable, but 7s and below were disappointing. We did not use letter grades, and I was not aware of a specific point below which you were failing. Some of the students made 6s and 7s, but I do not remember anyone with a grade below that. Nao, who led the class academically, had lots of 9s and 10s. I think that the teachers were fair in their grading and did not feel under pressure to give good grades. I think Japanese parents confronted with poor grades are less inclined to question the teacher's judgment and more inclined to urge the student to work harder. Gambate!

Learning Ethos

Tony: Let us talk about motivation. We have talked about drill, the students putting effort into studies, and more being expected of them. What happens in the classroom to get the kids going? Do you ever have competitions, like spelling or math bees?

Marie: No, we did not.

Frances: When our children started American school, we were very surprised to encounter the practice of constantly rewarding children with presents of toys and candy. At the end of the week or month or quarter, the child is rewarded for behavior, getting all his or her homework done, doing well on quizzes, etc. Did you experience that in Japan?

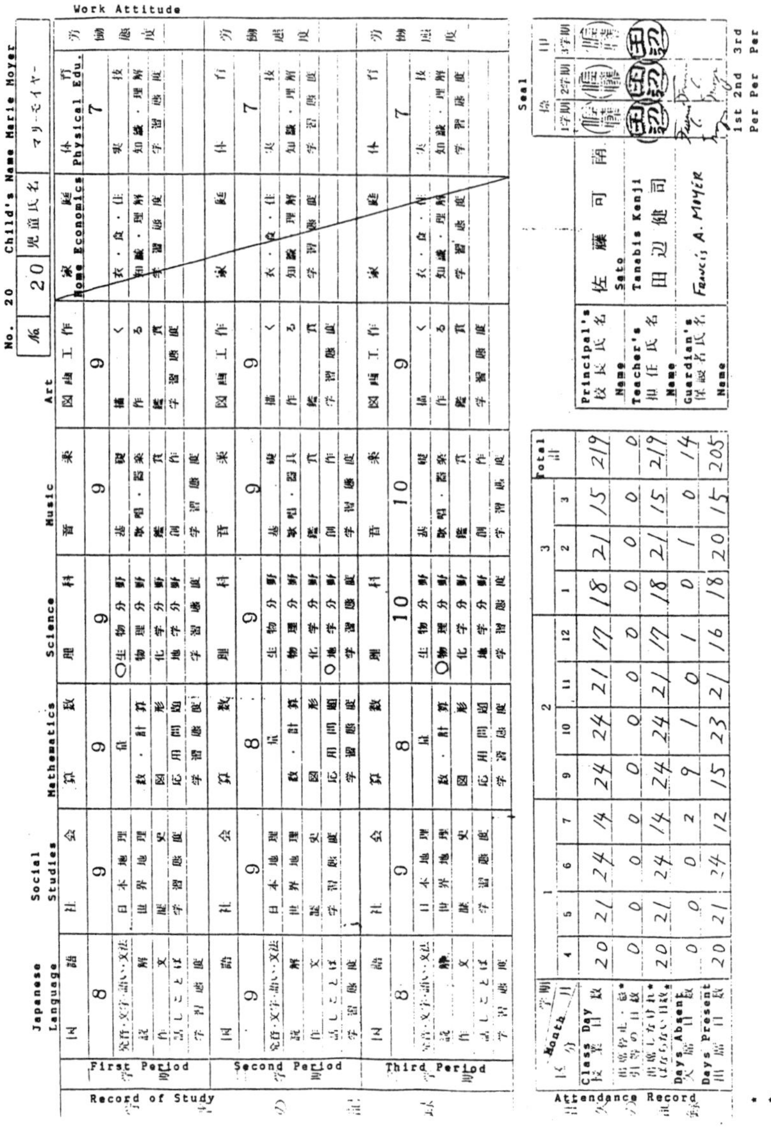
No. 20
Child's Name Marie Moyer
マリーモイヤー
Work Attitude
Japanese Language
Social Studies
Mathematics
Science
Music
Art
Home Economics
Physical Edu.
Record of Study
First Period
Second Period
Third Period
Attendance Record
Month
Class Day
Days Absent
Days Present
Total
Principal's Name
Sato
Teacher's Name
Tanabis Kenji
Guardian's Name
Francis A. Moyer
Seal
1st Per
2nd Per
3rd Per
Required Attendance Days

Figure 10.1.

Marie: No. Once in fourth grade the teacher gave us bookmarks for some exercise, but otherwise, no.

Frances: Did you have any contests, such as story writing or drawing contests such as we have in the American schools?

Marie: Those are fun, creative things to do. In our school we had only one such activity. The local fire department would bring an ambulance and fire engine to the school. Students would bring our sketch pads and draw the vehicles. One year Nao and I didn't want to draw the fire truck, so we decided we would draw part of the fire truck—the wheel.

Tony: What was the reaction?

Marie: The teacher was not amused.

Tony: Expectations are high with children approaching school as a serious task to be worked at and taken seriously. What do you think helps create this in a Japanese school?

Marie: That's tough. Otherwise, I am not exactly sure what makes Japanese kids take school so seriously. That is the way it is.

PARENTS AND COMMUNITY

Role of Parents

Frances: Let's look at the role of mothers in the school. In American schools there are room mothers who help organize parties or transport the children to some event. I do not think parents ever went along on outings unless they accompanied a handicapped child. Parents were never in the classroom, supporting the regular educational schedule. Here in the United States, we encounter tremendous pressure to volunteer time in support of the school system working with individual students, preparing materials for teachers, monitoring classes, participating in class trips, etc. In Japan, mothers were assigned many chores to do, but they were kept out of the daily life of the school.

Another issue is communication between parent and teacher. Each child had a "Communication Booklet," that the parent was supposed to check every day. The teacher was also supposed to check it daily. If you wanted to send a message, you wrote it in the book and dated it. The teacher would read it and initial it to confirm that it had been read. The same practice was used in reverse when the teacher wanted to send a message to us.

When Anna was in kindergarten, we also received extensive mimeographed communications every week. These described class activities, recounted interesting incidents, and even reported dialogues that the teachers thought were cute or interesting. There certainly was a strong commitment to communication being displayed.

Tony: There were periodic meetings with the teachers. There were two different types. Every quarter we had an individual meeting with the teacher that I used to attend. Less frequently, about twice each year, there would be a group meeting of all of the mothers in a class with the teacher.

Frances: I went to those and remember sitting in on the first one. Everyone spoke about their child. I quickly saw that you were supposed to run your child down. ''My poor little lazy child will not get up in the morning; I am sorry he is always so late,'' or ''My obnoxious child will not eat all of his lunch rice, and I apologize deeply for his slovenly manners and wasteful habits.'' When they were very young, it often focused on poor manners and the difficulty of getting them to do their homework. Later, it shifted to more academic inadequacies. You do not brag; you put your child down.

Tony: This is a cultural pattern in which you denigrate yourself and your family while praising others. By contrast, Americans tend to be very defensive of any criticism of their children's performance. There is a tendency to reject criticism and try to find an external cause for the child's poor performance. The teacher is inadequate, the textbook is at fault, or something other than the child is the problem.

Marie: But I find it so uncomfortable to have to praise myself. My sophomore year we had to identify three positive character traits in ourselves and write a paragraph about them. I had the hardest time doing that. It drove me crazy.

Frances: The teachers generally gave some bland comfort to the parents about their children, but I do not remember being struck by the teacher's response as much as by the mothers' public confessions of the children's shortcomings. The teacher would talk in general terms about the class and what progress they were making. But Japanese teachers did not praise your child to you. They liked the children and had a good opinion of them, but they did not praise them to the parents.

Tony: In addition to the group meetings, there were also one-on-one sessions scheduled each quarter. The parent would meet outside of class hours with the teacher. I usually attended these. These were conducted in the classroom and involved a brief review of how the student was progressing, a look at the student's desk, a look at a package of tests and other papers by the student, and a look at workbooks. There was time here for discussion of how the child was doing. There was also discussion of whether it was appropriate to be thinking about sending the child to Juku. Sometimes these sessions get a bit stormy often over parental demands that the teacher push the child harder. This reflects the intense concern about academic accomplishment on the part of Japanese parents, particularly the mother, who has the task of encouraging the best academic performance possible from her children.

The teachers would not only report on what went on in class but would collect information about home life. Has she been eating and sleeping well? Does she get enough exercise and play time? What kind of games does she play and with whom. What does she read outside of class? The conversations in Marie's and Anna's cases included curiosity about English language skills and their socializing with the other non-Japanese children in the neighborhood. There was also some curiosity about just why we were sending our girls to Japanese schools.

CURRICULUM

Reading and Writing

Tony: I wanted to mention that instruction in math and reading really focused on the basics the first couple of years. The American approach is to try to get children excited about science very young. That is not a bad idea, but the conclusion we drew from our Japanese school experience is that science can wait. You have to get the basics down first. Let's talk about academic instruction. Start with reading.

Marie: Each child would read the textbook by themselves during reading class. Our teacher and a specialist who helped first graders with reading would go around to each student individually and listen to them read aloud.

Tony: Japanese is written with two phonetic scripts of 48 characters each that represent syllables used to write all Japanese sounds. These are called *kana* and are similar to our printed and cursive scripts. In addition, Chinese characters, called *Kanni,* are mixed with kana to write mature Japanese. By the time students finish middle school, they are supposed to have mastered nearly 2000 *Kanji.*

Marie: In kindergarten you learn the first kana script, hiragana. Then you review it in first grade. There you learn the second kana, the angular katakana, and you learn 46 Kanji.

Tony: There is a national curriculum established by the Ministry of Education that specifies which characters are to be learned at each grade. The assigned list indicates 105 in second grade, 187 in third, and 205 in fourth. One advantage is that publishers of textbooks know what characters the children know at each grade level. You can find versions of books aimed at particular grade levels.

Frances: You had workbooks in which you had to practice writing characters over and over. There was a great deal of copying of characters.

Marie: Kanji are very easy at first. It is just rote memorization and you just get used to it. It is not all that hard until you get up into fourth and fifth grade; then it becomes challenging. We had Kanji workbooks with 10 or 20 characters on a page. We would copy the characters repeatedly. Then there were sentences in which we had to fill in the Kanji that we had learned.

Frances: I remember your grandmother being surprised at how small you were when you were required to write.

Mathematics

Tony: We were impressed by the fact there was a tremendous emphasis on drill and memorization of basic math facts as well as a concerted effort to help students recognize what they were dealing with in concrete terms. Can you talk about how math was taught?

Anna: In first grade we had workbooks that showed addition and subtraction using little squares. Along with the book we used matching tiles. Everyone was given five tiles that could be snapped together and broken apart. When we were used to working with those, we received five tiles permanently connected plus the five single units. We would use the tiles for adding and subtracting. The teacher would have a set of 5s and 10s.

Frances: This pattern of representation was replicated in their workbooks and went on all the way up to the 10,000s. When they were teaching different places, they would have drawings to illustrate the concepts in the same system—the same units. The student could see this is a block of 100 or 1000 or 10,000 squares, and this representation actually accompanied several pages of problems. It would help the child to visualize the numbers, and repetition would help impress it upon their minds.

Marie: There was a 10 × 10 grid with the single digits, 1−9 and 0 along the top and down one side. You would have to complete the grid drill by filling in all 100 squares with the correct answer, and you would have to time yourself. The goal was for the entire class to complete the whole grid without error in 2 minutes.

Frances: They started with much longer time goals and gradually increased the speed. I remember when she was working on the addition grid in the first grade, Marie was unable to make the final goal of 2 minutes. We drilled at home, as she was assigned to do, but could not break the 2-minute barrier. She kept putting the correct answers in the boxes but took too long. Ultimately we figured out the problem. She was performing most of the calculations. When we changed tactics and drilled her on memorizing the combinations, she quickly cleared the 2-minute goal. The critical lesson is to memorize.

Marie: I think it still helps my math. I have many calculations memorized and immediately available.

Tony: How did you feel about all of this drill and repetition?

Marie: I did not mind it. I liked math homework better than language. It came a lot easier to me. It was a lot more fun.

Oh, estimating was a problem. We did rounding in Japan but not estimating which was a big thing in my American classes. I hated estimating. It seemed to encourage vagueness after we had been taught accuracy in the Japanese school. It always made doing the problem itself so purposeless.

Tony: One criticism Americans have of the Japanese school system is that the Japanese are good at teaching facts but not at teaching thinking, problem solving, or creativity. There is a lack of appreciation by American observers of problem-solving skills that Japanese students learn. I think that they do learn some good problem-solving skills.

Marie: We did lots of word problems.

Tony: What about the expectations in class?

Marie: They are higher in Japan. The expectation is for the whole group to perform well. They do not divide the students into those who are better and those who are slower. Everyone has to keep up with the group. The material is a lot harder.

Frances: I think we should discuss the introduction of science and social studies.

Marie: We started in third or fourth grade, but in some schools, they start earlier. In social studies we learned about our city, the dumps, the factories.

Tony: It was very concrete, very close to home. I remember you making a very detailed map of the neighborhood.

Marie: Everyone did gardening all the way up to sixth grade. And we all did lots of science labs from the beginning.

AN AGENDA OF IDEAS FOR AMERICAN EDUCATORS

Tony: What lessons do we think American schools could learn from the Japanese? Remember that social differences make it difficult or impossible to transplant many practices. Marie, what do you think could be changed in American education, especially in elementary schools, to improve education here?

Marie: *Work ethic: Do not take time away for entertainment, construction paper exercises, and other things which take you away from class.* Give the younger grades periodic breaks to blow off steam and recess, and then when you sit down to study, work.

Teachers should also join the students in their games during recess and breaks. The students would see the human side of the teachers and develop friendlier feelings toward them that would help the relationship. One of Anna's teachers here has done that, and the kids love her for it. She is also strict during study times and does not seem to have difficulty with discipline, and it will help the teachers see a different side of their students.

Personally, I do not advise giving homework over summer vacation or shortening vacation time. Just use the time you already have in school more efficiently.

Frances: What about equipment in the classroom?

Marie: *Technology: I think access to computers in a computer class or lab is a good idea, and American schools are correct to teach students how to use them.* In the United States we have televisions and VCRs in class, and they can be very helpful with materials relating to classes. However, I think that having a computer in every class is a waste of resources.

As for calculators, they should be used in high school, but not until the students have really learned their math skills in elementary and middle school by lots of drills, memorization, and exercises. If you start early with calculators, you never really learn the your basics. People grow to depend on them too heavily. The Japanese approach of forbidding them in elementary and middle schools is right.

Frances: *Basic education: I would point out that the Japanese emphasis on basics, reading, writing, math, especially in the first two or three grades, is a good idea which pay dividends later.* I would recommend the practice of making basic math very concrete and using a consistent system to build that awareness from one grade to the next. And I think that we can move faster and expect more from our children in the basics.

The Japanese focus on basic skills, but they also have high expectations for music and art. I think that it is a shame that in American schools music tends to be shunted aside or left as an elective in middle or high school.

Tony: *Americans would benefit from cultivating more of a sense of social responsibility. We could do more to foster a sense of group identity.* I tend to view many aspects of Japanese and American societies as being at opposite ends of a continuum: Japanese group orientation versus American individualism; Japanese respect for authority versus American rebelliousness. Neither society should try to become like the other – they cannot – but I think that both would benefit from moving a little closer to center. And this goes for the schools as well. Uniforms are a hard sell in American schools, but can you issue some kind of badge or other symbol of belonging?

Marie: It would not be cool to wear it.

Tony: *Building responsibility: Cleaning the school and grounds might be good for American schools.* It would take little time, be a shared activity, and if students took care of the physical plant, they might be more careful about how they use it. Start from elementary schools and teach a rising generation of students to accept it. I also think it would be good for the custodian to supervise this. That contact and doing some of the work might teach the students more respect for people in service roles, and it would also teach greater responsibility for the school plant. I think that this would cultivate a sense of practical, active community membership, and the responsibility would cultivate in students a concern for social or environmental issues.

Marie: *Discipline: I would like to see some of the sense of teamwork that we talk about in sports transferred to the classroom.* I think a lot of

American students are very self-centered. Individuals throw their weight around and disrupt class for everyone else. I am not saying that this does not exist in Japan because they do have the problem with bullying, but in that case the individual is the victim of attack for not conforming. Here in American the individual can ruin everything for the rest of the class by being assertive.

Frances: *Respect for teachers: I think we need to cultivate more respect for teachers.* A lack of respect for teachers undermines education, and it certainly makes a teaching career less rewarding.

Tony: One area where the change can begin within the school system itself is for administrative staff to show greater respect for the teachers as professionals, especially in front of the children. Specifically, they should not interrupt classes at random times to make PA announcements. I have been in any number of classes when a class was interrupted by long, rambling PA announcements. That sends a message to the students about the relative value of the teachers' time and what they are doing in class. It shows a profound lack of professional respect.

Maybe we can also do some other things within schools to cultivate respect, not only for teachers but for all members of the school community. There is some value in the old drill of standing up when a teacher comes into the room. If that would not suit an American school, an emphasis on more polite language and behavior might help.

But this is also part of a larger social problem, and the schools cannot tackle it alone. We live in an environment that delights in tearing down any figure in authority, and teachers and education suffer from the fallout from these attitudes. Polite behavior and mutual respect do not mean that you have to be servile and abdicate the right to make personal judgments, but it does require that you approach others with some respect for them as individuals and for the role which they are trying to fulfill. The schools can work on this internally, but real change and the resulting benefits for American education depend on a change within the general society.

Frances: *Value of study: One last thing that should be emphasized is the stress on study as an endeavor of high value and purpose.* This is something else that must be grounded in the attitudes of society as a whole. Within the school there are some things that can be done. This frequent rewarding of children with sweets and other prizes sends a message that, ''While learning these lessons opens the world and the future to you, that is not enough to command your interest. Really what motivates you is the immediate short-term prize or sweet. You do not want to be here and we are asking too much of you, so I have to bribe you to apply yourself.''

Japanese children are looking way ahead to adulthood. Everyone around them is telling them this. Their futures depend on this. I think we have lost the will to really tell our children that they have to take a long-term view. We are inconsistent in the message we give about the value of education as a society. Japanese society is much more consistent about the importance of formal education and conveys that message very clearly.

Marie: It is like the athletes who make the ''Stay in School'' commercials and then drop out of college to play for the professionals. What is that telling students about the value of education?

RECOMMENDED ADDITIONAL READING

Shields, J. B., Jr., ed. 1989. *Japanese Schooling: Patterns of Socialization, Equality, and Political Control.* University Park, PA: The Pennsylvania State University Press.

White, M. 1987. *The Japanese Educational Challenge: A Commitment to Children.* New York: The Free Press.

A WORLD-CLASS ELEMENTARY SCHOOL: SETTING THE AGENDA

Not one of us alone is as smart as all of us together.
— Slogan hanging on a classroom wall, author unknown

Chapter 11 describes the authors' idea of a world-class elementary school, and it presents a portrait of an existing school, the Lord Lansdowne Elementary School in Toronto, Canada, which the authors' believe contains many of the essential features of a world-class elementary school. This chapter also provides three basic processes to consider when designing a world-class elementary school: (1) the staff development needed to begin the process of creating a world-class elementary school, (2) envisioning what a world-class elementary school could look like, and (3) setting the agenda for a unique world-class elementary school.

ENVISIONING A WORLD-CLASS ELEMENTARY SCHOOL

The educational leadership literature is replete with references to the power of vision. The development of a world-class elementary school should begin with some notion of what one would look like. The authors present their vision of such a school as a start to the reader developing a unique vision for his or her own setting.

Welcome to World-Class Elementary School (WCES). Looked at from the outside WCES is nothing out of the ordinary. The building may be old and timeworn — many of the world-class schools in other cultures can be several hundred years old! The parking lot is small because many teachers use mass transit to get to school. Early in the morning the streets team with parents holding children by the hand, walking short distances to the local

287

World-class schools do not require fancy new buildings. This Chinese school shows students practicing for a dragon dance in an urban school. Many of the world-class schools' nations report schools that are old and in relatively poor physical repair. What makes a world-class school is the dynamics of home, classroom, and learning (photo courtesy of the Ministry of Education, Republic of China).

school. Teachers and the head mingle among the community which comes to school, and the air is punctuated with the lyrical quality of children who are happy to be there. The visitor sees smiles on faces and senses the calm that only trust evokes. First names are used by teachers greeting children, parents talking to teachers, and by the head mingling with the gaggle of scholars sweeping toward the day of challenges that await.

In many ways, WCES is like the vision that first year teachers have as they go to school for the first time as a teacher. Instead of having dour "lounge lizards" castigate the dreamy young teacher, WCES makes the dream possible. The head approaches the visitor, anxious to share the school with someone wanting to study it. The visitor wants to study each brick carefully, so the tour of WCES is divided into various parts.

STUDENTS IN THE WORLD-CLASS ELEMENTARY SCHOOL

The WCES student charter is a blueprint for success at the fictional school. The charter starts with a definition of a world-class student, so that teachers and parents can help children learn the definition of success. The ingredients of success are goal setting, hard work, and achievement. The community expects students to feel good about doing well as opposed to feeling good about doing poorly. Preschool parents and day care agencies have a copy of the charter so that they can teach the definition of success to preschool children. The principal invites preschool children living within the attendance area to visit the school with parents so that they will be comfortable at school. The school staff believes that the parents are the student's first teacher and that their success makes or breaks the teacher's later effort at school. Teachers talk about the definition of a world-class student to students in kindergarten, and when students learn to read and write, teachers have students write about the definition of a world-class student, and teachers read stories about school successes. Students in the later elementary grades visit the younger children and talk to them about success. The school believes that success begets success.

The WCES student charter contains a "Bill of Rights and Responsibilities" for children enrolled in the school. Student rights focus on the opportunity to learn and be treated equally. Equal treatment includes a "no labeling" pledge by the school, and teachers cannot group students into any form of dummy groups. Student responsibilities include value statements about respect for self, other people, property, and hard work. The board of education approved the WCES student charter, and the principal consistently protects the integrity of the charter from parents who oppose the teaching of any universal values.

The principal, with assistance from teachers, parents, and children, published a code of conduct that all students learn in the early grades. Teachers teach students that self-discipline is a prerequisite to learning and that learning leads to success. Students receive praise from teachers when they obey the code, but the same teachers admonish those who disobey. Teachers send students who continually disobey to an alternative room staffed by specialists in child development, a counselor, a special education teacher, and a paraprofessional specially trained to assist with discipline. The principal and assistant principal are on call, but teachers do not send students directly to the office. The teacher calls the parent when discipline problems become serious enough to eject the student from the classroom. The principal becomes involved when students need to be sent home. The board of

The end of a hard day at school gets cheers from these happy Chinese students. Many will attend extra school ("cram school") before going home to homework. These children are happy with their success (photo courtesy of the Ministry of Education, Republic of China).

education, on request from the principal, removes students for the remainder of the year if they bring weapons to school or commit serious illegal acts.

Students assume a share of the responsibility for maintaining an orderly climate in the school. The staff trains older students to be peer mediators, and older students are peer teachers for younger students. Students have responsibility to keep classrooms, hallways, and the playground clean, and a cleanup period concludes the school day.

Teachers provide guidance about how students should spend time outside school. Television guidelines indicate programs of value, and teachers encourage limited television watching. Parents helped prepare the document and pledge to support its implementation. A homework policy exists that requires homework for all students. The policy includes guidelines for the amount of time students should spend on homework, as well as the types of activities that constitute homework. The school encourages participation in extracurricular activities but only during lunch or outside the school day. The school provides a basic extracurricular program for all students and cooperates with local government for the provision of additional activities.

Students at WCES expect similar high expectations to apply to all students. Those who take longer to meet the expectations work hard, and the school provides extra learning opportunities for them. Students with learning disabilities receive additional help from teachers trained to remediate the disability either in the regular classroom or in special classrooms. Inclusion is an option, not a mandate. Teachers pledge to initiate a special education referral only if the child's needs require intervention by a special teacher. The goal is to keep the labeling of students to a minimum.

TEACHERS IN THE WORLD-CLASS ELEMENTARY SCHOOL

The teachers at WCES are respected professionals, entrusted with the only next generation that the community has. Because they are professional, they are treated that way, and they both dress and act professionally as well. They use the title teacher with dignity and pride. The "teachers' room" is at the center of the school, and the teachers' desks are grouped in that room by planning teams. The head has made a concerted effort to minimize nonteaching functions so that teachers' time is devoted to planning, presenting, and reflecting on the teaching act. The visitor to the school is given a simple directory in which each teacher is pictured and their credentials explained.

At WCES teachers talk with each other a great deal. Planning occurs in teams, using the national curriculum as a base on which the best teaching methods are built. The teachers are glad to have a common base for planning so the discussions focus on the best teaching possible. At the early elementary grades most teaching time is devoted to language and mathematics lessons. The head actively teaches during the day and is involved in the planning and reflection phases as well. The teachers are pleased with that involvement because they know the head started as an excellent teacher.

Novice teachers at WCES are given special attention. Because the school is actively involved with a teacher training institution, there is a clear understanding of the mentoring role the school provides during student teaching and the first years of cadet teaching. The teacher training institution continues its involvement with the cadet teacher after graduation because it is responsible for the quality of preparation given to the graduate. Mentors are assigned and given released time to work as a mentor. The head sees that mentoring is a priority at WCES.

The teachers at WCES plan together but teach alone. Their rooms have more children than U.S. teachers expect, but the children are well behaved. The room's walls are colorful and stimulating, centers dot the room, and the room is inviting for learning. The day starts with a brief patriotic or civic exercise, lead by the head. Desks are in straight rows, and direct teaching is a whole class activity. The teachers appreciate the fact that once they begin teaching, there are no outside interruptions, because teaching and learning are number one at WCES. Although the parents have walked the children to school, some stay as volunteers, performing nonteaching duties to free the teacher to teach. During nonteaching periods (the teachers do not teach every minute, all day), the teacher may leave campus for personal business if need be. The head knows the planning is done, and teaching will occur on time.

The teacher is respected, and students are attentive while lessons are presented. There is very little disruption from the students. Some of the teachers at WCES have students stand and bow politely when they enter the room. When classes change, the teachers move and the students do not. The teachers expect students to have backpacks with them when they arrive at school, and the teachers check the packs for notes from the parents which are put in a special place in each backpack. The teachers know the parents will check the same spot for a note from the teacher when the child gets home.

The teachers work long days because they are involved with reteaching after school to help the ''slow birds'' keep up with their lessons, rather than slowing the whole class down. Then the teachers may be involved in sports programs or other activities as the school day stretches toward evening. When the teacher goes home, it all seems worthwhile because the community is proud to have a teacher in neighborhood. Besides, Teacher's Day is coming!

PARENTS AND COMMUNITY IN THE WORLD-CLASS ELEMENTARY SCHOOL

Perhaps the most important program at WCES is the preschool parenting program. The administrative staff conducted a census of all parents in the WCES attendance area who have preschool children. As parents move, the office staff removes them from the census, and office personnel add new residents to the list. The principal contacts the parents and tells them that they are officially adjunct faculty at WCES. The principal invites them to an adjunct faculty meeting at the school and stresses the important role they play as their child's first teacher. The principal invites them to attend future meetings where teachers and parent volunteers explain to the parents how they can prepare their children for school. Teachers stress reading aloud as well as game playing that can help preschool children prepare for future, similar activities at school. Speakers, faculty, and volunteers talk about disciplining the preschooler and the behavior expected of students in prekindergarten or kindergarten. Parents may borrow videos and written materials about parenting the preschool youngster and games to play with preschool children. The WCES faculty adopts the parents of preschool youngsters, because the faculty knows that students properly prepared to enter school will achieve and that the practice may be the most important practice adopted to earn world-class school status.

WCES uses a generous portion of Chapter 1 funds to offer prekindergarten classes to those youngsters who qualify for Chapter 1 programs. Students attend half a day, Monday through Thursday, for a year. Parents are an important cog in the program, for they must volunteer in the classroom and attend parenting classes. The school uses remaining Chapter 1 funds to provide follow-up programs for K−6 students.

Parental involvement during the child's elementary years is a commitment of the WCES faculty. Parents helped write a "parents' charter" that reiterates the parents' responsibility to the school and the school's responsibility to the parent. The charter encourages the parents' participation in school activities and the parents' participation in learning at home. The document lists school events that parents should attend and encourages volunteerism. The charter serves as a contract between the school and the parent.

With the charter, parents receive guidelines relative to television watching and homework. The staff also involved parents in the development of this document. The staff asks parents to limit television watching to 2 hours per evening with preference going to educational programs and family programs. The principals and teachers view homework as an extension of the curricula and ask parents to enforce the homework requirement at home.

At WCES, parents come to school on the child's birthday for a special conference. If the child's birthday falls outside the school calendar, the teacher declares a special day for the child. The teacher presents to parents a portfolio of work accumulated by younger children, and older children present their own portfolio to their parents and teacher, reflecting on the growth during the past year. The conference is a celebration of the child's accomplishments but is also a chance for the teacher and parent to establish goals for the child during the next year. Teachers request additional conferences when needed.

The WCES encourages business leaders in the community to release parents for conferences during the workday and to release other employees 2 days a year to volunteer at school. The principal looks for WCES and business partnerships that will enhance learning and bring children and adults together at school. The principal belongs to the chamber of commerce and visits business groups when requested. With the growing number of two-earner incomes, businesses understand their responsibility by providing time for parents to tend to their children's needs.

WCES has a plan to assist dysfunctional families. Principals and teachers refer parents to agencies that service families in need of assistance on health matters, personal matters, or child care. If the child becomes disruptive in school to the point where the disruption deprives other children of learning, the teacher sends the child to an alternative classroom or home if the problem is more serious. The philosophy at WCES is to help dysfunctional children as much as possible but not to tolerate disruption of the learning process. WCES constantly searches for grants that will provide alternative programs for elementary students, but the district uses local funds until grant money becomes available.

A citizen and teacher advisory committee with rather important responsibilities exists at WCES. The committee chooses staffing patterns for the school, advises on curriculum changes and budget, and advises the principal on other subjects initiated by the committee. The staff knows that formal involvement of parents and citizens delays the formation of political, informal groups that force their way into the decision-making process. The school remains committed to positive relations with parents and the community.

THE CURRICULUM AT WORLD-CLASS ELEMENTARY SCHOOL

The curriculum at WCES is important just as it is to teachers around the world. But the ministry of education outlines the basic curriculum and suggests the pace of instruction for WCES teachers, so planning the curriculum offers little in the way of a problem. The teachers know approximately how long to devote to each subject they teach, again because of ministry guidelines.

Putting the curriculum into practice is not a problem at WCES. The teachers are experts on the content due to their teacher training. Planning in groups with other experts allows for a polished lesson to be planned and delivered. The classrooms at WCES are mainly self-contained so the teachers have broad responsibilities with the curriculum. But a lead teacher in each content area assists the teaching teams when needed. This provides the teachers with assurance that students from lower grades are well prepared, and the portfolios will be passed up to the next grade so the teacher there has samples of earlier student work.

The textbooks are useful at WCES. The ministry provides most of them as new books are given out at the beginning of the year. Students own the books so there is no worry about what happens to them during the year. In some cases parents may buy the books, which makes them have added value to the parents. To the untrained eye the textbooks do not have much pizzazz. They are small and lightweight, more like newsprint for paper quality. Of course, the students take the books home each night which is why they are small and lightweight. When the students take notes at WCES, they often take them right in the text—more like college students do in the United States, but it makes the textbooks real learning tools for that reason.

Textbook adoptions at WCES are no problem. The books may be written by the ministry or approved for printing based on a large contract. There are no book shows or wine and cheese parties when books are adopted. In some cases the ministry simply sends the book; in others there will be limited choices made by the teachers from a small group of approved books. Because there is one curriculum all of the books are written to that curriculum, so alignment is ensured. Parents are supportive of the curriculum because they know the books and something about the curriculum, so they buy inexpensive workbooks to assist the student learning. But there is no confusion about who does the teaching, as parents assist learning at home.

Part of the learning day occurs out of school. Everyone expects there to be homework as part of the curriculum. There is a reading at home activity daily and then a set amount of additional homework. It is a direct extension of the teaching in class, and it is assessed as part of the mastery process.

The full curriculum at WCES is well rounded. The arts, physical education, and character education are all part of the learning process, but the focus is on language and mathematics. The emphasis is on teaching and learning the processes rather than rote learning other than basics such as times tables and sight words. WCES has computers but not in a laboratory setting. They are used to supplement mathematics and to teach the curriculum area of technology.

STUDENT ASSESSMENT IN THE WORLD-CLASS ELEMENTARY SCHOOL

The WCES staff favors national assessment aligned with national curriculum and lobbies the professional organizations to push for both national assessment and national curriculum. In the absence of national assessment, the WCES staff works with other elementary schools in the district to develop a comprehensive evaluation program.

WCES places most student evaluation in the hands of individual teachers. The exception is a comprehensive testing program for all students at the conclusion of the sixth grade. Teachers may make evaluation as authentic as possible by requiring portfolios, hands-on demonstration of competence, oral examinations, and teacher observations. However, the administration requires teachers to also test students in writing using a format that the student will come across later during the sixth grade test. Teachers, however, must include essay questions on each examination. The teacher grades the teacher-made tests and the test administered in the sixth grade. The school district does require all students to take a nationally-normed, criterion-referenced test at the end of the third grade, so that parents have an idea of how their child compares with a national group. The principal expects teachers to use their knowledge of testing to prepare students for all exams. The school does have an "Ethics in Testing" policy, however, that tells teachers what are ethical test preparation practices and what are unethical practices.

During the past 3 or 4 years, the staff at WCES worked to align the curriculum and the testing program. Teacher-made tests in kindergarten through grade 6 measure attainment of curricular objectives, and all teachers structured questions that will help prepare students for the exit examination in grade 6. The staff developed benchmarks throughout the curriculum to help teachers, parents, and students understand a student's comprehension of the curriculum. Teachers now know which students have mastered the curriculum objectives and which students remain behind. The staff offers help after school and in the summer for students behind in achievement.

The staff at WCES uses test scores to prescribe learning experiences for students and to evaluate teaching methods and the curriculum. Each teacher must review the status of each student and complete a written analysis made available to the student's next teacher. The local paper compares the results of the third grade criterion referenced test with national norms, but teachers stress the importance of the locally prepared tests and seem to survive the yearly comparisons. The third grade teachers meet with parents and explain the results of the national test but take care to explain to the parent the child's performance on other school's assessment devices. At the end of the sixth grade, the teacher meets with parents to review the child's test result and progress during the elementary experience. The conference includes a planning session to establish plans for the student's future schooling.

A World-Class Idea from Canada: Portrait of a World-Class School

When one enters the door of the Lord Lansdowne Public School in Toronto, Canada, one senses the beginning of a world-class experience. Displays of student work appear in the foyer where a few weeks earlier students had displayed projects that celebrated their national heritage. The location of the school is about 1 mile from the Toronto City Hall in a multicultural, multiethnic neighborhood. The school houses students in junior-kindergarten through grade 8. The students are primarily of Chinese descent, but significant percentages of Portuguese, African-Americans, and Caucasians are present. Five hundred two students attend Lord Lansdowne, but only about 20 percent live in the school's attendance area. The remainder are at the school because parents initiated a choice option. Parents choose to send their children to Lord Lansdowne.

The principal, Peter Friberg, is a man with a vision. He is as comfortable talking about the theories of Sergiovani as he is talking with teachers or students about their work. He prefers to make educational decisions within the confines of the school, while still adopting the regulations necessary in the bureaucracy of a large, urban system. Peter Friberg retired in June 1996 and was replaced by Elena Aleinitou. The assistant principal, Dr. Porter, is no longer the school disciplinarian. The administration has weaned the teachers away from sending discipline cases directly to the office, and, instead, a resource room exists where students must report if referred for disruptive behavior or simply if they need additional help. The school counselor and special teachers staff the room. The assistant principal is, therefore, a second instructional leader con-centrating on educational programs and people rather than dis-cipline. She left the school during the summer of 1995 well prepared to assume her own principalship.

Teachers teach the Toronto Common Curriculum. The Ontario Ministry of Education has also introduced a provincial common curriculum, so both the local school board and the provincial government share the value of a common learning base. The Toronto Common Curriculum comes complete with benchmarks, and com-mon testing is not far behind. The curriculum contains the basic elements of elementary curriculum found in all world-class countries. The staff does not hesitate to teach students basic values. Study of a second language begins in grade 4, and an extended French program begins in grade 7. A bilingual program exists to help those students who come to school with limited English skills. The principal schedules classes with multiage groupings so that every classroom contains students from two grades. Teachers, therefore, do not stream or group students. The staff expects all students to learn the common curriculum. Students who qualify for gifted programs may travel to another school for lessons, but the staff prefers to have them stay at Lord Lansdowne. The staff believes in enrichment for all. The principal describes the school climate as an ''efficacy for achievement'' and points to a well-endowed and open library as proof of the school's commitment to learning. Teachers model hard work and expect students to work hard, and all these expectations exist despite classes that vary in size from 22 in junior-kindergarten to 33 in grades 7 and 8. Special education teachers do what is best for each individual student, even if it means keeping them in a self-contained classroom.

The Ontario Ministry of Education requires all prospective teachers to complete an academic degree before enrolling in a teacher certification program, so teachers at Lord Lansdowne own a certificate that required 5 years of preparation. Because Lord Lansdowne is close to the University of Toronto, many student teachers observe at the school and complete their required semester of student teaching there. Teachers work 11 days when students are not in school, so the opportunity for extensive staff development exists. Teacher pay for Toronto teachers starts at about $32,000.00 and extends to $50,000 to $60,000, depending on experience and additional degrees.

The school climate at Lord Lansdowne appears disciplined but relaxed. Students attend school 185 days from 8:35 A.M. to 3:40 P.M. A remedial period offers slower students a chance to catch up. The staff requires the students to take responsibility for their own behavior and the behavior of other students as well. The "Code of Behavior Expectations" details (1) what the school expects of students, (2) what students expect of teachers, and (3) what happens to students when they exceed the limit. A document called "Safety and Security in the School" and another called "Violence Prevention" also deal with setting a safe and proper school climate. The staff trains older students to be "peer mediators." Two or more students having trouble can submit a grievance to peer mediation and avoid meeting with an adult. In the senior school (grades 6, 7, and 8), students belong to student advisory groups of approximately 15 students who meet daily with their staff advisor. Senior school students also have a sports program and interesting special activities. Because the school does not serve lunch, the principal permits older students to leave the school grounds.

The teachers at Lord Lansdowne expect students to do homework each evening, and the principal had parents write a homework policy for the school. Teachers also counsel students and parents about television watching. Students start school at an impressionable age 4, so junior-kindergarten teachers spend time on parenting issues. The staff makes parents welcome at school and approximately 80 parents volunteer at the school. Parents serve on the staffing committee that helps determine class size, teacher placement, and the school schedule. There is a parent-teacher association, and the school sends a newsletter to parents periodically. The inside cover of the school folder that contains information for the public says, "Education Is a Shared Responsibility." The school encourages parents to enter a partnership with the school that results in shared responsibility for the student's success.

The Royal Commission on Learning chose Lord Lansdowne Public School as the site for the official release on January 26, 1995, of its recommendations for the future direction of the Ontario education system. This honor was one of the first facts about the school related to the author during a visit to the school, and, needless to say, the principal related it with great pride. The Lord Lansdowne School is well along the road to world-class.

STAFF DEVELOPMENT FOR A WORLD-CLASS ELEMENTARY SCHOOL

A world-class elementary school will not result from spontaneous combustion; it must be deliberately crafted. Hopefully, the reader has gained new ideas about the world of school, but that vision must be shared to be of value. The authors have been in education for over 60 years, combined, and the work that has gone into this book has dramatically changed their ideas of education. The impact of looking at the world's schools is dizzying. How can the reader move from ideas to reality? Where should the development of world-class schools start?

To begin, review the two world-class rules that were mentioned in Chapter 1:

(1) Just because it is world-class does not mean U.S. citizens necessarily want it.

(2) Just because it is a U.S. idea does not mean that it is not world-class.

The authors firmly believe that the schools mirror what society wants its schools to look like. Some world-class ideas, such as a national curriculum or longer school year, will be met with skepticism at best and hostility as well. So the reader needs to approach the crafting of a world-class elementary school with a sharp eye on the community, planning the change process carefully.

A second step would be to share this book with others, beginning a discussion about the ideas of developing a world-class elementary school. This can be accomplished in a single school by having the informal leadership of the school reading the book and talking about it, or it can be accomplished system wide with other leaders reading and then discussing the book.

The school leader should approach the process using the best staff development methods. Sparks (1985) proposed a multistep process for most effective staff development. The process should be followed in order, with the leader expecting this to be a multiyear process. The stages are:

(1) *Readiness:* which starts with a supportive climate and interest in new ideas. A school that is accountability-paralyzed will have no tolerance for change because it can fail. Readiness could start with an awareness of what other countries do that is successful. One tidbit a day on the school bulletin could get people to thinking. From there, begin sharing the book, invite international students in to talk with faculty, etc. The availability of international students through exchange programs, in local colleges, through second language teacher contacts, etc., is amazingly accessible. The leader needs to be creative, using foreign churches, contacting English as a second language teachers, etc. The authors teach comparative education as a graduate course, and the impact of having the classes interview nationals from the world-class countries was profound. Developing an awareness of other ways to conduct school is a first step in getting the school ready to change. The process ends with the staff setting goals and objectives tied to school improvement and world-class school ideas.

(2) *Planning:* This is a crucial part of the staff development process. Once the staff is ready for change, a needs assessment is useful for planning, because it aligns perceived needs with new ideas. Learning styles, the climate of school and community, etc., need to be taken into account. Specific objectives and strategies need to be agreed upon, some taking as long as 3 years to complete. Facilitators and parents need careful screening and direction. The authors are frequently involved at this point as the overwhelming impact of so many ideas causes some leaders to lose direction.

(3) *Training:* This stage can take many forms. Often, a presentation on world-class schools begins the process. The use of action research teams and planning retreats are often used. The leaders need to establish a means of continuing the flow of new ideas so the excitement level remains high. Area media coordinators can help develop contacts with embassy personnel from various countries. There are several cost-free publications about other nation's schools, available

from selected embassies. One important part of the training stage is developing staff proprietorship of ideas so the staff selects what they believe will work rather than having the change mandated.

(4) *Implementation:* This part of staff development is commonly left out, and much of the failure of staff development comes from not having the new ideas supported as they are implemented. Peer coaching is a valuable tool to use at this stage. But planned support and further exposure to the change needs to be provided.

(5) *Maintenance:* A systematic plan for maintaining the change once in place is necessary to ensure that it continues. Tying professional development plans and school improvement plans to the process makes it more likely there will be some form of maintenance.

The reader is referred to the *Journal of Staff Development* as an ongoing means of providing effective staff development. Sparks (1983) provided a good review about effective staff development, which would be good additional reading prior to planning to develop a world-class elementary school.

DEVELOPING THE AGENDA FOR A WORLD-CLASS ELEMENTARY SCHOOL

The agenda is designed to become a worksheet for school administrators who wish to incorporate elements of world-class schools in a particular setting. The reader is advised to read the agenda items over several times. First, read the list to eliminate items that either are not feasible or not wanted. It is suggested that such items be crossed off the agenda, leaving only items that are feasible and desirable. Mark the lines along world-class standards which already exist, using a plus mark. They are a plus for the school. Reread the remaining list, numbering the items that remain:

(1) Indicates an item that can be accomplished quickly with relative ease

(2) Indicates an item that can be accomplished with time and study and perhaps with limited additional resources

(3) Indicates an item that will take study, substantial staff (and community) development, perhaps calling on significant resources not currently available

It is likely that the items coded 1 can be accomplished the first year, those with a 2, within 2 years, and those coded 3 may be accomplished within 3 years. Review the list, thinking about a 3-year plan to develop a world-class elementary school, and adjust the coding appropriately. Then copy the items into categories 1, 2, and 3 to be prioritized for each year. Those can be infused into a strategic plan or other school improvement model. Each item can be analyzed for staff involvement, training, resource and time allocation, etc. Once the agenda is set for the school, the reader is urged to keep abreast of other developments from the world of world-class schools.

(1) Curriculum:
- ☐ The curriculum is aligned with the emerging national curriculum frameworks.
- ☐ The community is consulted for input in the design of the curriculum.
- ☐ The curriculum reflects the purpose of this school.
- ☐ The curriculum is disseminated widely, articulated for teachers, parents, students, and the community at large. The curriculum is well understood.
- ☐ The curriculum (not the texts) determines what is taught at each grade level.
- ☐ The curriculum has an established pace and minimum teaching time per subject articulated. Language and mathematics dominate teaching time through grade 3.
- ☐ Character education is part of the taught curriculum.
- ☐ The preschool curriculum is reaching ever younger children, starting around age 2 or 3.
- ☐ There is a homework policy, stipulating estimated time for learning out of school. Teachers are trained in the use of homework; parents are aware of the expectation that homework will be monitored.
- ☐ There are select teachers who are leaders in subject-specific areas.
- ☐ Students who fall behind are taught out of school by the teacher, so they may catch up without slowing the whole class to the slowest student's learning rate.
- ☐ Teachers communicate regularly and clearly with parents about student mastery of the taught curriculum.

☐ The principal regularly teaches some part of the curriculum.

☐ The value of work as part of the learning process is modeled and taught.

(2) Teachers

☐ Teachers plan together in a "teachers' room" where they also reflect on the lessons taught.

☐ Teachers clearly know and follow the established curriculum.

☐ Teachers cooperate with each other, designing assessments to match the taught curriculum.

☐ The principal is a teacher with curriculum responsibilities, often teaching character education.

☐ The principal provides common planning time for teaching teams to work together.

☐ Teaching time is almost never interrupted with outside announcements, activities, etc., and the sanctity of teaching time is respected, with any interruption started with an apology.

☐ Out-of-school activities are part of school life, but they do not overshadow the learning environment of the school.

☐ Student attendance is stressed with makeup sessions being reasonable but mandatory.

☐ The school is proactively involved in teacher education programs.

☐ Teacher esteem is fostered with business cards, a school directory, teacher certificates and degrees clearly displayed. Teachers are acknowledged for extra work and additional schooling in front of parents.

☐ Teacher isolation is reduced to teaching time only.

☐ Nonteaching duties are removed from the teacher as much as possible, using teacher assistants and volunteers to maximize the teacher's concentration on teaching.

☐ Mentoring novice teachers is a priority with time allotted and other expectations reduced so the mentor can serve the novice first.

☐ There is an active attempt to make the public aware of the benefits of a longer school year and year-round schooling.

☐ There is support for greater teacher license-reciprocity among states, and support for manageable national teacher license.

☐ The research on class size is understood by the faculty.

☐ Teachers are treated as respected, dependable professionals.

☐ Faculty meetings start with teaching and learning issues first, and there is ongoing dialogue about best teaching methods.

(3) School Governance

☐ The school understands the use of a national ministry of education and national funding of schools. Although that is not feasible in the United States, there is support of equitable funding among schools and districts.

☐ There is a school charter for the governance of the school and a local school board of governors.

☐ There is a student charter of rights and responsibilities.

☐ There is a charter of parents' rights and responsibilities.

☐ There is a charter of educators' rights and responsibilities.

☐ There is an effort to increase school efficiency without cutting necessary personnel.

☐ Strategic planning and site-based management are used to direct the school.

☐ District offices of the state education agency are accessible to the LEA.

☐ Principals are trained in school administration and supervision skills, and they are drawn from among the ranks of the best teachers in the district.

☐ Parent choice and involvement are encouraged in the school.

☐ The school is governed to include parents in their child's education, and it is "parent-friendly" with schedules designed to meet parent workloads.

☐ Accreditation involves having a team of expert teachers audit the school, reporting publicly on the audit.

(4) Student Assessment

☐ All student assessment tools are aligned with the articulated curriculum.

☐ There is a clearly understood statement about ethical testing practices that is adhered to by all school personnel.

☐ There is support and a public education effort to align national testing, both commercially prepared standardized tests and national assessment of education progress testing, with the national curriculum frameworks.

- ☐ Those involved in designing the frameworks should be involved in designing the tests of it.
- ☐ Multiple choice and true-false tests are discouraged, using essay testing as of grade 1 and more authentic sources of assessment of student progress.
- ☐ Identified benchmarks for student assessment of mastery are available starting at kindergarten, and a final benchmark at the end of elementary school should measure overall student mastery.
- ☐ Reteaching opportunities should be widely available.
- ☐ Grade inflation should be discouraged.
- ☐ Using tests for comparisons of students and groups should be discouraged, testing for assessment of mastery and to determine further needs would be encouraged.
- ☐ Teachers are trained in the skill of writing proper test items and in interpreting the results.
- ☐ The frequency of testing should be monitored with it being taken seriously.
- ☐ The school should have an accountability plan that includes, but is not limited to, test results.

(5) Students
- ☐ Students are taught the characteristics of a successful student and encouraged to emulate that success.
- ☐ There is a student mediation program to reduce school distractions.
- ☐ Peer and cross-age programs and peer tutoring programs exist.
- ☐ Advisor-advisee programs include character education modules.
- ☐ Violent or otherwise disruptive students are placed in alternative programs so the learning of the majority of students is not disrupted.
- ☐ Students know and follow the homework policy.
- ☐ School guidelines for television viewing are developed and disseminated to parents. Television viewing as part of education is encouraged with care.
- ☐ Student participation in extracurricular activities is encouraged, but not on school time or in lieu of homework.

☐ Grouping, "streaming," or otherwise labeling students is discouraged. Cooperative learning is encouraged.

☐ The staff includes a child development specialist.

(6) Parents, Home, and Community

☐ Preschool parents are active participants in school life prior to sending their child to school. They could be appointed as adjunct faculty as of the birth of the child.

☐ Preschool parents should have access to developmentally appropriate materials with which to stimulate the child. Parenting training and preschool coordination is stressed by the school that provides it.

☐ Parents should have copies of the parents' charter, exercising both their rights and their responsibilities.

☐ Parent-teacher conferences should be scheduled at a time and place where working parents can be involved. These sessions should be interactive and user-friendly. Teachers may need training in how to conduct such sessions.

☐ Community businesses should be involved in making working parents available for conferences and able to volunteer in school.

☐ School board meetings should rotate among district elementary schools.

☐ Linkages should be forged and strengthened among the elementary school and related child service agencies such as Head Start and Department of Social Services. Joint staff development programs could foster such efforts.

☐ Benchmarks for adult literacy should be established. Opportunities to remediate those in need should be offered.

☐ Parents should provide a place for students to study while doing homework and should monitor student television watching, following school guidelines.

☐ Dysfunctional families and children should have help at the school, but dysfunctional students should not keep others from learning.

☐ The main lobby at the school should have academic trophies prominently' displayed for the community to see.

This checklist should be expanded, adding other ideas that occurred to the reader and other features of the text. Make this book a beginning rather than an end. Reach into the community for other ideas and to contact foreign nationals who can add to the rich brew needed to make world-class schools. One final thought: world-class schools are just that because they are unique and fitted to the community they serve. The journey to world-class status starts with the leader who shares the vision of high achievement, hard work, and love of education constantly. As the Brits say when leaving a good friend: "All the Best!"'

REFERENCES

Sparks, Dennis. Circa 1985. "School Improvement through Staff Development,' Alexandria, VA: Association for Supervision and Curriculum Development, videotape.

Sparks, Georgia. 1983. "Synthesis of Research on Staff Development for Effective Teaching,' *Educational Leadership,* 41(3):65–72.

This is the second book by the authors who work together in the Department of Administration, Curriculum and Instruction, College of Education and Allied Professions, Western Carolina University.

Richard M. Haynes is Associate Professor of Education. He also serves as Director of Field Experiences. Dr. Haynes has written seven books for young adult readers. He served as a supervisor of humanities and assistant superintendent of curriculum and personnel in North Carolina systems and was an instructor at both the public school level and community college level in Florida. His undergraduate degree came from Florida Southern College, his master's degree came from Rollins College and his doctorate came from Duke University in 1978. Dr. Haynes and his wife, Dianne, have two daughters—one a university student and the other teaching in the public schools while pursuing her master's degree.

Donald M. Chalker is Professor of Education. In addition to teaching school leadership courses, he directs The Office of School Services and The Alliance of Business Leaders and Educators, the sponsor of the world class research reported in this book. Dr. Chalker previously served the public schools in Michigan and Ohio as a teacher, counselor, assistant principal, principal, assistant superintendent and superintendent of schools. Dr. Chalker holds a bachelor's and a master's degree from Kent State University and received his doctorate from Wayne State University in 1981. He

315

and his wife, Harriet, have four adult children and four grand-children.

The authors present their research on world-class schools internation-ally and consult with schools seeking world class status. They may be contacted at Western Carolina University, Cullowhee, North Carolina 28723 (Phone: 704-227-7415).